PAUL SCOTT
A Critical Study

PAUL SCOTT
A Critical Study

by Francine S. Weinbaum

 University of Texas Press, Austin

First Edition, 1992

Requests for permission to reproduce material from this work should be sent to
Permissions, University of Texas Press, Box 7819, Austin, Texas 78713-7819.

∞ The paper used in this publication meets the minimum requirements of
American National Standard for Information Sciences—Permanence of Paper for
Printed Library Materials, ANSI Z39.48-1984.

Library of Congress Cataloging-in-Publication Data
Weinbaum, Francine S. (Francine Schneider), 1941–
    Paul Scott: a critical study / by Francine S. Weinbaum.
        p.   cm.
    Includes bibliographical references and index.
    ISBN 0-292-76539-8 (alk. paper)
        1. Scott, Paul, 1920–   —Criticism and interpretation. 2. India
in literature. I. Title.
    PR6069.C596Z94   1992
    823'.914—dc20   91-28317
                                                                              CIP

Frontispiece: Paul Scott, photograph © Mark Gerson, 1970.

*For my husband, Marvin,
and my children, Peter, Meg,
and Ted*

Contents

Preface

When I first picked up *The Jewel in the Crown* in 1973, the last volume of *The Raj Quartet* had not yet been published. Although there had been rave reviews of the first three volumes (Orville Prescott wrote in the *New York Times* that *The Jewel in the Crown* "may be one of the finest novels about India since E. M. Forster's *A Passage to India* and . . . will certainly be one of the finest novels of any kind published this year" [July 29, 1966]), Scott had received no academic recognition. After reading the novels, I was surprised to find no literary analysis of the work of a writer who was clearly a major novelist. I decided then to do my research and doctoral thesis on Paul Scott's works. When I needed the final volume of the *Quartet* to complete the critical study, I wrote to Paul Scott and eventually received a proof copy from his English publisher. It was the beginning of a lengthy correspondence over a three-year period and a friendship which began when, with the support of my advisors and various campus units, I arranged for him to give a public lecture at the University of Illinois at Urbana-Champaign. He also spoke to students in my introductory fiction courses who were reading *The Bender*, his novel about the meanderings of a lonely middle-aged alcoholic in London. Additionally, he agreed to do several television and radio interviews in connection with the publicity for his just-finished novel which concluded the series, *A Division of the Spoils*.

While I was writing the dissertation, two articles were published, "Paul Scott's Raj," by Benita Parry, which to Scott's chagrin criticized the novels as sentimental, and a flattering review of the novels, "The End of the Raj: Paul Scott's Novels as History," by the eminent historian Max Beloff. When I finished my work, I had the opportunity of presenting a copy of it to Paul Scott in New York in August of 1976. I was pleased when Scott wrote that he was "proud and flattered to have been the subject of such an excellent thesis."[1]

In 1977 I wrote an essay, published the next year in *Critique*, which contrasted Scott's vision of love to that of Dante's *Paradiso* and introduced his subject as an idea of thwarted love or union on three levels: historical, social, and psychological. I was later amused to learn during an evening in New York with Scott that one of his English publishers, Roland Gant, had affectionately accused him of writing "the Gospel According to St. Paul."[2] In a fine introduction to the novels, Patrick Swinden does not speak of love but about "a sense of personal integration and belonging" when he names Scott's subject a paradise lost.[3] In the course of my discussion I will identify two kinds of paradises to which characters aspire in *The Raj Quartet*, one based on love and union, the other on power and mastery, true and false paradises for Scott and both ultimately illusory.

K. B. Rao in *Paul Scott* has written the Twayne publication life and work. There are perceptive insights but too much plot summary, and the discussion of *The Raj Quartet* is partly derivative. M. M. Mahood, in "Paul Scott's Guardians," writes of the contrast between "the would-be guardians" embodying the crumbling English proconsular ideal, and "the true guardians . . . all seers," embodying "love without power."[4] Janis Popham and Janet Tedesco in *An Introduction to The Raj Quartet* have done a moralistic study which makes no mention of the literature but which provides good insight into Scott's characters and identifies Scott's use of light-dark imagery broadly as good and evil. More recently, David Rubin, in his excellent survey *After the Raj: British Novels of India Since 1947*, compares Scott's fiction dealing with Anglo-Indian relations favorably with that of his contemporaries and with Forster's; he argues convincingly that Scott takes "all the stock material of the Anglo-Indian novel—India and sex, the transposed racial identity, the value of the British mission (the white man's burden), India's power to confer illumination as well as destroy—and transforms it into highly original fiction."[5] *Paul Scott's Raj*, Robin Moore's very useful account of Scott's creative process in the India novels, and *Paul Scott: A Life*, Hilary Spurling's admirable authorized biography, have just been published.

Scott's reputation as a major writer is still young. The University of Tulsa McFarlin Library collection of 6,000 of his letters as well as his correspondents' responses and typescripts of his lectures on the novel, sometimes containing more than one version, was catalogued in March 1987. The other large collection of his writing, consisting largely of his working manuscripts, is at the Harry Ransom Humanities Research Center at the University of Texas at Austin. A collection of his essays, *My Appointment with the Muse*, was published in London in 1986 (and in New York in 1987 as *On Writing and the Novel*).

Scott's winning of England's prestigious Booker Prize in November 1977, not four months before his untimely death and just short of his fifty-eighth birthday, probably did more than anything else to enhance his reputation as a writer. But it was the Masterpiece Theatre presentation of *The Raj Quartet* as "The Jewel in the Crown" that captured the imagination of audiences in Britain and the Commonwealth in 1983–1984 and the United States the following season. It was that production that convinced me to revise extensively my analysis of *The Raj Quartet* and do a more broadly based study of Scott's novels.

While Paul Scott was in Illinois and after he died, my overwhelming curiosity was about his creative process. Francine Ringold, a writer and teacher of creative writing, published an informative interview of Scott while he was Writer-in-Residence at the University of Tulsa in the fall of 1976. Even more revealing is Scott's demonstration of his creative process in *The Corrida at San Feliu* and his description of it in several of his essays, most notably in "The Architecture of the Arts: The Novel," "The Form and Function of the Novel," and, specifically in regard to *The Jewel in the Crown*, "Method: The Mystery and the Mechanics." I shall rely on these essays as I trace the antecedents of *The Jewel in the Crown* in Scott's own experience.

Even more than I wanted to know how Paul Scott wrote his novels, I wished to understand how this man who looked, when I first met him, as though life had beaten him down, could metamorphose into the author of the magnificent *Raj Quartet*; I wanted to comprehend the alchemy of the transformation. E. M. Forster has written of the impossibility of touching the artist because he or she becomes, in a sense, another person the moment someone comes into the room, and although I spent three days interviewing, introducing, dining with, and shepherding Paul Scott around campus, I felt the frustration of not being able to understand the connection between the man I met and the artist who had written *The Raj Quartet*. It was not until after his death, when I had an opportunity during the summer of 1979 to interview his editorial director, Roland Gant, his elder daughter, Carol, and his U.S. literary agent, Dorothy Olding, that I began to intuit a connection between his life and his fiction, a connection confirmed for me by a later reading of several of the novels that seem to be inspired by the character of Scott himself.

Scott appeared to be a man of acute sensitivity. He probably had, as Henry James has described his own, "an imagination of disaster." Certainly, he could jump too quickly to conclusions. He occasionally seemed to suffer from a preternatural suspiciousness, often followed by a relief that his fears were unfounded, much like District Commissioner White in *The Jewel in the Crown*. Roland Gant describes Scott as "quirky" and "diffident" and as a man who abhorred and liked to mock pretentiousness of any kind.[6] Like Count Bronowsky in *The Raj Quartet*, Paul Scott was a man of many faces.[7] A friend who knew Scott in the Indian army saw him as two different people, a grave reserved man from whom another, livelier character was trying to escape.[8] Each daughter had a different father, according to Sally Scott; for Carol, he was a "hail fellow, well met" sort of person, for Sally a more quiet, intellectual companion sharing books and music. During his lifetime, Scott developed a close platonic relationship with a number of middle-aged women. Each woman to whom he became close knew only one side of him, depending on what she brought out in his personality.[9] Although he was a loner by choice, he had an uncanny ability to project himself into the psyche of the person with whom he was engaged in conversation. Perhaps this is obvious to anyone who has read the novels and marveled at the array of characters created with a degree of realism not often found in fiction. In this, as in many other ways, Paul Scott is like his novelist Edward Thornhill, in *The Corrida of San Feliu*, who "has this terrible facility for looking at a man, making judgments about what he is thinking and feeling, and then continuing to look, with an eye open for the expression or gesture that alters the whole picture" (207).

Like Alec Guinness, who likes to imitate people's walks, Paul Scott would memorize people's expressions and gestures, almost mimicking them, as though the key to a person's psychological makeup was to be found by donning his or her physical coat. My impression was that he did not like to be observed doing this. ("It may be that stealing is a metaphor for taking over people's personalities," says Kram in a short, unfinished manuscript, "The Appointment.") Scott knew his characters so well that not only did he provide many of them with lengthy and fully believable life histories but would occasionally refer to what happened to them after the novels ended. He wrote to me on December 31, 1975—before *Staying On* had been published—that Sarah Layton and Guy Perron had been married in 1948 but that he had never gotten around to that year in the *Quartet*.

As a writer he revised extensively, and in a lecture delivered to students at Swanwick Writer's Summer School, confessed to dreading his daily appointment with the muse: "I see no reason why a writer shouldn't suffer from the same nervous tension, the almost-hatred of what he is about to try and do, that the actor feels waiting in the wings" (MM 72). At Urbana, he dreaded giving his talk and was relieved as well as disappointed when he thought, mistakenly, that no one had shown up to hear it. Outwardly confident, inwardly anxious, [10] he thought he would be a terrible teacher, but my English students were intrigued by him, as were his students later at the University of Tulsa. His method was to elicit response rather than attempt to have the students accept his view.

I once asked him who the model was for George Spruce, the main character in *The Bender*. I was startled when he said that, actually, it was himself. Instinctively I said that it was not. He liked that. What I did not understand at the time was that Paul Scott was constantly redefining himself. I think it is fairly clear that he is also, among others, the inspiration for Edward Thornhill, and for the publisher's reader, David Chalmers, in his barely begun and unpublished novel, "Mango Rain." It seems logical that my discussion of the early novels should be in part a search for the character, the inner nature of Paul Scott. This kind of critical focus, of course, has its dangers, as does any critical approach. However, when essentially the same characteristics and quests reappear in several novels, and when certain autobiographical elements are clearly present, critical attention is inevitably drawn to the identity of the writer. Scott was a very private person and might consider intrusive some of the suggestions in the concluding chapter. I have had to weigh my qualms against my desire to understand the interrelation of the novels, the creative process from which they emerged, and the mind of the writer.

The writing of this manuscript has been a lengthy process, and I am grateful for University of Illinois Research Board funding which enabled me to travel during the spring and summer of 1988 to the University of Tulsa McFarlin Library to sample the sizable collection of Paul Scott's papers and to New York and London to speak with his family, business associates, and biographer. I owe special thanks to Paul Scott's widow, Nancy Edith Avery-Scott, his daughters, Carol and Sally Scott, his brother and sister-in-law, Peter and Eileen Scott, his Heinemann publishers, former editorial director Roland Gant and former managing director Charles Pick, his former New York literary agent, Dorothy Olding, and his authorized biographer, Hilary Spurling. Additionally, I want to thank University of Tulsa McFarlin Library curator Sidney Huttner and his staff, particularly Milissa Burkart, for their assistance, as well as then provost Thomas Staley and Scott's creative writing student, Sally Dennison, for meeting with me in Tulsa.

I owe a debt to Leon Waldoff of the Department of English at the University of Illinois for his kindness in reading large portions of the manuscript and offering helpful suggestions. Additionally, I want to thank Zohreh Sullivan, Shari Benstock, Dale Kramer, Eleanor Feinberg, Betty Fish, and Kathryn Seelie-Fields for their contributions. For their suggestions for earlier versions of *The Raj Quartet* section of the manuscript, I also owe thanks to my dissertation advisor, Bernard Benstock, and to John Frayne, Blair Kling, William Archer, and John Friedman; I am especially indebted for the assistance given to me by the late Robert Schneider. Most of all, I am grateful for the loving support and encouragement of my husband, Marvin.

Abbreviations

AA	"The Architecture of the Arts: The Novel"
AS	*The Alien Sky*
AW	"Aspects of Writing"
B	*The Bender*
BP	*The Birds of Paradise*
CLP	*The Chinese Love Pavilion*
CSF	*The Corrida at San Feliu*
D	*A Division of the Spoils*
ES	"Enoch Sahib: A Slight Case of Cultural Shock"
FF	"The Form and Function of the Novel"
IPF	"India: A Post-Forsterian View"
J	*The Jewel in the Crown*
JS	*Johnnie Sahib*
MA	"Meet the Author: Manchester"
MC	*A Male Child*
MM	"Method: The Mystery and the Mechanics"
MW	*The Mark of the Warrior*
RQ	*The Raj Quartet*
S	*The Day of the Scorpion*
SO	*Staying On*
SR	"Scott's Raj—or India Returned"
T	*The Towers of Silence*
WS	"A Writer Takes Stock"

PAUL SCOTT
A Critical Study

1. Paul Scott: A Biographical Sketch

Paul Mark Scott was born at home at 130 Fox Lane on March 25, 1920, in Palmers Green, North London. He was the younger son of Thomas Scott (1871–1958), a commercial artist who did fashion plates and left the raising of the family to his wife, Frances Mark (1886–1969), a gifted and ambitious woman who is supposed to have written novels before her marriage, hiding in a closet to do so and burning them on the night before her wedding in 1916.[1] The family, particularly his working-class mother, was proud of a connection on his father's side with Thomas Bewick, the nineteenth-century naturalist and engraver, and with his well-off cousins, the Wrights.

His father's unmarried sisters[2] lived about a mile away in a "larger . . . more elegant house" that was the envy of his mother (SR 6). Tom Scott paid half the rent for Wyphurst and worked there up to twelve hours a day. Although his father was a quiet, gentle, reserved person, seldom raising his voice in anger and friendly with everyone, according to his son, Peter Bewick Scott (b. 1918), it was difficult to know what he was thinking.[3] Domineering Frances was often critical of her husband, who turned a deaf ear, and adored her younger son, favoring him over her husband and his elder brother. His mother had glorious ambitions for Paul, although he was unable to reconcile her split vision of him as a "wayward poetic genius with the world at his feet" and "a safe, dependable breadwinner who would redeem the family fortunes."[4]

Scott writes that his side of the family was "quite poor."[5] Exaggerating for dramatic effect their infrequent visits to their well-to-do relations, he adds, "Weekends in Richmond (a Rolls, a chauffeur, menservants and a nanny) were set off against years in Southgate (shanks pony, the 'bus, and making do)."[6] His father's family looked down on his mother, who had a sister in service and came from South London ("Really Black Town that" [SR 5]),[7] and all his life he would show enormous sensitivity to people low on the social scale.

"In Palmers Green we were as aware of social distinctions as they were in Mudpore," he would later say (SR 25), identifying the social strictures of his boyhood with those of British India. From the beginning, as it seemed to George Spruce in *The Bender*, the malleable world of the imagination must have seemed more attractive than the real world. Scott later spoke of his "early lesson about the flatness of life and the rotundity of art" (WS 195).

From an early age, Paul, who used to enjoy mimicking people with his brother, Peter, and later with Clive Sampson and Roland Gant,[8] wanted to be a film director, an actor, an artist, or a writer, and found plenty of opportunity to stimulate his imagination. With the first film he saw at the age of six, he became "a dedicated, fanatical film fan" (WS 195). From age nine to thirteen, he created illustrated films with his brother's assistance, an experience that perhaps played a part in his view of the novel as a series of images. They used as models films of the same genre as *Beau Geste*.[9] Paul would draw pictures of people he had met or else trace close-ups of the leading characters from photos of movie stars. They used India ink on tracing paper or strips of greaseproof which they gummed together and passed through a cigar-box projector, the lens taken from an old pair of binoculars. "The business of creating a plot and characters seemed to come perfectly naturally," he said. "Unconsciously I had absorbed the lessons of the cinema and also of the many books I had now read" (WS 196). By the time he was fourteen, he was becoming more interested in "the power of words without pictures" (WS 196) and wrote lengthy compositions for school when only a few pages would have sufficed.

At first the future had seemed bright. With his photographic memory, Paul "won every prize there was to win"[10] at the small private school he attended with his brother in North London, the Winchmore Hill Collegiate. He was expected to win a series of scholarships that would have sent him to a grammar school and then Oxford, and eventually made him part of the upper-class Establishment. However, his father's financial difficulties intervened when Paul was fourteen, and he was forced to leave school to find employment; at the age of fifteen he began training as an accountant.[11] The dashing of his hopes must have been made more painful by his mother's grandiose dreams for him and his father's indifference,[12] and he would later immortalize the shock in the devastating educational and career frustrations of his heroes, most memorably portrayed in William Conway's experience in *The Birds of Paradise* and Hari Kumar's in *The Raj Quartet*. The tragic sense in Scott's novels of personal and historical aspirations as "illusions; as dreams, never fulfilled, never to be fulfilled" (D 598) stems in part from this educational and social frustration.

During the time of his financial difficulties, Tom Scott moved his family in with his sisters at Wyphurst. So fierce were the conflicts between his mother and his aunts when Paul was thirteen that he felt it had affected his ability to express his emotions, "except in writing. Which is a form of expressing it to yourself" (SR 6). Perhaps of equal significance, it was at this juncture that Frances turned for full emotional support from her husband to her younger son.[13]

Paul did well in accounting despite the educational disappointment, managing to win at seventeen a Silver Medal from the Royal Society of Accountants. He worked for C. T. Payne, studied bookkeeping at night, read whatever literature he could get his hands on (Zola, Hardy, Walter Scott, and Trollope, among others), and in his spare time wrote plays and poetry in the style of Rupert Brooke. While he sought to make up for the education he was denied, auditing enabled him to meet people "against the background of their work."[14] One of the Payne clients he met was Gerald Armstrong, who took his aesthetic and worldly education in hand and with whom he had a homosexual affair. During this period he read Oscar Wilde and was fascinated by *The Picture of Dorian Gray* and its portrait of a divided self.[15]

Paul's second mentor was Clive Sansom, a poet who (with his wife, Ruth) became his lifelong friend and introduced him to Isherwood, Auden, C. D. Lewis, Stephen Spender, and, most important, T. S. Eliot. For Scott, writing was a sacred profession,[16] and *I, Gerontius*, the poem he wrote in 1940, is grandiose and bombastic. In later years, he preferred to forget it and the rest of his wartime verse, which appeared in the Resurgam series of poetry broadsheets and in anthologies and magazines such as *Poetry Quarterly*.[17] During the war *Pillars of Salt*, a play he had written on the fate of the Jews in Europe, was submitted to the Anglo-Palestinian play competition of 1945 and was one of four selected for publication.

Scott had joined the army in 1940, the Royal East Kent Regiment, and served at home as a noncommissioned officer in Brigade Intelligence. His sexual preference gave him some difficulty in the army, and his biographer suggests that he was involved in an incident not unlike that between Merrick and Pinky in *A Division of the Spoils*, which left him with "a lasting grudge against authority" and an interest in fiction in "the punitive connection between an obsessive authoritarian officer and the youth he selects as his victim."[18] The experience was a shock, and Scott would repress the sentimental dandy side of his personality in favor of "the soldier and realist with both feet on the ground."[19]

In 1943 he was commissioned into the Indian army and served in India, Assam, and Malaya. His command of an air supply unit in Bengal, Imphal, and Malaya provided the setting for his first published novel, about one officer's taking over another's job in an air supply unit during the advances of Wingate's second campaign. In the Indian army he was a sergeant (returning a captain), like historian Guy Perron of the fourth novel of *The Raj Quartet*. He knew nothing of India before his arrival in 1943. Like District Commissioner Robin White in *The Jewel in the Crown*, he became physically sick; and like Daphne Manners and Hari Kumar in the same novel, he was also homesick for England. But in the three years he was there, his "dislike" turned to "fascination" (IPF 116), and Christmas of 1945 found him pulling strings in Singapore to avoid a posting that would have taken him out of India to Malaya. Scott could not get enough of India, and the lengthy correspondence with his Bombay hostess, Dorothy Ganapathy, makes this clear; the country was "not so much a political territory abandoned as a continuing province of the heart."[20] He kept no journals, but his prodigious memory enabled him later in his novels to present British India of the 1940s in minute, realistic detail.

In 1941, while stationed at Torquay, Paul Scott had met and married Nancy Edith Avery (b. 1913), a nurse. Like his guilt-racked novelist Edward Thornhill in *The Corrida at San Feliu*, he had proposed to his wife, known as Penny, while she was engaged to someone else. As his mother had, Penny adored him and believed in his great talent. She worked and waited in England during the three and one-half years Paul was in India and Malaya. They had two children, Carol Vivien in 1947 and Sally Elisabeth in 1948. In their life together, Penny shouldered the family responsibilities while Paul took care of the financial arrangements, doling out housekeeping money and, as his father had, spending most of his time engaged in his work. Although there were communication problems (Paul was silent much of the time, as his father had been with his mother), they loved each other, and Penny, who was never sure which side of him she would see, both worshipped him and feared the part of him that was like his mother.[21]

When Scott returned home from the war in 1946, he was a somewhat cynical, brooding, and reflective man, his youthful fervor gone.[22] He resumed his accountancy studies and became a bookkeeper and then eventually company secretary[23] to Falcon and Grey

Walls Press in Crown Passage. Here, also in 1946, he met Roland Gant, who was then working in the publicity section. (They both wanted to work in the editorial section.) Gant, with whom he shared a hilarious sense of fun,[24] would later become his closest friend as well as his publisher, first at Secker and Warburg and then at William Heinemann.

Falcon and Grey Walls Press was run by Captain Peter Baker, who had published some of Scott's poetry in wartime broadsheets. In 1950, when it was clear that Baker's fiscal irresponsibilities were endangering the firm (Baker was later imprisoned for forgery and fraud),[25] Scott resigned, abandoning accountancy to become an eventual director and partner of a firm of literary agents. When Pearn, Pollinger and Higham split, Scott remained with David Higham Associates. Roland Gant writes that Paul Scott established an excellent reputation during the ten years he spent as a literary agent, as he was able to offer his clients artistic as well as placement advice. One of his clients was novelist and friend Muriel Spark; another was John Braine, whose best-selling *Room at the Top* Scott placed;[26] a third was Molly Miranda Kaye, the wife of a general in the Indian army and the grand-great-grand-niece of the official historian of the Sepoy Mutiny.[27] Kaye deeply admired his work and would later write *The Far Pavilions*, a romantic bestseller with an Indian setting, for which he was the publisher's reader.

Scott's correspondence shows his wonderfully detailed artistic suggestions for people for whom he acted as literary agent and, later, in a purely friendly capacity. Roland Gant writes that while Paul Scott was a literary agent "we had what we called the most incestuous literary relationship in London. Paul was agent for my novels, he was agent for my wife Nadia Legrand (also a novelist), and he placed novels by his wife, who wrote as Elizabeth Avery, with Michael Joseph, of which house I was editorial director at the time. Only one thing remained to round off this family circle. One day I must publish Paul Scott."[28] The friendship lasted more than thirty years, until Scott's death in 1978.

While Scott was at Falcon and Grey Walls Press he was writing plays for the stage which remained unperformed until he wrote on an Eastern theme in 1950. During that year he left his accounting position to become a literary agent for Pearn, Pollinger and Higham, and his first radio play, *Lines of Communication*, was accepted for production by the BBC. The novel was for him, however, "the most exacting form of literary composition there is." The first novel he completed, *The Gradual Day*, retitled *The Dazzling Crystal* (both titles based on quotations from Stephen Spender, whose poetry he loved so well), had been rejected for publication seventeen times, and he eventually destroyed it. But Eyre and Spottiswoode, on the basis of that novel, indicated an interest in his future work and published *Johnnie Sahib*, a novel that expanded *Lines of Communication*. The BBC then commissioned a television version to coincide with the publication of the novel. *Johnnie Sahib*, which was initially not published in the United States and which was out of print six months after its 1952 publication, nonetheless won Eyre and Spottiswoode's Literary Fellowship Award, a prize that embarrassed Scott in his new role as literary agent.

During the time Scott worked in this capacity, he wrote for publication by Eyre and Spottiswoode four additional novels: *The Alien Sky* (1953), also adapted by Scott for radio and television and published by Doubleday in the United States as *Six Days in Marapore; A Male Child* (1956), published in the United States by E. P. Dutton; *The Mark of the Warrior* (1958); and *The Chinese Love Pavilion* (1960), published in the United States as *The Love Pavilion*.[29] Associated Rediffusion performed a television version, and the BBC a radio version of *The Mark of the Warrior*. And with this novel William Morrow became Scott's U.S. publisher. Morrow generally published Scott's novels two to four months after their London appearance, enough time to gain the benefit of the British reviews.

Scott was always experimenting with form and content and generally considered any novel in progress more difficult than its predecessor. *The Chinese Love Pavilion* had taken him nearly three years to write; sensing that he might lose ground, he decided, at the age of forty, to become a full-time writer. It was a risk, both for him and for his publishers. In England one or more of the books had managed to sell about five thousand copies, and in the United States none of the hardbacks had even met costs.[30] However, sales of *The Chinese Love Pavilion* were promising: fifteen thousand over two years in England, plus a lucrative New American Library paperback sale in the United States.[31] To his desire to write, Scott sacrificed his financial security and his ten-year career as a successful literary agent, along with the likelihood of his becoming senior partner and editorial director (WS 207).[32] On April 1, 1960, backed by a three-year guarantee from William Morrow of eighteen hundred pounds per annum against all income from writing and free-lance editorial work, Scott, with his wife's encouragement, resigned his position and directorship at David Higham Associates to devote himself full time to his writing.

After his next novel, *The Birds of Paradise*, was published in 1962 by Eyre and Spottiswoode,[33] Scott left that publisher for Secker and

Warburg (a member of the Heinemann group), where Roland Gant had gone with Charles Pick after resigning his editorial directorship at Michael Joseph. *The Bender* was published in 1963,[34] *The Corrida at San Feliu* in 1964, and neither book sold well. (The latter had sold fewer than five thousand copies by the end of the year.) The fact that Scott had no full-time job aside from his writing may have contributed to the sense of burnout that progressively deepens in these novels.

Scott was by this time a serious alcoholic, stemming from the shock of his unfortunate army experience at Torquay. But he held his liquor so well that many people were unaware of the problem. He would drink around the clock to "releas[e] and subdu[e] the unruly warring selves whose conflict would in the end deepen and enrich his most most ambitious work."[35] He needed drink to release the bold, decisive side of himself.[36] Alcohol could release wit and charm but also an intense self-loathing, which once led to his slashing his own army portrait and raging around on all fours, much as Sutton does at the end of *The Chinese Love Pavilion*.[37]

The correspondence demonstrates that Scott and his publishers, editors, agents, and friends were always waiting for the breakthrough, for the recognition of a major talent and the financial rewards that would follow. Gant suggests that Scott's avoidance of London literary cliques was a reason for the belatedness of his recognition.[38] However, Scott was elected a fellow of the Royal Society of Literature in 1963 and presented a lecture in 1968, which was entitled "India: A Post-Forsterian View"; it was later collected in the Royal Society of Literature publication *Essays by Divers Hands*. He also received an Arts Council Grant of one thousand pounds in 1969.

In early 1964 Secker and Warburg funded a six-week trip to India for Scott, the object of which was "either to recharge the batteries of his interest in a country that he'd often written about, or prove to him, and to his publishers, that he had nothing more to say about it."[39] Through their distributors in India, Allied Publishers, Heinemann arranged for Scott to stay with middle-class Indian families. He became close friends with some of the people with whom he stayed, most notably with Dorothy Ganapathy, to whom Scott later dedicated *The Jewel in the Crown*. Ganapathy was the widow of an Indian civil servant and daughter of Sir Hary Singh Gour, the Edinburgh- and Cambridge-educated founder of Saugor University.[40] Critical to Scott's creation of his masterpiece was his survival of a primitive Indian village experience after experiencing her strong, supportive personality.

On Scott's returning home to England, Roland Gant took him to

Paris to be treated for an illness that was diagnosed as an amoebiasis that had been first contracted twenty years earlier.[41] The symptoms, shared by Ian Canning in *A Male Child*, were lethargy, indifference, stomach problems, a low-grade fever, and depression.[42] The depressed tone of the pre-*Quartet* novels may well have been influenced by the disease, and Roland Gant suggests a connection between Scott's amoebiasis and the "eroded will" and "stop-and-start methods" of Scott's novelist, Edward Thornhill, in *The Corrida at San Feliu*.[43] But with the amoebiasis treated and feeling revitalized by his visit to India, he began work on what would become the first novel of *The Raj Quartet*, *The Jewel in the Crown*. The novel was published in mid-1966 by William Heinemann, where Gant had become editorial director. It was, Gant rightly predicted, "the definitive novel, beyond Forster, of the British-Indian relationship."[44]

After the publication of *The Day of the Scorpion* in 1968, Scott returned to India in early 1969, funded in large part by five hundred pounds from Heinemann, to research the Indian National Army trials in the Red Fort in Delhi and again in early 1972, on a postponed British Council speaking tour celebrating National Book Year (1971) at Indian universities in Bombay, Poona, Baroda, Ahmedabad, Jaipur, New Delhi, Calcutta, Madras, Bangalore, Calicut, and Dharwar.[45] *The Towers of Silence*, which won the Yorkshire Post Fiction Award, was published in 1971; *A Division of the Spoils*, the concluding volume of *The Raj Quartet*, in 1975; and an afterthought, *Staying On*, in 1976.

A month or two before the publication of *The Jewel in the Crown*, Heinemann negotiated for the rights of all eight previous novels to bring out a special Collected Edition over the next two years. There was an advance of seventy-five hundred pounds as well from Mayflower/Granada Books for a complete paperback edition. Both series were advertised together in *The Bookseller* at Scott's suggestion—to his surprise and delight, since he thought his friend Gant had dropped the idea. Small wonder that Scott, with the help of Dorothy Ganapathy, had picked as his literary colophon Ganesha, "the fat little elephant with four hands and two feet . . . who clears away difficulties . . . if you invoke him."[46]

He had high hopes for the reception of *The Jewel in the Crown* and, despite the fact that plans for a U.S. paperback edition fell through, was encouraged by "rave" reviews on both sides of the Atlantic. The initial New York printing of ten thousand copies sold out and met costs within six weeks of its July 1966 publication.[47] Its successor, *The Day of the Scorpion*, was selected by the Literary Book Club, and on September 18, 1969, Scott wrote to Ivan von Auw, director of Harold Ober Associates, that the novel was holding its own in England "as the third most bought novel in the so-called charts of best sellers." It also met costs in New York within six weeks of publication despite the fact that, as a sequel in the United States, it went virtually unreviewed. Yet sales in London and New York were not spectacular.[48]

Scott was in financial difficulty for many of his most creative years. During the writing of the first three novels of *The Raj Quartet*, he had a guaranteed advance of two thousand pounds per annum from Heinemann, paid quarterly, plus two thousand dollars from Morrow, paid semiannually at his request. In addition, sales of his translations, readings for publishers, reviews, and occasionally lectures to writers' groups brought in extra money.[49] There was, necessarily, a time lag, as Scott felt he needed eighteen months to write a novel. Although Heinemann had inherited, in his estimate, a dismal financial picture from Secker and Warburg because of poor sales of *The Bender* and *The Corrida of San Feliu*, finances were not so much a problem during the writing of the first two novels of *The Raj Quartet*. Scott did not have large advances to pay back from earlier years when he was earning his living as a literary agent; additionally, he could count on twenty-four hundred pounds in Eyre and Spottiswoode credits and occasional paperback rights.

However, the writing of the novels progressed more slowly than he would have wished or could afford, the last two novels of the *Quartet* taking three years each to complete (at least double the time of the first two) and selling fewer copies.[50] Scott often underestimated the time needed to complete a novel. In a September 29, 1965, letter to David Higham, after a summer delivery of the completed manuscript of *The Jewel in the Crown*, Scott estimated that he would have three novels completed by the end of December 1969 (at the time he envisioned a trilogy). In fact, it was 1974 before he turned in the manuscript for *A Division of the Spoils*. Delays were caused by the increasing length and complexity of the novels, the detailed reading he had to do to achieve the amazing historical verisimilitude he was attempting, his increased reviewing responsibilities, and the severe depression and suicide attempts of his younger daughter during his work on the last two novels.

Yet some of the financial stress was self-imposed. Although his publishers would have given him as an advance however much money he needed, he chose to live within the strict limits of his earnings and paid back everything before he died.[51] He took an accountant's pleasure in calculating his earnings in a double-entried ledger, stretching his advances over as long a period of time as possible in order to enable him to write the kind of books he wanted to write. He tried as much as he could to keep deliveries of the novels to his publishers ahead of their quarterly or semiannual payments to him. This became increasingly difficult during the writing of *The Raj Quartet* over a ten-year span.

By 1972 Scott became so discouraged about his financial situation that he seriously considered once again returning to publishing on the editorial side, either as a chief editor or again as an agent, a move that he knew at the age of fifty-two would be very difficult to accomplish. In a sad letter to the managing director of Heinemann, he wrote, "For the first time since leaving Higham in 1960 I am becoming a red-figure author, in the true and substantial sense. This is not the atmosphere in which I find it easy, or even possible, to work. I had always hoped, naturally, that *The Raj Quartet* would establish things satisfactorily to enable me to continue entirely as a writer. This may eventually happen, but the sequence represents . . . the best I can do, and that best is, professionally, obviously not good enough."[52] Although Heinemann adjusted his advance accordingly, he was not freed from the need to take out occasional end-of-quarter advances against his advances. As late as February 1976, six months after the New York publication of *A Division of the Spoils*, he wrote to Gant, "Although not in debt, I'm about to be broke."[53]

Scott was energized by his September 1975 visit to American universities, coinciding with the August publication of *A Division of the Spoils*. There was as yet no interest in him in British academic circles, and he spoke jestingly in his correspondence of emigrating to the United States. His visit to the University of Illinois in September 1975 was part of a tour of several campuses that included the University of Texas at Austin, Montgomery College in Washington, D.C., and the University of Maryland. The trip to Illinois led to his becoming Writer-in-Residence at the University of Tulsa during the fall semester of 1976 (he returned for the fall of 1977). Scott was paid twelve thousand dollars for the semester, a sum that seemed generous, even after expenses, to a writer trying to eke out a living on an annual amount not equal to half that. Yet there was probably a factor other than finances in Scott's decision to teach at the University of Tulsa. Thomas Staley, then a dean at the university, writes of his impression, "through his polite reserve and quiet formality, that [Scott] wanted the position very much. His decision seemed settled before we met. . . . I knew it wasn't simply the prospects of a new challenge."[54] It must have seemed an ironic fulfillment to Paul Scott to have achieved academic recognition and a faculty position after being denied a university education.

At Tulsa, Scott made a lasting impression on his students, who in 1988 published a short collection of their memories of him, *After Paul: Paul Scott's Tulsa Years.* The literature course he taught was entitled "The Exotic Heresy and the Insular Tradition." He considered himself a part of this exotic heresy, very conscious as a novelist that he required "a broad canvas, an exotic milieu."[55] The stay at Tulsa represented the beginning of a reversal in his financial affairs. He won the five-thousand-pound Booker Prize for fiction in the fall of 1977 for *Staying On,* and the end of 1977 saw the sale of *The Raj Quartet* and *Staying On* to Avon for paperback publication. (All of his books were in paperback in the United States by 1984.) Also at this time Heinemann and Morrow jointly published the four novels of the *Quartet* in one omnibus edition.[56] But by this time Scott was terminally ill.

In the early fall of 1977, after exploratory surgery, he discovered that he had cirrhosis of the liver and colon cancer. The cirrhosis could probably have been cured, in his doctor's view, but the cancer had metasticized. His elder daughter, Carol, went to Tulsa to nurse him after his surgery and back in London in November accepted the Booker Prize on his behalf.[57] He found it ironic that he won the award not for his masterpiece but for a comic, sad afterthought, *Staying On.*[58] Although anxious to get back to England and his wife, who he hoped would be waiting for him and who returned to nurse him after a seventeen-month separation, Scott would not leave Tulsa until he had discharged his responsibility; he waited until the end of the semester. Not two and one-half months later, on March 1, he died at Middlesex Hospital in London. He was not yet fifty-eight years of age.

2. The Early Novels

Johnnie Sahib

Paul Scott's first published novel, *Johnnie Sahib* (1952), is a character study of a charismatic officer, Captain Johnnie Brown, in charge of one of Wingate's air supply units in Burma, and Jim Taylor, his conscientious second-in-command, who has difficulty replacing him first when Johnnie is on leave and later when he loses his job because of insubordination. The five parts of the novel, Comitarla, Prulli, Tamel, Pyongui, and Mandalay, correspond to stages in the advance of British and American troops south through Burma during World War II.[1] In the highly autonomous unit, Johnnie has been given free rein to direct his men as he wishes by a character we know only as "the Major." It is symptomatic of the egotism that brings him such good results that Johnny believes—with reason—that the men are working not so much for the war effort as for him. "My way's the only way," he says. "The war for them begins and ends in what Captain Brown does, what he says and how he says it" (102). Johnnie enjoys breaking the rules as well as developing a cult of personality. He gets into difficulty when the small, highly individualized unit is inevitably expanded and depersonalized, put under the command of an administrative arm, RAMO (Rear Airfield Maintenance Operation), which is ignorant of air supply procedures.

His resentment first takes the form of refusing to do the increased paperwork, something for which his second-in-command can cover. But Jim can do nothing when, for the second time, Johnnie refuses to obey an order to wake his men in the middle of the night to reload a plane. Annoyed that his unit was not apprized of the malfunctioning plane hours earlier, Johnnie gambles on the probability of its replacement not departing until morning, and loses. When Johnnie is dismissed, Jim reluctantly takes over Three Section. The men were devoted to Johnnie, but they do not care for Jim, a man who must

fight the tendency to let himself be "run around." Jim's strong principles will not allow his unit to falsify their loading figures when
their performance is less than adequate. Consequently, the men are
reprimanded with the coolie job on the ammo dump and the Major's
supervision.

Jim Taylor is the first of many Scott characters who are conscientious, yet suffer from a sense of emptiness and seek love: " 'If there is
nothing, then there is room for love.' . . . There was the emptiness of
Marapore, the emptiness of all India, the emptiness that he had
sought to escape and had succeeded in recreating" (192). At one
point he feels "his will destroyed by the impact of the timelessness
of time" (97). Jim finds in work a creative responsibility to counter
these feelings; we see this when he thinks, as Johnnie goes off on
leave, "It's a new beginning; it's the end of stagnation and futility"
(45). At the same time that Jim needs to carve out his own identity
as a commander, he feels revitalized by Johnnie, probably because of
his warmth and boldness in doing what he wants to do rather than
what he thinks he should do.

Whereas the men loved Johnnie because he had "spoke[n] and
acted from the heart," they think of Jim as "formal," "correct," and
"cold" (92). Though he admires Johnnie, Jim feels that he is living in
his shadow. The situation is exacerbated when two of the men are
killed in a plane crash. Jim blames himself because he had forced
one of them to fly because "it seemed a way of beating [Johnnie's]
ghost" (198). He is on the point of requesting a transfer when he encounters Johnnie's former Anglo-Burman girlfriend. Nina says that
although Johnnie loved her while she was there, he lost interest in
her when they were separated by her posting orders. In the same
way, losing his unit and the men who were so devoted to him has not
been the total disaster for Johnnie that people expected; he is happy
doing something entirely different from working in air supply, and
his love for his former unit has somehow become entirely unselfish.
The ghost is exorcized. As Johnnie had helped dispel Jim's sense of
emptiness, Nina relieves his sense of guilt at taking over Johnnie's
unit. Jim decides to stay on as captain of Johnnie's men, who can
now become his own.

Scott's ability to re-create the setting and explore the psychology
and relationships of his characters is apparent from this first published novel, which is very strong in portraying the nature of Johnnie's charisma and intuitive command of his men and in recapturing
the sticky and uncomfortable nature of the backwater places in
which the men are stationed. The novel is not successful, however,
despite its winning the 1951 Eyre and Spottiswoode Literary Fellow-

ship Award. (In later years, Scott called it "bloody awful."²) That is because Scott had not entirely decided what he wanted to say. Consequently, Johnnie appears both admirable and irresponsible in resisting RAMO and seems not so much to love unselfishly, as Nina believes, as to possess shallow feelings. It is not clear whether Johnnie is an immature egotist whose actions are dictated by a fit of pique at imposed authority, a man who "take[s] all; give[s] nothing, who had been "selfish, arrogant, childish and bitter" (166), or rather a person who is willing to sacrifice his career for his principles and what he believes to be the interests of his men. ("He resisted things changing and losing whatever it is that makes men believe in them" [173].) The reader constantly wonders which is the real Johnnie.

Nonetheless, *Johnnie Sahib* is interesting as a thematic and technical precursor of the later novels. It reflects Scott's sense of love and work³ as central to human identity ("This is what makes us stick together. Work. Without it we could be lost" [59]). All of Scott's novels are quest novels—for meaningful purpose that in the early and middle books remains largely elusive. His people are seen in the context of the work they perform—how this work impacts upon their characters and sensibilities, sometimes forcing unpleasant moral choices upon them. Many of his protagonists, MacKendrick, Conway, Canning, their work inadequate to their desire for self-actualization, suffer from a lack of purpose and a sense of loss in human relationships. In Scott's own words, his characters "invariably move from one disenchantment to another. The people they love and the work they do inspire them, certainly, but almost inevitably betray them too."⁴

Johnnie Sahib is also Scott's first exploration of the behavior of and consequences for a man who crosses an established role boundary. Captain Johnnie Brown is the first indication of Scott's interest in the unconventional embodying the loving. But whereas we seldom have anything but admiration for characters in *The Raj Quartet* who abandon their roles to transcend, for example, the community separation of English and Indian or of Hindu and Muslim, it is difficult to make up our minds about individualistic Johnnie. Some of the ambivalence we feel about him is due to the necessity in a military situation for role to dominate over personality, as it does in the case of the Major, a man so taken up by his role that he no longer feels a sense of personal identity. This problem was to be further and more successfully explored in Scott's fourth novel, *The Mark of the Warrior*.

Again, the themes that Scott would develop with such success in *The Raj Quartet* and *Staying On* are present in *Johnnie Sahib*. The man or woman who chooses to risk everything rather than compromise principles, to break rather than bend, is here present in the Major's view that Johnnie had perhaps "seen and understood how he could have saved himself [but] for some reason, emotional perhaps, refrained from saving himself or letting others save him" (173).

There is already an interest in people being misplaced by change, a sense of "mediocrity" rather than ability "scor[ing]" (170), and a sense of the organization (RAMO here rather than the Raj) running away with things. Additionally, there are insurmountable communication problems as Moti Ram and Johnnie stare at each other "across the gulf of time and change, which they were powerless to bridge" (144). The theme of love unexpressed until too late, a choric refrain of *The Raj Quartet,* is here demonstrated in terms of the feelings of the Indian soldiers for Johnnie: "the tears could fall unseen as they had not fallen since the day Johnnie Sahib had gone and it had been too late to say those things, too late to breathe warmth into the cold words that were said when they faced each other in the darkness . . . for the last time unknowingly" (160).

The beginnings of Scott's concern with race and class are present as well, although they do not figure significantly in the plot. Johnnie has a Cockney accent and comes from a lower-class background, and his girlfriend, Nina, and the soldier Johns, who pathetically pretends to a childhood in Buckinghamshire but is treated kindly by the men, are Scott's first characters of mixed racial background. Unquestionably Scott was interested in those of mixed race, and his heroes are often involved in a romantic relationship with them: Johnnie and Nina; Joe MacKendrick and Dorothy Gower in *The Alien Sky;* Tom Brent in his brief, immature fling with the "dusky Eurasian girl" (26) and more seriously with Teena Chang in *The Chinese Love Pavilion;* George Spruce in his attraction to his brother's Anglo-Indian girlfriend, Anina, in *The Bender;* and Edward Thornhill's character, Bruce Craddock, whose first marriage was to a sheltered Eurasian girl who committed suicide after she discovered the world's cruelty to those of mixed race. As we shall see, Scott was intrigued not only by those of mixed race but others who found themselves caught between two worlds—Hari Kumar (of mixed cultural identity) in *The Raj Quartet* or Tusker Smalley in *Staying On.* Johnnie Brown's difficulty is the first instance of this kind of problem: before RAMO his willful, individualistic style is manageable, even desirable; after RAMO there is no place for him in the company.

Scott's circular sense of structure, so evident in *The Raj Quartet,* is present in his first novel. The book opens with the departure of Nina and the visit by Lieutenant-Colonel Baxter from Calcutta, preliminary to expanding the air supply unit and putting an administra-

tive arm over it. Both reappear at the end of the novel. Like Brian
Saxby in *The Chinese Love Pavilion* and Hari Kumar in *The Raj
Quartet,* Johnnie disappears from our direct view well before the end
of the novel. What we know of him is largely from other people's
views, another Scott technique that, further developed in later novels, would overcome the ambivalence of this early portrait and succeed in giving the reader a clear view of the character portrayed.

There is a crisis in all Paul Scott novels, and *Johnnie Sahib* has a
physical disaster, the first of a number of deaths by fire in Scott's
fiction. A plane crashes and we see emerging from it "a burning
cross," "a moving pillar of flame" (191), "the image of a man cru-
cified, consumed by fire" (193). The disaster comes, typically in a
Scott novel, just as a character is on the verge of accomplishing
something positive—here Jim is freeing himself from Johnnie's
ghost by forcing Jan Mohammed to go with the airsick Ghosh on the
plane, deliberately taking away the privilege of not flying that Johnnie had given him. ("You can't touch me any more, Johnnie. You
can't interefere" [191], he thinks immediately before the crash.) But
the later novels would better juxtapose the physical disaster with the
psychological crisis; later Scott might have juxtaposed the deaths by
fire with Johnnie's refusal to follow orders and the consequent loss
of his position, ending in a sense of the tragic and some kind of death
or diminution for him. Here, however, the crash is little more than a
plot device that revives Jim's sense of emptiness and Johnnie's ghost
before Nina finally dispels them. Scott had yet to learn to extract
full dramatic and psychological significance from episodes of natural or manmade disasters, a technique that he would use brilliantly
in *The Raj Quartet* with repetitive, emotionally charged scenes
drawn in tableaux.

The Alien Sky

The Alien Sky (1953) is a novel about a man's search for his deeper
self which he hopes to find in India but is somehow incapable of
grasping. For this subject the Eyre and Spottiswoode title, with its
suggestion of remoteness and of the unconscious, seems more appropriate than its Doubleday counterpart, *Six Days in Marapore.*

Joe MacKendrick, an American businessman, has come to Smith's
Hotel and the Marapore cantonment in June of 1947, just before independence, ostensibly to check up on the Bombay and Calcutta
branches of his father's agricultural machinery business. Actually,
he has come, for reasons which are at first obscure, to find his dead
brother's rejected mistress, Dorothy Gower, having become ob-

sessed with her photograph and love letters to his bullying brother, Dwight, recently killed in the war. Dorothy is married to Tom Gower, editor of the *Marapore Gazette,* owner of a model farm at Ooni, and a vulnerable, vindictive idealist of poor political judgment. After writing abstractly in an editorial, "Let us embrace the fact of Pakistan" (84), Gower is humiliated on a public platform by Vidyasagar, a Laxminarayan College Hindu student radical to whom he is about to present a sports award. To add to his difficulties, his wife (whom he adores) tells him she hates him more than any man she knows and will not go to England with him if he decides to return (90).

MacKendrick, meanwhile, disappointed to find Dorothy cold and distant, is about to leave Marapore when he learns from the Eurasian girl Judith Anderson, cruelly baited at a party for her mixed blood and her British pretense, that Dorothy's mother was Eurasian. This knowledge, which explains why Dwight had left her, has an electrifying effect on him; Dorothy, he feels, shares his sense of being an outsider, and he suggests in an intimate conversation that they go away together.

Meanwhile, there is a strike at the model farm, which the youthful manager, John Steele, stops by intimidating its leader, Dass. Afterward Dass is beaten up by Hindu radicals, implicating Steele. The workers leave the farm, which is then burned down by students from Laxminarayan College. MacKendrick's servant, Bholu, who has used Dorothy's secret from her husband to blackmail her (he thinks mistakenly that she had a prior relationship with his master; she thinks he has found out she is part Indian), is shot and killed by Steele, who believes he is at the head of the rioters who are about to attack him. So terrified is Dorothy of having her secret discovered that she and MacKendrick, who is lacking in moral courage and always "fearful that a false move of his would leave him stranded with his own inadequacy" (190), persuade Steele against his better judgment to return her money and picture. If these items had been found on Bholu's body, the servant would probably have been incriminated, providing a defense for Steele in the Indian mind. Gower then suggests an inquest by the district magistrate to clear Steele's name. As he is going into the inquest, Steele is murdered in a vengeful act by Vidyasagar, who later in prison smugly tells the visiting Gower that the British will leave India before they can hang him.

Unable to think of another reason for his wife's behavior, Gower had concluded that Steele was her lover. Gower's consequent aggressive, irrational behavior toward him contributes to the circumstances under which Steele kills Bholu and is himself slain. When

Dorothy tells Gower that she may go away with Joe, Gower realizes his mistake, confronts MacKendrick, and then tries to kill himself by slashing his wrists when she leaves. Although he has courted Dorothy, Joe has mixed feelings about her decision to come away with him. He is afraid of the relationship (201) and, learning of Gower's suicide attempt, appalled at her indifference to his despair. Additionally, and despite his conscious intentions, the man who thinks of Steele's unborn mixed racial offspring as an "obscene . . . growth, a canker" (187) cannot help feeling a certain uneasiness about her race (204). Joe's attempt at lovemaking with Dorothy ends in his impotence and her contempt, and she decides to return to her husband. As the novel concludes, MacKendrick leaves India, presumably to return to the shallow life he despises (153).

The questions that must be asked in an analysis of this novel center on why MacKendrick has come to India. For what is he searching? What does he hope to find in Dorothy Gower? Why has he cuckolded Tom Gower in his heart before he has even met Dorothy?

MacKendrick is in many ways a closed, unappealing character, like Gower, an ineffectual loser and one who, like Jim Taylor in *Johnnie Sahib*, suffers from a sense of emptiness and must counter his own tendency to "get put upon" (JS 56) or be "pushed around" (AS 130). He is looking for kindness ("Somewhere in the world, then, there was gentleness" [52]) but wants to incorporate some aspect of the identity of the brother who had treated him with such cruelty during their formative years. In a revealing passage, he sees goodness as weakness: "We'd all be like Dwight if we knew how, but because we don't we cook up a lot of hooey about truth and honour and decency and fair play when all the time the only thing that adds up is our own goddam selfishness" (79). This statement, a variation of which is developed at great length by Scott's fictional writer Edward Thornhill in the 1964 novel *The Corrida at San Feliu*, is indicative of a character who, like Thornhill, does not understand himself.

In Dorothy, another of Dwight's victims, he sees a potential secret sharer. Although she is contemptuous and indifferent, MacKendrick is enormously moved when he discovers her secret, the source of her defensiveness: "The barriers collapsed and she was naked before him, so that her wounds, her scars were close enough to touch, to heal. All her pride and fear were there for his eyes to see, his heart to respond to. And out of his response would surely come hers?" (114). He too has been psychologically wounded, not only by a sadistic brother but by a mother of frightening silence and "vicious controlled anger" (25). His unconscious need for these eyes of contempt, under which his real self lay buried,⁵ is an important component of his attraction to Dorothy Gower.

It is not perhaps the cruel and ruthlessly self-interested side of Dwight that MacKendrick finds appealing so much as the independent, masterful side that would never have let himself be "run around." MacKendrick appears to be confused, therefore, between aggression and assertion. Where Dwight was in control, MacKendrick appears easily enraged and humiliated. Where Dwight was sexually unrepressed, Joe appears to suffer from a severe mind-body dualism; his flirtations (with Cynthia Mapleton, who finds him attractive) are only for show, and he is "repelled by the physical hunger" he awakens in Dorothy. Consequently he becomes embarrassingly impotent at the end of the novel because "the fever had been in his mind, not in his blood"— "he gripped her shoulders and pressed his mouth on to hers, not in physical passion but in a desperate attempt to show he was not afraid of her or of himself, to show that he could make a decision, take control, smash down opposition" (205).

In some ways the relationship between Joe and Dwight MacKendrick is duplicated in the relationship of Tom Gower, owner of the model farm at Ooni, and its youthful manager, John Steele. Both Joe MacKendrick and Gower (who has an excellent relation with his servant) bear, as MacKendrick realizes, "the smell, the taint of defeat" (73), both embodying perhaps the perception that love, though desired, is the value of weakness. In contrast, Steele is, as was Dwight MacKendrick, a self-assured man of action, in control of himself and the situation at hand. And toward these latter two also, Scott is ambivalent. Dwight was masterful yet cruel; Steele has physical courage, and his relation with a young Indian girl and eventual victimization make him a forerunner of the later tragic figures. Yet there is a suggestion that he is devoid of love, having been deprived of it in his childhood (191). He is also a predecessor of the trigger-happy characters of some of the later novels.

The characters, then, are polarized; the weaker, more thoughtful ones envy and hate the stronger, whom they are unable to emulate. MacKendrick's wish to be free of the inhibition of aggressive, independent impulses, then, reflects a desire for an unrepressed self. That he is searching for himself is made clear immediately after he discovers Dorothy's secret:

He walked across the level crossing into the town. He saw nothing that registered on his mind, but he was grateful for the strident music which came from the shops, still open and bright and evil-smelling and vicious and pitiless. Sometimes faces were pushed close up to his own and hands grabbed at his clothes and there was laughter, bitter and merciless laughter and voices which derided and begged and scolded and threatened and pleaded so that it seemed a whole world to which he was forbidden entry revolved before him like a shining fairground wheel: and *somewhere in the centre of the wheel was understanding and love. Somewhere in the street there was himself to be found.* Was it there, beneath the gaunt breast of the beggar with twisted limbs and feverish eyes? Or there, smug and smooth like the folds of the white dhoti of the man cross-legged upon a wooden charpoy set under a tree; or there, in the eyes of the little naked boy who ran by his side and begged for dimes or food or offered women? Or here . . .

MacKendrick stopped, dazedly, in the middle of the tumultuous road: A Brahmini bull, its eyes like liquid fire as it gazed at the open, brightly lit shop, barred his progress. Slowly it moved away. He looked at the shop. Naphtha lamps purred and beneath their light an old man squatted and slowly wrote what another man dictated. As though mesmerized the younger man gradually turned his head until his eyes met MacKendrick's.

It was Bholu.

For a few moments they looked at one another, and then MacKendrick turned back and went along the way he had come. It couldn't have been Bholu, he thought. Bholu is not here. The road back was strangely deserted. He passed along it like a man watched from windows, from behind doors. Not here—the voices shouted. Not now—the music sang. (112–113; italics mine)

There seems to be something about the atmosphere of India, with its "evil-smelling shops" and "strident music," its aggressive beggars with "twisted limbs and feverish eyes," its dung nuzzled by starving pariah dogs, that brings MacKendrick closer to his core. India has an effect on him similar to what Dorothy feels about men and women working in the fields: "There are times when I look at India and know, it's inside me as it was in my mother, and her mother, and her mother's mother. Failing a different sort of love, there's always that sort to be looked for and found" (152).

In India MacKendrick senses the possibilities of a more unrepressed self. The freedom he seeks is equated with a life with Dorothy, and at the same time that he yearns for it, he fears its emptiness: "Was this how it would always be? Himself and Dorothy cut off from the living, dining always in lonely rooms, in empty rooms, in rooms held together by nothing but hope and memory; was this, indeed, drifting? Was this the reality, the cold and unforgiving reality behind a dream of freedom? Get back! a voice cried. Get back! There's comfort in bondage" (202). The desire for flight from and a return to

bondage can be seen in psychoanalytical terms as flight from and return to a symbolic mother. There is emptiness without the mother,
emptiness because MacKendrick lacks the sense of independence
needed for a mature relationship with another human being. Clearly,
he never internalized in childhood the stable image of a loving
mother, and this handicap affects his relationships with other
people, whom he keeps at a somewhat unreal distance.

The passages quoted above demonstrate the curious dynamic of
reality and illusion that marks a Scott novel. The first instance of it
is when MacKendrick, seeing the discovery of himself in mystical
terms, encounters his ordinary world in the form of Bholu (who has
undoubtedly gone to the bazaar to get a scribe to write the blackmail
letter) and does not believe that he has seen him. The juxtaposition
of the startlingly real with elements of the mystical is another technique Scott would perfect in *The Raj Quartet*. In the latter instance,
MacKendrick appears afraid to fall out of the dream into reality because he fears that reality would be disillusioning. The dream in
which he lives is one where images take the place of reality, where
he can fall in love with Dorothy's photograph without ever having
met her. That he lives in a defensive cocoon of images which he substitutes for actual relationships is evident when he must tell himself
on first meeting Dorothy: "You aren't dealing with images but with
people who exist outside you and in spite of you. You may know the
image backwards but you don't know what's behind it or within it.
You don't know [Dorothy] in the way you knew Dwight. You've set
an image against a man and you've judged" (65).

In the end MacKendrick remains in that world of shadows rather
than take the plunge into reality, which India represents. In a tone
that effectively echoes the ending of the lengthy passage quoted
above, the novel describes his thoughts as his departing train moves
out of the station:

> He heard doors banging and the bell and the mournful call of the boy
> selling tea, and over it all the fierce music from the bazaar.
> Now it was going. Oh, hold it, his heart cried, oh, enter it: dig deeply
> with the hands into it and raise out of it all the love and pity and com-
> passion the music sings of. But now it is going. The light in the sky is
> going. The singing is fading. And the train is moving into the plain
> where night holds and the deep silence is broken only by the muffled
> drumming of the wheels and the distant cry of the jackals. (208)

In that final paragraph India is again a symbol of an opportunity
for a richer life that MacKendrick remains incapable of grasping. At
the end of the novel he is left with the dream which he has failed

to grasp and make real. The problem with the novel is that a richer life is also identified with Dorothy, who, though passionate, is in so much psychological pain that she is totally self-involved; contemptuously indifferent to the fates of others, she is indirectly responsible for the suicide attempt of her husband and for the death of Steele. The use of Dorothy as a standard—that is, someone who can offer a life of meaning—does not work very well. Her hostility and underlying aggressiveness make her a poor symbol of what should be attained, of an India which still calls to MacKendrick when he leaves. The failure in the relationship appears to have been his failure, his psychic and physical impotence, but it may have been impossible for anyone who was not brutal and domineering to have a decent relationship with Dorothy Gower.

Scott had not yet found his voice. Although Gower loses his promised position with the maharajah of Kalipur because of difficulties in the Princely States, what Scott wants to say in this first study of the British-Indian relationship is not altogether clear to him. He had not yet had a chance to read much of the history. The novel contains the universal values found in *The Raj Quartet*—there is the acceptance of the Other (whether racial or national) by characters with whom we sympathize, as well as the suffering that insularity causes in the psychological torment of the rejected and the riots that kill Bholu. But MacKendrick and Gower are not appealing characters. Attracted by the same distant and contemptuous woman, they are here weak-willed and ineffectual, and vindictive Gower, who wants to shoot Steele and then MacKendrick because he believes first one then the other has been cuckolding him, is overcome by inertia at a time when police protection is required to keep the farm at Ooni from falling into the hands of the rioters.

The novel develops Scott's interest in cross-cultural relationships barely demonstrated previously and again shows him profoundly interested in displaced people like Gower, who suffers from a feeling of "formlessness, an almost negative despair which was at once part of him and outside him, suspending and sustaining him between two worlds as it were" (140), or like Cynthia Mapleton, an impoverished war widow who, in the time present of the novel, has nowhere to go. That Scott treats empathetically this disagreeable character, "the sort of woman who frightened [MacKendrick], taut, skinny, calculating" (23), is a demonstration of his extraordinary gift. For she viciously humiliates the obviously Eurasian Judith Anderson (who aspires to marriage with a distasteful English officer). Scott is already a master at recapturing the cruel barbs of social ostracism, and the question of race plays a critical role in the drama. In a variation of the words used in *The Raj Quartet,* Dorothy tells Joe, "Underneath all the so-called trust and understanding between white and black, there's mistrust and dislike" (150). At the same time that MacKendrick cannot help feeling that a person of mixed race is freakish, he also envisions a relationship with such a person as an ideal. This latter notion would be somewhat transformed in the mixed cultural identity of Hari Kumar in *The Raj Quartet* and further developed in social and historical terms.

A Male Child

A Male Child (1956), set in London in 1953 and dedicated to "my mother and father, Frances and Tom Scott,"[6] examines some of the same themes as *The Alien Sky* and demonstrates significant emotional growth. Joe MacKendrick had searched for himself in a foreign land, whereas the narrator-protagonist Ian Canning searches for himself on his home turf. Where MacKendrick was psychologically incapable of grasping the richer life of which India was the not fully realized symbol, Ian Canning, with the help of his friend, Alan Hurst, is more successful. The subject of Scott's highly original "turn of the screw" is no less than recovery from neurosis, a formidable task for any novelist. Alan, the freer character in this novel, is not selfish and sadistic like Joe's brother Dwight, but kind and caring, "brimming over with life and vitality and sound common sense" (33). Where the role of love is limited in *Johnnie Sahib* to charisma and in *The Alien Sky* to MacKendrick's wistful yearning, *A Male Child* spells out how love provides meaning and cure. The novel is divided into three parts, "Seed," "Gestation," and "Parturition." Stella Hurst's pregnancy is, in short, a metaphor extended over the body of the novel for Ian's psychological rebirth; in both creations, Alan plays a parental, guiding role. A leap forward in terms of Scott's value system, the novel presents his first unambivalent association of the relatively unrepressed with the moral and the loving, a juxtaposition seen again in *The Birds of Paradise* and *The Raj Quartet.*

Ian Canning, an intellectual introvert and disillusioned liberal who suffers some of the same psychological inhibitions and inertia as MacKendrick and Gower in *The Alien Sky*, has been sent home to London from India with a malarialike fever, unable to pursue the military career he had sought in India as an escape from his orphaned past. Sick in body and spirit, he is on the verge of suicide when he encounters a good-natured, nonintellectual extrovert, Alan Hurst, whom he had first met as an officer cadet on a troop ship bound for India. Alan, intuiting his despair, invites him to spend a few weeks with him at his mother's home at Aylward and functions for Ian as an alter ego. Both men are separated from their wives, who have in common their unhappiness and search for independence.

Ian has been working as a literary advisor and a publisher's reader, in which capacity he advises Brian Selby against the publication of a novel, *Opal*, by one Isobel, who turns out to have been Alan's dead aunt, Isabella. Although her husband, the parasitic, womanizing spendthrift Rex Coles, never shows him any open anger ("his capacity for making you feel a bit of a rotter was his most effective weapon" [54]), Ian learns that Rex has been angered by Ian's recommendation against publication. *Opal* had started as a light romance before its character was changed by Isabella's marriage to Rex; her illusions were shattered by his ongoing affairs with barmaids and his persistent demands for money. This, however, is a subplot, one whose details seem too weighty for the minor role they play in the novel.

Alan, who had abandoned his accountancy training, is on the verge of leaving for Assam to plant tea when Stella, his estranged wife who is now pregnant, decides to return to him. At Aylward Ian is disturbed by Alan's mother, Marion, a vindictive, meddling, possessive, pretentious yet pitiable woman. Drunk, she mistakes Ian for her son Edward, killed in World War II, and then desires to re-create Ian as Edward. For Marion, Edward yet inhabits the house at Aylward, and at one point Ian also feels his presence.

Aylward (one cannot miss the play on "ail") turns out to be a house inhabited by the dead, both in the sense of ghosts and of the living dead. It is an appropriate place for Rex Coles, who uses people and then discards them and who keeps his sister-in-law supplied with liquor. It is also an appropriate place for Ian Canning, haunted as he is by the "ghost" of his ex-wife, Helena, who has published a novel and, to Ian's dismay, had an abortion. But Marion herself is the emotional center of Aylward. With "sunken eye-sockets and cheeks," "thickly applied paint and powder," (60) and the "strange, glowing redness of her dyed hair" (48), she can be taken for a specter; her body is so wasted and cadaverous that she appears to be a richly vibrant, disembodied voice. Her uncanny ability to read Ian's mind is unnerving, as is her belief in the existence of Edward in the house and his exaltation together with the denigration of her second son, Alan. For narrator Ian and the reader, she sets the tone of the house, as is apparent when Ian enters the drawing room immediately after meeting her and finds that "the furniture, the pictures, the knickknacks: all had acquired an air of being possessed. I appreciated what had so far escaped my conscious thought, that in this one room were collected most of what remained of more spacious days. When she entered the room she gathered them round her. She protected them, and they her" (61).

The juxtaposition of reality and illusion, the sense of straddling two worlds, is more developed in this novel and is found mainly in Scott's unusual use of the supernatural. The question is not, as it is in Henry James's *Turn of the Screw*, whether the ghost exists or the woman is paranoid; we come to accept that Edward does exist. We do so at the point at which Ian, an apparently reliable narrator, feels Edward's presence in his room, formerly Edward's bedroom. His existence is also confirmed when Mrs. Voremberg, a spiritualist tenant at Aylward, tells Ian that she lost control of Edward on only two occasions, one of them the very same time that Ian felt him in his room. Edward appears to Ian when he is in his most depressed state, that is, when a returning attack of the fever again leads him, alone in his room, to wonder whether he was foolish not to have ended his life. He muses about

whether the time would ever come when raising a window would be the first step of a leap into darkness. The windows gave: gave on to air and freshness and the buoyancy of space.

And it was in that instant that I knew, without any doubt whatsoever, that Edward was there. There was nothing unpleasant or frightening about it. I did not see him, but unmistakably he was there, quite close to me, the whole of him making itself known in a resigned exhalation of breath which I heard, and felt upon my cheek; and there was something so melancholy about it that I was filled with an overwhelming sense of loss.

I knelt on the bed for a few more moments, but the manifestation had taken its course. It was over. I leaned forward and pulled the window down again, and turned my back on it. Gradually I could feel the warnings of fever abating. I was retreating from them, retreating from the fever itself as from the edge of a deep chasm; withdrawing myself from it, withdrawing myself from death and from Edward.

I understood, then, that the sense of loss had been a sense I shared, briefly, with him. For that moment we had come together and I had been touched by it; his loss, his sadness; moved, too, by his grief that, whilst I might join him, no power of mine or his could ever help him to return to that state of grace which was my ignorance of the world in which he moved, that gulf which separated us and now grew wider and wider until, with a quieter mind, I rose, and took possession of my room at Aylward. (89–90)

In this passage the manifestation of Edward is coincidental with the return of the fever, its abatement with Edward's moving off. If we take the physical as suggestive of the psychological, the manifestation of Edward is a demonstration of neurosis, his moving off an indication that Ian is moving toward a rebirth of physical and mental health. Edward, of course, does not appear to Alan Hurst; the supernatural can exist in the novel only for those figures who represent varying kinds of death-in-life. Edward and Alan pull Ian toward two poles. Edward represents the most powerful of the forces (selfishness, indifference, unreliability, weakness, depression, nastiness) pulling Ian toward neurosis and death. Alan, with his "code of upright dealing [and the] charitable understanding [it] demanded" (208), represents those forces pulling him toward emotional strength and life: "[Alan] came closer. The light from the lamp-post was on me, so that I could not see his face clearly. He put out a hand in greeting and I took it, not knowing whose hand I shook, but feeling it warm and firm and friendly in my cold one, knowing it different from the probing professional hands of doctors, the waxen hand of the old man in Wendover, the limp hand of Selby, the flabby hand of David, the clawlike hand of Peggy. It was a hand reaching out to hold me back from the darkness to which all these other hands had pointed so that I might see and enter it alone" (32).

That Alan functions for Ian as a stabilizing breath of fresh air is also evident later in the novel when Ian talks of returning to a nursing home. Alan asks him:

> "What good's a nursing home ever done you?"
> "You think I ought to go to a nut house?"
> Slowly he grinned at me. "My dear old Ian," he said. "You're in one."
> For a few moments neither of us moved. Then the absurdity of the situation overwhelmed me. I laughed because it seemed as though I had surfaced from a submarine world into one of wind and wave and sky.
> I felt that what he offered me was life and sanity. (136–137)

At the end of "Gestation," Ian finds the "world miraculously transformed by sunshine" (169) and tells Stella that he has turned his back on defeat and fear. Aylward is losing its effect; as he walks toward it, the house appears to vanish with the daylight. In the "Parturition" section of the novel, Aylward no longer has any effect on Ian, indicative of his state of health. It no longer seems to him "dark, melancholy, full of ghosts, unbidden memories. . . . It was as if the windows had been widened, heightened. Perhaps it was the effect of the snow reflecting light. I noticed the shabbiness of everything;

threadbare patches on the carpet in the drawing room; an uncleaned, uncared for look which might once have depressed me. It was too matter of fact to do so now. You saw it, registered it. It had no special effect" (197).

What Alan has given Ian is not only recognition of neurosis but freedom from its inertia-producing guilt. Like Jim Taylor in *Johnnie Sahib*, Ian adopts too easily another's point of view, and so is easily put upon when his temporary renter, David, wants to keep Ian's apartment. Alan, on the other hand, is assertive when he needs to be: " 'To hell with David and Peggy. If I wanted the place I'd tell 'em to clear off.' He spoke almost angrily" (40). Living with his mother, he sets an example for Ian because, secure in his code of caring and upright dealing, he remains refreshingly (and unbelievably) untouched by her neurosis, her accusations, and her contempt; it is she, in fact, who appears to be afraid of him.

So healthy does Alan appear that Ian at first mistakes his background as "normal," leaving him "confident, unscarred" (42). In fact, the world "from which Alan had sprung and to which I was a stranger" (41) seems very much like the world from which Ian could have sprung and Edward did spring. Beginning with Marion's mistaking Ian for Edward, there has been, throughout the novel, an identification of the two, as though Edward had returned to Aylward. They both have the same opinion of *Opal*, that Isobel had her eyes opened while she was writing the novel. They both have an interest in writing and, in Marion's view, have the look of men of letters. It had been Edward's desire to write a biography of Isobel, and for a while—at Marion's request and against his better judgment—Ian contemplates doing so. Additionally, says Marion, Ian is the sort of man Edward would have liked to become. Marion's wish, Ian believes, is that he should feel himself and Edward one. His reaction is a mixture of feeling imposed upon and a strange excitement as though looking into a mirror to find a face not quite his. The identification between the two (Scott's first superimposition of past on present) lessens as Ian gets healthier ("You're not really like Edward at all. Edward wasn't much use to anyone but himself" [112].) But Ian, in one sense, is another aspect of Edward, one that with Alan's help moves toward a redefinition of self. If the novel is about the psychological rebirth of Ian, symbolically Edward[7] is dead because Ian has rejected this part of himself and, when the novel opens, is looking for a new identity to fill the void. According to Adela, Edward was dependent and smothered by Marion, subject to fears and inhibitions and nasty to Alan, who never held a grudge. Clearly Edward had suffered from Marion's attempt to live through him ("I knew every thought of

Edward's. Every hope. Every plan. Every ambition. He kept nothing back. Nothing" [131].) Marion used to long to draw off some of Alan's strength to give to Edward. The subject of the novel, then, is the re-creation of Edward-Ian into a strong, positive character, or Ian's independence from the kind of mental state, symbolized by Aylward, that Mother Marion and Edward represent.

We see Ian's recovery from neurosis in several ways. One of them is that his view of Alan does not remain ambivalent, as the portrait of Johnnie Brown did for the reader in Scott's first novel. At first Ian is confused by Marion's distorted view of her sons and does not know what to think. Since Ian is the narrator (Scott's first use of a first-person narrator), neither does the reader. Ian first sees Alan not as a whole person but as an "amalgam of what I believed him to be and what others believed him to be" (118–119) and wrestles with the problem of Alan's identity. Is he the insensitive man Marion sees who deliberately brought Ian home to hurt her by his resemblance to Edward, who is indifferent to anything outside of his immediate gain and who might have pulled his father back from his death under the wheels of a bus; or is he the caring man who extended his hand when no one else would to save another on the verge of suicide? Gradually, Ian learns to protect himself from Marion's negativism; he "had developed a special sense to deal with her tendency to hint at sharpness or greed or lack of generosity in others. It was necessary to do so if you were to keep a sense of proportion" (139).

In due time, Ian comes to see Alan unequivocally. He has learned much from Alan; he finds curative Alan's honesty, openness, un-selfishness, and sincerity. He looks in vain for mere politeness on Alan's part and is moved by his desire to give freely, without impos-ing on others and creating in them a sense of obligation. Alan teaches him, with his benevolent silence, that "he trusted me not to think badly of him, in spite of what I might hear" (94) and to "ignore a [physical] condition which could not be diagnosed" (135). He is the first Scott character who embodies selfless love. His unselfish giving of himself is stated unequivocally at the end of the novel. With the birth of his child, Alan, who would not be removed from his wife's side during labor and delivery (unusual in the 1950s), "suddenly cov-ered his face with both his hands and sobbed as if his heart would break, as if the joy he felt, the physical proof of his convictions were more than he could bear" (220). Scott would expand his technique of ambivalence followed by resounding truth in *The Raj Quartet,* in the many versions of the circumstances of the Bibighar affair ending in the truth illuminated in Daphne Manners' diary.

Influenced by Alan's positive spirit, Ian has gained his mental health and is able to give to others something of what Alan has given to him. He pulls Stella out of her depression, brings Marion out of her alcoholism and into the present where the ghost of Edward can be put aside, and even provides some small degree of comfort for his own bitter, driven ex-wife. No longer haunted by her "ghost," he feels sorry for Helena and responds to her attacks in the positive spirit he has learned from Alan. And he finds his situation and David's reversed. David's conniving to take his apartment from him had at the beginning of the novel added to his suicidal depression; now he pities David, both for his shallow values and his deceptive girlfriend and tries to help him overcome disillusionment about his career. An image here effectively conveys that in attempting to help, Ian is doing with David what his friend Alan Hurst had accomplished with himself: "The light from the streetlamp fell on his face. Mine, I knew was in shadow, as Alan's had been that night . . . not so many months ago" (187).

In *A Male Child* the freedom-bondage dichotomy, described in *The Alien Sky*, is resolved in bondage undertaken freely for the sake of love. Where the searching MacKendrick sensed the emptiness of freedom as defined by a life with Dorothy, Alan goes voluntarily into bondage because he comes to believe that love places restrictions on personal freedom. The conversation which follows is between Stella and Ian:

> "Alan has no inhibitions, Ian, he feels himself utterly free. Free to cut loose at any moment he wants to—"
> "The way a man should feel."
> "The way he should! Why should he?"
> "So that he can assume his bonds voluntarily, as Alan does."
> She clicked her handbag shut. "And what bonds has Alan got?"
> "He has you. He has the child. A home to hold, mouths to feed. The ghosts of Aylward to live with. A longing for sun and sky in place of electric light and dust and ledgers. . . ."
> "Why should he go voluntarily into prison?" . . .
> I said, "He goes voluntarily into prison, Stella, because that is where love is." (211)

The change in this novel is in the perception of love, which has become a value of strength. If love here represents a voluntary and positive kind of imprisonment, living in an ideal past represents a negative imprisonment and an illusion. "We're all forgotten, Canning," says Rex Coles. "We're all back numbers. We live in the past, old chap, and it's nice to think of the past as something comfortable and pleasant, which it wasn't of course, but still . . ." (146). The novel is a predecessor of the *Quartet*'s insistence that the past is dead and must be buried; using a broad canvas, the *Quartet* would substitute for individual neurosis represented by Marion Hurst, the embodiment of Aylward, a collective neurosis of the British community.

Although a dramatic step forward, *A Male Child* is not one of Scott's best novels, and in 1965 he considered nothing that he had written before *The Mark of the Warrior* worth reading.[8] While the reader is made to live in the claustrophobic atmosphere of Aylward, the story yet lacks the tension between reality and hallucination of *The Turn of the Screw*; we must somehow suspend disbelief and believe with Ian that the ghost of Edward exists. The dramatic situations do not bear the weight of the novel's melodramatic details (such as Marion's theatrical would-be suicide attempt), which occur in passing and do not hold our interest. Additionally, "meaningful" props such as the swastika that Stella takes from an Aylward tenant, Mrs. Vorumberg, to help overcome her fear of the future do not work very well. Scott had not yet learned to combine dramatic with psychological climax, and the novel is not very well integrated. Dramatic development of a few incidents without the melodramatic references would have been preferable. Scott achieves these improvements in technique in his next novel.

The Mark of the Warrior

In contrast to *A Male Child*, where a number of incidents appear largely irrelevant to the plot, *The Mark of the Warrior* (1958) is a spare, organic novel in which every part has a purpose. The book is enhanced by a taut poetic prose. Like its predecessor, the novel has a highly original theme and is a novel of psychological development; the London *Times* called it "a novel more powerful and more frightening than many of those which run with blood."[9] *A Male Child* sought to regain psychical energy by divorcing it mainly from the depressive effects of the past, succeeding through the development of an ideal behavior of love. *The Mark of the Warrior*, conversely, is concerned with the opposite impulse, pursuing aggression at the expense of one's humanity. Not surprisingly, there is a parallel investigation of remorse. Conscience and the repetition compulsion of the death instinct in an attempt to gain mastery over anxiety and guilt is what inspires this story, somewhat reminiscent of Hawthorne's "Roger Malvin's Burial."

The setting of much of the novel is the jungle, suitable for a study of aggression. In "The Prologue," dated May 1942, what is left of an

Indian rifle company, led by its commander, Major Colin Craig, is moving northwest toward Imphal across the hills of Upper Burma. Crossing a river, their raft disintegrates, and the column loses mainly their nonswimmers and four of an advance party which has been fired upon, including a subaltern, John Ramsay. The death of the subaltern becomes an obsession for Major Craig, next seen in the novel as the self-involved commander of an Officers Training School [10] northeast of Poona. The appearance of Bob Ramsay, John's brother, as a cadet in the training school eventually leads to a replay of the circumstances in which John was killed.

"Part One: The Forest / January to April 1943" takes place at the training school. Craig cannot escape his feelings of responsibility in John Ramsay's death and suffers recurrent nightmares. Having discovered his leadership inadequacies in the jungle, he had depended on John to carry out what should have been his own role. From the beginning Craig is afraid of Bob Ramsay because "he is his brother all over again" (33), and the stage is set for a repetition of the disaster when Sergeant-Major Thompson persuades Craig that a training session in the jungle instead of on the plain is the best way to prepare the cadets for jungle warfare.

Going with Thompson and Esther (Craig's wife) to scout out the Chota Bandar hills, Craig overcomes his fear of the jungle to scout out the river alone. Returning after he imagines himself to have been lost, he sees in Thompson's face an expression which is a revelation and a clarification of his purpose. As he tells Esther, "I saw Thompson properly for the first time. You remember—you didn't hear me coming. He was down in the river bed, and did hear me coming. When he looked round I saw that he was alone in the forest and wanted to be alone in the forest because he was in the forest to kill" (58). The passage continues:

> He smiled. "Whereas I and most of the men I remember were in the forest to live."
> She said, "Most of the men?"
> "Yes. Except John Ramsay. He was in the forest in Thompson's way. It's like a mark on them."
> "Them?"
> "Men like Thompson. And Ramsay. It was strong on Ramsay."
> "You said he was the finest soldier you'd ever known."
> "He was. They are. The rest of us are nothing. The rest of us are dressed for the part." (58–59)

Craig believes that a man who is in the forest not to survive but to kill has a sixth sense which enables him to sense another's presence in the forest. Sensing the killer instinct in Ramsay, Craig admits to a certain fear of him but determines to enable Ramsay to develop this instinct, on which the rest of them depend for survival. Cadet Ramsay, meanwhile, senses that Craig wants him to find something in himself and is aware, when he goes off limits to explore the jungle area, that the journey is as much Craig's as his own. The journey is both physical and psychological, and Scott presents a totally believable development of the psychologies of both men in tandem.

There is a simple narrative progression, and the chapters alternate between Craig's point of view and Ramsay's. The younger man's view of the elder as an authority will change, as Ramsay progresses from innocence to knowledge and Craig from teacher to a man confounded by the warrior he has helped create, "a hunter wounded by the thing he hunted" (160). When this happens, Craig, who has watched the development of Ramsay as his creation, can no longer follow his reasoning. The end of the first section of the novel is presented as the end of Ramsay's link with humanity.

"Part Two: The River / May to June 1943" consists of the enactment of the training scheme Ramsay has developed for jungle warfare in the Chota Bandar hills. A new character, Blake, is introduced, borrowed with his Indian infantry battalion to be commander of enemy forces and Ramsay's foil. The section is most interesting for Scott's familiar play on reality and illusion. The situation is least real to Blake, who never takes the exercise seriously and is probably not aware that his putting a spy in the water truck (which in a real warfare situation would be replaced by air supply drops) constitutes cheating. Craig insists to Blake that what they are doing is "more than an exercise" (93), but it is Ramsay who, as Craig realizes, "had truly crossed the barrier which separated one reality from the other" (162). Since the fictional world is more real to him than the real one, he puts his men through severe hardship, enforcing discipline by denying them water in the evening and force-marching them many miles a day. Discovering the spy, Baksh,[11] in the water truck, Ramsay turns him into an enemy villager spy who is treated to some of the same physical and emotional privations as a prisoner of war. He does this so that Baksh will have the motivation to escape later and provide Blake with the wrong information about his plans.

Scott's handling of the mock military situation is masterful, as is his treatment of the emergence of the warrior instinct in Ramsay. With Craig's help he develops into a killing machine whose personal identity extends to include all of his men. Ramsay's development is already beginning, as Cadet Lawson observes, when he does not notice people anymore, only things, and is instinctively drawn toward isolation and the hills of the Chota Bandar where he can give his instinct free play.

In the forest and the jungle, he feels exhilaration in his own emerging powers together with a belief in his invincibility. His identity progresses from human being to military machine, concerned logically and without feeling with the harmonious functioning of all of its parts. In this state, he is burdened by an extended self, a development of the Major's consciousness in *Johnnie Sahib* (65–66).

In imagery reflecting Scott's concern with psychological imprisonment and later with unfeeling systems, he thinks, "He and Blake were prisoners within the separate patterns of safety they had each devised and they had no choice now but to bring those patterns into conflict, no choice but to keep their own patterns secure. I am one hundred men, he thought, but I am not in myself a man. There is nothing honourable in what I do. I am myself the heart of a machine that has no heart. I am one hundred links in a chain which is only the image of a chain. I must preserve the image of the chain. If the image is destroyed I am also destroyed. I am nothing without the image and the image is nothing without me" (177). Although he longs to break his extended image and retreat into himself, Ramsay is imprisoned by it, by his men's need of him.

The novel uses a second measure of Ramsay's progression to military machine. From being a green cadet moved by his brother's courage and sickened by his wound, he progresses to the belief in the second part of the novel that he would have killed John because he was going to die anyway. He goes further when he realizes that he would have shot John when he asked to be shot because John would betray the men under torture if caught, and killing him would look like mercy to the men. Then, at the height of the intuitive powers that accompany his feeling of extended identity, he concludes that "John bodged the raft on purpose . . . to get rid of the weaklings" and tells Craig, "I'd have shot the bastard. . . . Because he'd murdered himself. He couldn't face up to the weak links. He broke the pattern deliberately. He broke his own image" (178). Paradoxically, because he defines himself as an unfeeling extended mechanism ("They were not men he went to save, but links in the disrupted pattern without which the pattern was lost forever with the image of himself" [183]), he dies in a herculean effort to save his men, jumping in to save them just when his strength is gone and he is weighted down by two backpacks.

The creation of a warrior is at best an ambivalent task because it is done, as Scott presents it, at the sacrifice of that person's humanity. Although Craig worries that he is destroying Ramsay as a man, he has a hidden agenda—an overwhelming need to rid himself of the obsessive anxiety (a quality that makes Blake smirk and even Esther momentarily withdraw) which began with John's death. By the successful completion of circumstances similar to those in which John was killed, Craig hopes to rid himself of his recurrent nightmare. It is not so much guilt that motivates him, although guilt plays a part. The creation of Bob Ramsay as a warrior is a creation of the man that Craig as a commander should have been ("It should have been your pattern and your image" [178–179]), a re-creation of John Ramsay and a justification for Craig's having abrogated his own responsibility on the battlefield in favor of dependence on the superior warrior.

Craig's prime motivation, however, is his need to create a parental omnipotence in Ramsay to protect himself and his men. The need is to delude himself that he will be creating a leader "who is past destroying, beyond survival, a man stronger even than John Ramsay" (118). The omnipotence is of course illusory, and Ramsay dies on a mock battlefield preserving the illusion of his extended self, as Teddie Bingham in *The Raj Quartet* would die on the battlefield in an ultimate ironic comment on the illusory parental projection of *man-bap.*

Perhaps one mark of the writer is the ability to clothe external situations, abstract philosophical questions, and psychological dilemmas in situational garb that dramatizes the writer's internal conflicts. One associate wrote of *The Mark of the Warrior:* "No one could read this novel without realizing that . . . it developed out of your inner being."[12] There is a conflict, even sometimes a confusion of the impulses of love and aggression, areas of ambivalence which the novel presents but cannot resolve. The conflict is evident when Craig feels contempt for himself for having not finished off John Ramsay but left him to die slowly and in agony. Its inverse is seen when Ramsay feels contempt for himself for denying his humanitarian impulse by insisting that Baksh go without certain basic necessities. Both men are caught between their love and aggressive impulses, and the reader responds with an ambivalent view of both men.

The central issue is the need to destroy a man in order to create a protective killing machine. Ramsay is destroyed as a man because the urge to kill his enemies, with Craig's help, becomes stronger than the desire to live. We have seen that, as part of this development, he gains an identity mechanistically devoid of feeling ("You make it all sound very mechanical, as if people weren't involved at all" [117]) and extended to include all of his men. The problem for the reader is that many of Ramsay's acts, though calculated, seem

strong and kind. (The exception is his harsh treatment of Baksh.)
When Ramsay sees that Everett is on the point of collapse during the
forced march, he gives him water from his own canteen (Everett,
against instructions, has exhausted his own supply) and carries his
pack for him. It is difficult to see as a destroyed man one who gives
the water he needs to another, or one who risks his life to save his
men. Ramsay acts not in his own interest but in the combined interest of all of the men, and this is what kills him. But this sense of
imprisoning extended identity is also a definition of the highest
form of love, and we have seen it developed in *A Male Child*. Ramsay is presented as devoid of feeling, but his thought, midway
through the novel, that he would have granted his dying brother's
wish and shot him, can be interpreted as humane. Craig, however,
sees Ramsay's willingness to entertain the idea as a crack in the mirror of his humanity and hastens to assure Esther, who distrusts
Ramsay, that he himself did not finish off John. Esther, who walks
beside Craig in his dreams "in all the guises of love" (151), functions
as the moral norm of the novel. The reader is therefore perplexed
when his not finishing off John Ramsay is presented dramatically
not so much as a humanitarian act but as an act of self-interested
dependence:

> John said: Finish me off: but I did not finish him off because while he
> lived there was hope for us of the forest and when he died there were
> left ourselves and death, and only luck dividing us from it, or mercy,
> divine providence, what you will. A man could not trust in luck, or in
> mercy. In the forest he could trust only in the destroyed man, the man
> who beat and hammered and shaped the senses of living men into a
> single weapon to demonstrate his will and knowledge of the enemy.
> (152–153)

In this context, Craig's not finishing off John can be seen as cowardly
and unnecessarily cruel.

Craig is as calculating in his way as Ramsay is in his and appears
to be more of a predator than Ramsay as he deliberately refrains
from giving Ramsay what he needs to develop the human side of
him ("He felt the emptiness of his hands and turned away because
for all their emptiness he could not bear in them the weight of all
the things he had not given" [175]). He is not unaware of the predatory nature of his relationship with Ramsay ("When I enter the forest today I shall be the hunter, he the quarry" [152]). After Ramsay's
death, torn by guilt, he needs and begs forgiveness from Esther; he
needs reassurance that Ramsay was not killed as a result of his own
hidden aggression. Her response becomes the last words of the novel:

"For what? For what?" (188). But the reader, who has followed Craig's "game of chess"[13] in a way that Esther has not, is not convinced of his innocence. If one takes away the military trappings, the fact that it is part of Major Craig's job to develop the killer instinct in his men, the story is one of dependence and predatory anxiety. However, judgment of Colin Craig is modified by the fact that Craig's treatment of Ramsay might appear justified by his role. Clearly, Scott's purpose was to ask the questions, not provide the answers.[14]

3. The Middle Novels I

The Chinese Love Pavilion

The Chinese Love Pavilion (1960) represents the beginning of Scott's mature philosophy. It explores in yet another way the symbiotic nature of reality and illusion, further incorporating the relationship into the texture of his novel. Philosopher Stein's memorable line from *Lord Jim*, "In the destructive element [the dream] immerse," is considered and regretfully rejected as the path to madness. But striving to free himself from illusion, narrator-protagonist Tom Brent discovers that the real world is also destructive. Additionally, Scott continues the exploration he began in *The Mark of the Warrior*. He sees as inimical to happiness the aggressive impulse in people he would later call "the spoilers," a theme developed fully in *The Raj Quartet*.

The novel begins with a preface; "The Door by which men enter" refers both to the start of the novel and the entrance to the Chinese love pavilion. A description and tragic history is presented of the fanciful pavilion which we sense will take on symbolic meaning as the story progresses. The legend of the pavilion involves the story of Lieutenant Hakinawa, a gentle Japanese officer driven to suicide during the war, either by the ghosts of the garden or by his love for Teena Chang. The novel begins in a typical Scott manner, as a quest for meaning through occupation (or human relationship) by a protagonist who has gone to India to follow his grandfather's tradition of service. After a year of working for an Indian merchant, he is disillusioned over the sour Indian reaction to his egalitarian idealism and envy of his nationality; he is about to return home to England when he encounters Brian Saxby, ten years his senior and a philosophizing adventurer of some means. In the first section, "The God Hunter," Saxby advises Brent to immerse himself in his dream, what he identifies for Brent as a dream of earth. On Saxby's advice Brent farms with Greystone, a rebel who resigned from the Indian Civil Service to set himself the hopeless task of the rehabilitation of a barren valley. But whatever it means for Greystone, Brent finds with satisfaction that farming has plunged him not into the dream but the real world. Several years later, visiting Saxby in Singaputan, Malaya, Brent finds a changed man. Saxby, who has mortified his body, has apparently given up the search for his own dream; he believes that he exists in the physical sense only, a mere mechanism, and is therefore waste. When Saxby, aggressive and self-centered, treats him with contemptuous indifference and then tells him to leave, Brent does so, a decision he is to regret for the rest of his life.

The next section, "The Garden of Madness," begins six years later, immediately after the war, and is largely concerned with Brent's relationship with Teena Chang, an enigmatic prostitute of mixed race (Dutch, French, and Chinese). Brent, seriously wounded in the war, finds himself again in Malaya at the request of a Major Turner, the only person aside from the guerillas who may be able to locate and identify Saxby, who is no longer a nonbeliever but has unfortunately found his dream. Saxby, working with the Communist (Kampong Malim) guerillas during the war, had captured four Japanese soldiers in a raid on a Japanese outpost. He had bound, gagged, and burned them alive in mad revenge for the burning of the deserted Sakai settlement in which Saxby had been living. This and other fiery acts were met with serious reprisals, and the guerilla leader was killed. Major Turner wants Saxby now because he is suspected of indulging in a private vendetta in the unexplained deaths of people whom he deems to have collaborated with the Japanese. Turner sends Brent to Bukit Kallang, scene of the last assassination, to begin his search for Saxby by meeting with Wan Lo Ping, the guerilla leader, who has worked with him. A Major Reid, the commander of the Indian rifle company overseeing the effort to control bandit trouble outside of Bukit Kallang, is to arrange the meeting.

Brent stays with the obsessively masculine Reid and his trigger-happy company while he searches for Saxby. Reid is another version of the destroyed man of *The Mark of the Warrior*, although he is a much less sympathetic character than Ramsay. He has a simplistic, macho psychology, the purpose of which is to make his young men feel "six feet tall" ("I've turned them from boys who wouldn't hurt a fly into men who'd as soon plug you as look at you" [166]). Their unnecessary slaughter evokes a dislike on the part of the reader that was absent in *The Mark of the Warrior*, where the lack of any serious consequences to others coupled with the extraordinary care shown his men kept the idea of Ramsay as a killer abstract and the reader's feelings about him unsettled.

To keep his men sexually satisfied, Reid has contracted with Teena Chang, who runs a sophisticated bawdy house in the Chinese love pavilion. The pavilion is artfully arranged, with yellow, green, and red rooms, and with silken robes matching in color for the girls and their men. Reid, who (he confides to Brent) is impotent, gives Teena of "the Scarlet Room wherein the Setting Sun lies sleeping" to Brent, who falls in love with her. Discovering that Saxby wants to kill her for her refusal to betray her Japanese clients at the time of her wartime affair with the gentle Lieutenant Hakinawa, Brent surmises that Saxby is responsible for Hakinawa's suicide. Hakinawa must have killed himself instead of Teena when Saxby crept up behind him one night and made him believe she was working for the guerillas. Brent's presence at her house keeps Saxby from killing Teena one night, but he is knocked unconscious by Ah Choong, Saxby's right-hand man.

The title of the final section, "The Flower Dreamer," is again named for Saxby. Although Brent is concerned about Teena's safety, he also worries that Reid and his men will find Saxby and kill him so that they can feel like "a giant" who can "punch a hole in the sky" (247, 248). Mac has already "dropped" an eighteen-year-old Japanese having a bath, and Chop and Suey unnecessarily kill an old Chinese man who is peacefully fishing. The murder of the boy and the fisherman by Reid's men is in keeping with the final tragic ending of the novel, both in terms of their being too quick on the draw and of Reid's ultimate responsibility.

Forced to hunt for Saxby with Reid and his men, Brent manages to lose them and find Saxby's cave, where he discovers his notebooks (a device of revelation like Daphne's diary in *The Raj Quartet*) and the rationale for his madness. He discovers too that Ah Choong would have killed him that night on the road outside Teena Chang's house if Saxby had not intervened (he had not wanted his old friend's blood on his hands). Brent is concerned to find him before Reid and his men can kill the wandering madman. Consequently, he acts in a manner that risks his own safety, and Reid saves his life by killing a few more Chinese, including Ah Choong. On a telephone tip from Turner, Brent finds Saxby dead in Singaputan, surrounded by his plants.

When Brent returns to Bukit Kallang, he finds Reid proud of his accomplishment in having saved his life and in having exposed his own protégé, Toby Sutton, to "what sten-gun fire could do to the human body" (289). Sutton is a young man who has "a strange, innocent, violent face" (277) together with "the tight-wound unresilient look of someone packed with explosive" (209). Drunk and feeling that Brent no longer deserves Teena, Reid assigns her to Sutton so that he can prove himself a man. This happens just when Teena is to tell Brent whether she will leave the pavilion to go away with him. In her Chinese mood and wearing a mask, Teena is frightening to Brent; he imagines that she has rejected him and does not fight for her. The next morning, she is found stabbed to death by the kris that Brent had given her to arm her with his love. Sutton acts like a dangerous madman and claims that she killed herself in despair because Brent had abandoned her.

In "The Door by which men go—," the exit from the pavilion and its illusion of happiness, and the end of the novel, Brent wonders years later whether there was not another possibility, that Sutton killed Teena because she was the only one who could have betrayed his impotence. He does not know which of the two occurred, just as he cannot be sure whether Teena loved him or was just doing what was good for business, and whether she would have gone away with him; the novel retains these ambivalences. Brent also concludes that Saxby indirectly succeeded in killing her.

In later years Scott was not proud of this novel.[1] Only in the last third of the book does the story become gripping; as a whole *The Chinese Love Pavilion* lacks the power of the later novels or even of *The Mark of the Warrior*. There are "signs of a creative burst,"[2] as friend, critic, and fellow novelist Peter Green wrote, but Scott was attempting the dramatization of a complex metaphysical idea, and the book takes off in too many directions. Although the details appear a better fit to the overall scheme than those of *A Male Child*, the novel contains disparate parts that are not well integrated. The narrative seems contrived, its structural skeleton showing. The first part, Brent's quest on Greystone's farm, seems to have little to do with the rest of the book in dramatic terms. Additionally, there is an uneasy shift of focus from the relationship of Saxby and Brent to the romance of Teena and Brent. Saxby, however, remains Scott's real interest; Teena exists only as an emblem of an enigmatic ideal. But although two of the three sections of the book, "The God Hunter" and "The Flower Dreamer," are named for Saxby, the dramatic climax of the novel is Teena's murder and Brent's unfulfilled relationship with her. The relationship of Teena and Brent does not appear developed enough to support its tragic implications, and the story is melodramatic. There are tautly written insights, but the prose is at times awkwardly sentimental.

The image uniting the disparate sections of this novel is, of course, the love pavilion, and the novel began in Scott's imagination with the image of a man walking across an open space, away from a pavilion.[3] The unifying idea is that of the relationship of the dream, the heart's desire represented by the pavilion, to the real world. The pavilion is a place of pure fantasy, and the ambivalent, artificial nature of fantasy is presented by the use of the pavilion as a bawdy house and as a symbol of a true paradise. That it exists in a dangerous relation to the real world is hinted in the preface, where a view of its fanciful dragons and golden roof, the four corners of which were "curled up like the shoes of Aladdin" (12), was the last sight of Japanese victims of execution.

Because the pavilion is emblematic of the heart's desire, the human heart is compared to the pavilion in an image that seems contrived, the beginning of a zoom into focus that does not quite work: "And that heart was in its complexity, as strange and mysterious as the pavilion with its chambers of different colours, its doors to come in by and its doors to go out of, its strong supporting pillars awrithe with dragons. But within it there was always the illusion of the occasion found" (210). The occasion found is one of love, illusory both because it may be merely the semblance of love and because it will pass.

The real danger comes for Scott when one is about to actualize one's dreams, when one stands somewhere between reality and illusion. The place of execution was in the space between Bukit Kallang's Eurasian-style house and fanciful oriental pavilion, just as the danger for Teena is in the pavilion, as she is about to tell Brent whether she will leave to go away with him. There is a similar pattern in *The Jewel in the Crown:* Daphne Manners encounters disaster when she crosses over from the world she knows in the MacGregor House to a moment of perfect happiness in a sexual relation with the Indian man she loves in the Bibighar pavilion. In both novels, the tragic histories of the polarized houses and pavilions set the tone for a tragic renewal in the body of the text.

When Brent wants to turn the illusion of happiness into reality by making his relationship with Teena a permanent one, Teena senses the impossibility of doing so:

"The door that only open [*sic*] inwards, that is called the Door by which men enter in anticipation of Desire. But the little door opens outwards, that is the door by which men go in memory of loving."
Was she cautioning me, warning me that however often a man entered

the pavilion he could not stay there, that the time would always come when he had to go?

"Must a man go out by that door, Teena?"

"There's no other door."

"He could stay here. He need not go at all."

"You said it was a magic cave."

"Yes."

She smiled again. "You would have to be a magician always to live in a magic cave."

I caught her arm. "Ah, but I am," I said. "I am. Watch." (216–217)

Teena is doubtful, telling Tom sadly that he is like poor Lieutenant Hakinawa: "You think the world is big. But it is very tiny. For us it is no bigger than the pavilion" (242). In the Chinese love pavilion, Scott has found a metaphor for the illusory, or transient, quality of happiness. This idea will be further developed in *The Raj Quartet*, where at the end of the novels a Hari Kumar abandoned by the English in India sees his past happy days in England as unfulfilled dreams.

What ties the pavilion and the tale of Teena and Brent to the story of Saxby is the close relation between reality and illusion. (This relation is also captured in Teena's realistic European mood and her enigmatic Chinese mood.) Saxby's advice and Brent's response to it pose the question—whether to immerse oneself in dreams or in the real world. Over an Indian curry, Saxby sees a romantic in young Brent and, summarizing Stein's advice in *Lord Jim*, urges him to follow it: "Directly a man is born he's flung into his dream as if into the sea . . . he would suffocate if he tried to climb out of his dream, out of the sea into the air. . . . Commit yourself to the destructive element and by the exertion of your arms and legs keep yourself up. . . . The realist may swim in the sea but he won't find a dream in it or recognize it as a dream at all. Your romantic will" (41).

Although under Saxby's influence Brent had at first thought of himself as "a man who sought mystical union with earth for the promise it held of leading him straight to the truth" (53), he came to believe that "it was life [he] had been flung into in Bayswater, not a dream, and life was a perfectly ordinary business" (58) where he did useful work and kept physically fit.

Yet Brent notes the symbiotic nature of reality and illusion when he does hard physical labor on Greystone's farm only to get a mystical feeling of land, and Saxby notes it when he discovers that without its dreams, the processes (the body) die (82). The question is which element should be placed first in Saxby's equation: "My body plus what?" or "What plus my body?" (47). Saxby takes the way of the romantic and puts the unknown first, while Brent attempts the way of the realist. The message that the novel will work out is that the dream cut off from reality is the way of madness, and Brent sees early in Saxby "a curious lack of balance . . . a kind of weight-lessness as though he had cut himself adrift from moorings, thrown overboard whatever urge it is we have that acts as earthly ballast and keeps us from soaring heavenwards before our time" (42). Con-versely, dealing with the world realistically in an attempt to actu-alize one's desires may be healthful to the psyche, but it is ulti-mately frustrating (Greystone is driven mad). Scott appears to be saying that people are imprisoned between a dream of their relation-ship to God, which has no known basis in fact, and the acceptance on earth of a lesser, more practical reality. The consequent ambiva-lence in Brent, the yearning of the romantic together with his com-promise with the real world, is expressed by Saxby's refrain: "You have the face of a sahib . . . but then in your heart you heave coal" (43).

The problem for Saxby is that he has no dream of his own, no im-age into which the search for the truth can transmute itself (and this is why he has a need to develop the dreams of others). He tells Brent: "I sometimes think I was flung into no dream at all. Perhaps my exertion is to scramble into it," and wonders, "Will it suffocate me? I mean if I find a dream to keep myself up in" (41). This is precisely what happens, and when Brent visits him in Singaputan, he has al-ready entered the world of illusion, his plant collection playing the symbolic part of suffocating him by shutting out reality.[4] Having de-cided that a vision like the apostle Paul's on the road to Damascus is granted only after hope has been abandoned (63), Saxby had given up hope to provoke one. And provoke one he did. Improving on the dream of his shaman, he dreamt of his five souls imprisoned in five flowers, and of their location nearby (199). After they are trans-planted in the Sakai aborigine village where he is living, they are de-stroyed when the Japanese burn down the deserted village, and the impact on Saxby is profound. "Five were burned that could not be moved" (200) is the reason that he in turn burned alive four Japanese soldiers. For Saxby it was not simply a question of revenge: "*[The Flowers] were the medium through which He and I were able to watch each other.*" After the flowers are burned, Saxby "cannot see God any longer, and He cannot see me. It is to burn away this dark-ness that I have done what I have done" (269).

There are ways in which the mad Saxby is like Ronald Merrick, the catalyst of the central tragedy in *The Raj Quartet*. He too has red hair and is the sole connection (aside from the narrator) among the three parts of the novel, just as Merrick connects the four novels of *The Raj Quartet*, once planned as three. Like Merrick, who disguised himself as a Pathan (for his nocturnal homosexual foragings), Saxby dressed as a Sikh and went into the forest, in his case to look for his souls. But the most important connections between Merrick and Saxby are those of power and the dichotomy between the dream and the real world. When Brent tells Saxby that he has never had a dream of his own to fall into, one thinks of Merrick standing metaphorically high and dry on the riverbank instead of, like Daphne, jumping in, actualizing a dream to live fully. Merrick and Saxby have an overwhelming need for mastery as well as a distinct sense of superiority, however defensive. Saxby's hostility to Brent develops when he can no longer control him. When Saxby had wanted Teena to murder the Japanese officers with whom she slept, make a list of collaborators, and send the information to the guerillas, he told her: "You'll do this . . . because I control the situation" (173). When he discovered he could not dominate her, she, like Ah Choong, became the devil for him.

Brent is drawn to Saxby at the same time that he is appalled by him because Saxby carries to a logical conclusion the romantic search for a self-image that "shows clearly how and where you've been touched by God, in what manner He has wrought you to make you more than mortal, more than a speck of waste in a wilderness of waste" (79). Saxby, the "god hunter," devotes his life to hunting for his soul. He is in search of a dream into which he can immerse himself because "it's only in dreams you get anywhere near the truth," in which God has "got your soul tucked up" (44). As a sign of God's special favor, he wishes to discover eternal truth while yet alive. Although Saxby is an obnoxious character, "a bloody hulk of a man with a flaming red beard who seemed to think he was God and made you feel like dirt" (96), Brent is unable to dismiss him. He has ideas that Merrick never shared, and the narrator finds something of worth in his mad search. Saxby is "dogged[ly]," "ludicrous[ly]," "pitiful[ly]" "nosing through the undergrowth of a forest all of us were lost in." He "so much impinge[s] on the darkness, the emptiness" (64) because he is attempting to find answers to questions Brent knows must be ignored or taken on faith.

Brent's own yearning for a solid knowledge of the ontological, probably what makes Saxby consider him a romantic, appears to be identical with Scott's. Not only does Brent adopt almost without realizing it Saxby's search for a piece of eternity but so does Reid. Brent tells us he would have found such an image of himself symbolized by the pavilion: "The pavilion was the place which seemed to have been waiting for me all my life, the logical end to days and years spent looking for a sign that God had touched me in some fashion" (313–314), he says when instinct tells him it is too late to save Teena. Reid has found his image in that of a man made six feet tall by killing but now wonders whether the image was sent by the devil and not by God (247).

Scott does not spell out what Brent means by this statement; the novel lacks a certain control and proportional emphasis. But we can draw our own conclusions. Reid, who considers himself punished by the gods ("It's . . . like a mark on me" [232]), tells Brent two-thirds of the way through the novel that the gods are not punishing him yet. The implication is that they will: "If you weren't scorched by [the gods] . . . you wouldn't give a fig about Saxby" (232). This statement is indicative of a certain ambivalence regarding Brent. He has sustained a serious shoulder wound, emblematic of a man who has come to terms with reality and who is yet psychologically wounded. At the same time that Brent tells himself he cannot have it both ways, he sees the championing of Saxby in the highest terms; he berates himself not for risking Teena's life to save Saxby but rather for, early on in Singaputan, abandoning obnoxious Saxby to the mercy of his plants. Brent is a man who generally places caring and conscience above his own self-interest and regrets it when he does not. Therefore, reality is destructive for Brent in large part because he cannot ignore the call of the dream, the ideal.

The concluding passage throws the book off balance as Brent loses himself in sentimental admiration of Saxby:

> One thing I am certain of. I would have had Saxby no different. He
> seems still to tower up in the darkness to which those times have gone
> and I would not have spared God a single jab from that hard elbow, one
> tap on the shoulder from that peremptory finger. Knowing him, I feel
> myself to have been with him if only for a short time and vicariously in
> his business of importuning Heaven, of not being prepared to accept that
> showing you believed had to be a one-sided affair. I would rather have
> had Saxby's brand of doubt than my own brand of faith which is, per-
> haps, no more than the belief that in the love of one human being for
> another, whether that love be returned or no, there is all the glimpse on
> earth that God will grant us of our souls before the time comes for us to
> go barefoot to hold them to the light and see what's left of them. (326)

Because Brent is the norm of the novel and Saxby is generally detestable, the reader has difficulty with lines such as "I would have had Saxby no different"; remembering Saxby's view of himself as waste and the cruel crimes he committed "to burn away the darkness," we are skeptical about Brent's statement: "I would rather have had Saxby's brand of doubt than my own brand of faith." Still, Scott does succeed in creating something beautiful in the mad, obnoxious Saxby; despite his grandiose delusions, Saxby lives only to communicate with God, and something is implied about his greatness of soul. On one occasion Brent encounters him dressed as a mendicant speaking in Hindustani: "There was an air about him so remote and yet so gentle I fancied that were the moon to shine more clearly on his face I should have seen upon it an expression of beatitude" (225). Saxby's face of beatitude, reflected as well in the oriental pavilion, will become in *The Birds of Paradise* exquisite dreams (symbolized by the birds) which, too rarified for the real world, die as soon as they hit earth.

Brent's dream of earth, his hunger to work with his hands, can be seen as symbolic of his desire to live deeply. What Brent wants is the same thing that MacKendrick felt and avoided in *The Alien Sky*, and the image of one's self in eternity for which Saxby, Reid, and Brent are searching to a greater or lesser extent has evolved from Mac-Kendrick's simple longing for a deeper self that eludes him. Brent, however, is a much less repressed character, and we have moved from a novel where a repressed and relatively unappealing protagonist experiences a kind of nonlife to one with an attractive protagonist of generally good judgment who is open to experience and therefore to tragedy. However, for whatever different reasons, Brent, like MacKendrick, Hari Kumar, and William Conway in *The Birds of Paradise*, is left with the dream of ideal happiness which he had failed to grasp and make reality.

One last point—the novel presents a sense of the complex contingencies leading to the death of Teena Chang and the thwarted relationship between her and Brent. None of these factors would have been enough to cause it—Reid's psychology of killing and Brent's reaction to it, Brent's desire to help Saxby, Reid's arbitrarily assigning Teena to Sutton, Brent's gift of the kris, her choosing to return it to him that night, or his failure to fight for her:

> Sometimes I think that Saxby, in the end, did not fail in the business of killing her. Sometimes I think she was doomed in that few seconds it took me to unbolt and open the door of the hostel in Bombay to which Saxby had come to find shelter, or even in the fewer seconds it took me to accept his invitation to eat curry with him. There are so many occasions to which you could point as the one decisive moment for Teena: the occasion when I thought, To hell with him. . . .
>
> But none of these occasions was significant in itself and they only arose because Saxby was what he was and I am what I am and they are

only fallacious arguments that would produce a pattern out of the sad jumble of our dreams (325–326).

This retrospective sense of causal complexity would be repeated in *The Raj Quartet* on social and historical levels. Although the ending of this novel denies that there is a pattern of events responsible for the disaster, Scott in the *Quartet* would root the pattern for disaster in human psychology. And he would make the objective of the narrative the tracing of responsibility.

The Birds of Paradise

The Birds of Paradise (1962), narrated from the island of Manoba in the South Pacific and taking place largely in Scott's Indian states of Tradura and Jundapur, is a complex, highly symbolic novel about the retrospective search of a London businessman for "meaningful occupation" amidst shattered ideals that appear illusory. In retelling the details of his search, the protagonist attempts to uncover the truth about his own life and in so doing provides a dramatization of the limitations of memory and perception. *The Birds of Paradise* laments a lost intensity of experience where the richness of physical sensation was once united with a sense of devotion religious in nature; it is a more richly textured exploration of the symbiotic relationship between illusion and reality than Scott had achieved in *The Chinese Love Pavilion*. The novel shows great philosophical and technical progression from *The Alien Sky*, also about a businessman's search for meaning in one of the Indian states. In that novel the American MacKendrick's search seemed childish, largely a compulsive need for an involvement with his dead brother's Eurasian mistress whom he had never met. *The Birds of Paradise* foreshadows *The Raj Quartet* in its careful incorporation of specific political aspirations in British history and in its shattering of them on the political as well as personal levels with some explicit metaphorical correspondence between them.

The narrative opens with William Conway, the forty-one-year-old narrator, on Manoba, where he has gone on his "sabbatical year" in 1959 to see the birds of paradise and be with the drunken old doctor, Daintree, when he dies. Living on this island with his own personal bird of paradise, Melba of Paraguay, a parrot (which gently mocks his own aspirations), Conway writes the narrative, an experience which must be seen as part of his search for meaning. When Melba sings to him, Conway gives us in the first section a clue to the novel's meaning: "There is contentment in her singing, happiness in recollection and a mature acceptance that so much of her youth was maya, so much of it illusion; and . . . when she . . . squawks my name: William Conway! and, Wurrah Yadoor-a! I feel that it is my youth she has been singing and not her own" (19). Structurally and thematically the novel consists of tracing beliefs and consequent disillusionments in his own life and lives that touch his.

In Book One, "The Wheeling Horsemen," Conway reminisces over his childhood days when his father was the political agent in Tradura. There he made two close friends, the English girl, Dora Salford, whom he loved, and Krishi, the young prince of the neighboring state of Jundapur, and he determined to devote himself, like his father, to a life of service in India. His favorite subject is the history of the British in India, and, at an early age, he learned that the paramountcy of the British Crown was represented for Tradura and five other states by his father's person. Being invited to the palace annually on his birthday to have tea with Maharajah Ranjit Raosingh only served to "increase my loving awe of Father, who told him what to do" (39). His governess, Mrs. Canterbury, and then his tutor, Grayson-Hume, help set his occupational aspirations, "to go on helping these people to live better lives" (29), and give him the sense of a superior calling. Scott very well captures in young Conway and the father after whom he attempted to model himself a condescending self-righteous quality based on an ideal of service that was part of the empire mystique for the British. Despite the death of his mother when he was four and the terrible beating ordered by his father for his misadventure with Dora and the Kinwar tiger during Shikar Week, his boyhood was idyllic, made so in large part by a sense of importance emanating from the consular power of his father's position and his own special stature as his heir. His father does not permit dogs, so he takes his imaginary dog Digby with him wherever he goes, a touch that is somehow appropriate for a boy whose most cherished beliefs will turn out to have been illusory.

Book Two, "On the Banks of the Water," takes place at Four Birches, his Uncle Walter's house in England where he has been sent to complete his education. Uncle Walter and his lower-class wife, Aunt Ethel, provide a warm home for him, but he keeps some distance, reserving his affection for his father, who writes brief, infrequent letters and who never sends for him to come to India for the summer. He has many memories of and fantasies about his life in India on the banks of the place called "The Water," and there his dreams are abruptly shattered when his father comes to visit. He is not to have a career in the Indian Civil Service but go into business in England with his Uncle Walter; with the British certain to leave

India, there would have been either no career for him or one cut prematurely short. He is bitterly disappointed by what he sees then as his father's "astonishing betrayal" (113). There is an occasional forward to recollections of his later ostentatious and adulterous marriage and of his son, Stephen, who prefers his materialistic mother to his undemonstrative father and who has also been brought up in a world of illusions.

Book Three, "The View from the Terrace," describes the deepest negative of the reality experience and asserts the final burial of the old Conway world in a Japanese prisoner-of-war camp, Pig Eye. It takes place immediately after the war as Conway returns to Gopalakand (where his father, knighted, is now Resident) to slowly recover on the terrace of the Residency from three and one-half years of horrific experiences as a prisoner of war of the Japanese in Malaya. Whereas Book One described the illusions of his childhood and Book Two his personal disillusionment, Book Three sets up the parallel political illusion and dilemma of the princes together with the diminishment of the British represented by his father, who seems smaller and in need of justification. Independence having achieved the status of a benevolent myth, the princes refuse to believe that when Britain ceases to be a paramount power, its protective treaties will be worthless and the Princely States will be at the mercy of the independent, democratic Indian government. The elder son of "Dingy Row," the maharajah of Gopalakand, urges William to stay on under contract. His blind trust in the British is much like that of the child, William, in the greatness and wisdom of his father. When William is feeling somewhat better, he tells Aunt Sarah something of the medical doctor, Cranston, who had once given up everything to work for Daintree in Java and who had saved his badly burned feet and his life at Pig Eye. This provides the rationale for the next section of Book Three, which moves backward to describe Conway's ghastly experiences of capture by the Japanese and the inspiration that Cranston provided with his mobile dispensary around which Pig Eye literally grew up.

Book Four, "Against the Wind," explores the symbolic meaning of the birds of paradise, which fly in this direction to prevent entanglement in their long, trailing plumage. Recovering from a failed marriage and disgusted by his view of himself as no more than a consumer, Conway visits Cranston, who is now director of the Muzzafirabad Laboratories in India. Attempting to contact Dingy Row's son, who has succeeded to the gaddi in Gopalakand, he is coldly rejected and through his own reading learns what part his father played in the British abandonment of the princes. He visits

Krishi—after independence and the lapse of paramountcy, a maharajah without power—and finds Dora, ungainly and middle-aged, visiting at the palace. Both are unhappily married, leading useless lives; each is sorry for the other, and both are seeking in each other a clue to the meaninglessness of their lives. The three friends once again visit the caged, stuffed birds of paradise on the lake isle. Then, with Cranston's blessing, Conway goes to Manoba to perform the duty that will give some small measure of meaning to his life: to be with Daintree when he dies, a broken man whom he has never met, and to see the living birds of paradise.

As in all Scott novels, the plot is an explication of the central image, the birds of paradise. There is no sense of a disjointed connection of the strands of the novel, as there was in *The Chinese Love Pavilion* or *A Male Child*. Textually this novel is Scott's finest pre-*Quartet* achievement, a dense, organic whole that impressively merges form and content. Like *The Raj Quartet*, *The Birds of Paradise* is a lament, not just for the past but for its idealization, in this case for the expectations of William's childhood (and, by implication, of all childhoods) which were not actualized. For William, 1929 was a time of anticipation and adventure, "the year of the great hunting party, the year of the Kinwar tiger, the year I met Dora, the year of the birds of paradise in the cage on the lake isle at Jundapur" (42). His hero worship of his father and expectations of following his career of service are at their apex; the sense of a higher purpose is mixed with feelings of omnipotence and the awakening of his sensuality, which melts into the year's lush, dreamy magnificence. The object of his interest is Dora,[5] who represents an ideal mixture of sensuality and spirit that he would later find lacking in Laura (whose name rimes with Dora), a cold, superficial woman who marries him for his money.

The loss of his childhood illusions causes a spiritual emptiness in Conway that he can fill only temporarily. This loss is foreshadowed for the first time during the maharajah's Shikar Week procession. Passing through a village on an elephant and enjoying the tribute paid by the villagers to members of the maharajah's entourage, the child, William, was suddenly devastated by the appearance of an old woman in rags. She knelt at the side of the road, palm outstretched, destroying the feeling of splendor by making the procession look "suddenly . . . unreal and tawdry," a tawdriness and artificiality that would be repeated in the dead, stuffed birds of paradise. He says, "The way I would describe it now is to say that in the midst of the magnificence I saw the face of damnation" (58). The image of the

beggar woman calling the lie to the reality of the magnificent procession has something in common with that of the suffering, unknown Indian missing from the artificially rosy picture, "The Jewel
in Her Crown," in *The Raj Quartet.*

The magnificence of the maharajah's procession is emblematic of
the life of high purpose that William intends to lead, a world where
right is victorious and where his own role in achieving it is of prime
importance. When Conway refers at the end of Book One to "the
prison of my Indian boyhood" (83), it is because adults tend to place
their children in a world of idealistic illusion where "tokens of love,
honour, courage, defence of the good against the bad, of the weak
against the strong" masquerade as "rules instead of exceptions" (94).
As one of these exceptions, William fights Krishi for calling his father a coward, although neither of them had attended the killing of
the Kinwar tiger; when he wins, he finds himself "trembling from
the exertion and excitement of finding that life was just as they said
it was in books" (66). But he discovers abruptly, on the banks of the
water, that life is not a fairy tale.

This conflict between noble desires and the real world, between
justice and power, is the very essence of Scott's mature novels. For
although Scott's novels demonstrate that he did not believe in a
creed, his sensibility is profoundly religious. We see this in several
ways. The first is in the most memorable incident in the novel, pre-
adolescent William's attempt to kill the Kinwar tiger by himself,
aborted because of the intensity of what one critic terms "a natural
religious experience."[6] Waiting for the tiger with Dora in the *machan,* the tree-fork observation post, he sees the tiger emerge from
the shadows and stare at something that had caught its curiosity. Instinctively, William turns and sees, instead of what the tiger saw, or
fancied it saw,

> Dora's profile: the small speckling of sweat on her upper lip, the partly
> open mouth and lowered jaw, her perfect stillness, the isolated pulsing
> movement of a vein in her neck; her appearance of being bewitched and
> totally unafraid.
> At once the waves of her enchantment made themselves manifest in a
> faint vibration, a sawing of the air all about the *machan;* a compound of
> our breathing and the tiger's breathing. The tiger stood quite in the open
> now, but I made no move to bring the gun to bear on him. He made a
> perfect target. The phrase "perfect target" was in my mind but there was
> something wrong with it and presently, when quite unexpectedly he lost
> interest in whatever it was he had been looking at or listening to and
> moved to a patch of dappled sun and shade, lay down and began to lick

his paws, I knew it was the word target that was wrong. There was no target in that place, just myself and Dora, the surrounding forest and the tiger washing himself.

And then it was not a question of being awestruck by the tiger's burning bigness or of seeing in it a kind of savage nobility. . . . It was a question of being awestruck by something quite other than these things: by the realisation that it had a right to be where it was, as much right as I and Dora; not *more* right, but as much right.

My lust for the animal's blood drained away. It left a sediment behind and I felt soiled by it. (63–64)

His intense experience of the Kinwar tiger, his most significant childhood memory, unites physical beauty with a sense of religious devotion, the real world and the ideal, "my body plus what" (CLP 47). It is reflected in his love and awakening desire for Dora. With an integrated sensibility he understands that he does not want to kill the tiger, nor does Dora want him to, an intuitive demonstration of the rightness of the sensibility of love or at least tolerance[7] over that of power and aggression.

Awed by the tiger's majesty, William finds the youthful belief in his own omnipotence succeeded by a realistic consideration of the danger to Dora, something that had not entered his calculations before. But emotional development is not permitted him naturally, independent of aggressive intrusions. Powerful forces in the form of the will of his father intrude, just as they would later intervene to prevent the fulfillment of his dream of service. He is cruelly beaten for his part, although whether the beating is for endangering Dora and himself or for later acting as a coward might—by giving up his place at the kill—is not clear. His bloody underpants, hidden in the rhododendrons, the private place of his awakening joy in the world, foreshadow the beating of Pig Eye and his general disappointment in the real world, where he keeps his joy in sensuality but loses his sense of specific, idealistic purpose.

"The illusion of my life," he says, "had been that a man should love his job, be dedicated to it, born to it" (148). In Pig Eye some years after his disillusionment on the banks of the water, Conway thinks he has recaptured his sense of purpose under the tutelage of Cranston, the only man he has thus far met with a burning sense of mission. Cranston was a civilian volunteer who, coming upon some badly wounded men in a truck in Malaya, "saw it as his duty to tend the sick, succour the dying, and await capture" (144). After his badly burned feet are healed, Conway becomes Cranston's assistant and feels once again that a life of high service is before him.

But Conway's devotion to the medical profession is a form of "gate fever" that does not survive Pig Eye. In a sense Cranston's fire, his creative purpose, does not survive Pig Eye intact, either. As a boy at school, Cranston told Daintree that he wanted to be a doctor because he wanted to feel alive. Yet, years later, when Conway visits him in India, he has become a medical organization man, the head of the well-endowed, spiritually sterile Muzzafirabad Laboratories. The job is easier; the diseases are all on slides, and he sits "wait[ing] in the middle to be fed" (184). The sense of heroic dedication is gone, replaced by a new acceptance of the status quo. Taught by Daintree, Cranston of Pig Eye had been in search of his "own burnt offering, . . . a job that could be offered up like a sacrifice" (149). His colleagues in the medical profession hated and envied him, he perceived, "because they knew he was . . . 'closer than they were to what medicine was all about'" (149). The contrast between the old Cranston and his new organization, with the reading of *The Raj Quartet* behind us, brings to mind the difference between Sister Ludmila, who goes about Mayapore collecting the destitute dying, and the Sisters of Charity, who embody the form rather than the actuality of caring. The brief mention of the people in his organization shows them smug, self-satisfied, and superior, concerned mainly with their image and the sterile sense of their own importance.

As a corollary of the concentration on sterile appearance, Conway has become obsessed with the notion of modern man as consumer rather than contributor. Cranston, for example, "had changed beyond recognition, had become reconciled to his own role of consumer" (183). The man who had once been willing to withstand torture to achieve his purpose is now "ready to consign the Muzzafirabad laboratories—outwardly perfect but inwardly no doubt already short of essentials—to the heap of brand new rubbish that seems to surround us always" (183). Daintree had dedicated himself to finding the cure to yaws, only to find when released from the prisoner-of-war camp that he had been rendered obsolete by penicillin. It had all been done; it was no longer possible to find yourself "somewhere remote where nobody in his right mind wanted to go . . . [and] make your burnt offering" (149). Daintree on Manoba laments that men who go it alone are finished ("Ah, God, if I threw myself into cancer these days I'd still have to be a cog in the bloody wheel" [191]), and drowns his disappointment in liquor.

Thus the individual becomes a member of a fairly meaningless organization, like Dora's husband, Harry, who tries to impart to the fertilizer he promotes some spiritual value (211). Or like Conway, who goes "about my dead Uncle Walter's business doing what every man I knew was doing; manipulating other people's money, biting off a chunk of it for myself, giving as little as possible in return" (174). Ironically textured into the novel is the idea that consumption has replaced devotion; the Manoboans have now succumbed, for example, to "the religion of goods, what are called consumer goods, what is sometimes called cargo—a cult rather than a religion; the cult of the happiness that must follow in the wake of the tins of Kwikkaffy which have already made the white man rich and powerful, and lie on the sands, the paths and the tracks, like shiny manna fallen from heaven, gone rusty, but no less potent for that" (15).

In *The Raj Quartet* Sarah Layton and Ahmed Kasim live a mutual objection to "a *received* life," a life of conformity. In *The Birds of Paradise* to consume, to receive, is to ride "with the wind," to be like William's former wife, Anne, cold, materialistic, inwardly vacuous, metaphorically "suck[ing] and munch[ing] her way steadily through life in the company of other suckers and munchers" (233). By way of contrast, to devote oneself to a worthy cause regardless of cost is to have one's own fire, one's own creative altar of sacrifice, to fly, like the birds of paradise, "against the wind." Conway feels himself to be a man like Cranston, possessing "a demon of unrest, a disturbance of the spirit" (147), which leads him to find satisfaction only in riding "against the wind." In Cranston's case, it "seemed to have been harnessed to the business of healing the sick; in mine, to nothing" (147). He fears that there has not been much to him after all and that (like George Spruce in *The Bender*) he has been "content to drift in whatever direction the wind blew me": "Hadn't I been compensating for the revelation of an empty hold by scratching around for memories of rich, impossible cargoes?" (170). With his dream of service in India destroyed and with Pig Eye behind him, he is unable to find a higher purpose to which he wishes to devote himself.

Going to Manoba to provide some small comfort to Daintree when he should die of alcoholic excess is Conway's only constructive protest against consumer life, which substitutes (it is implied) for the lack of meaning at the heart of things. People use ideals, which he considers imaginary, to "forget that if they suddenly closed their eyes and listened the only real sounds in the world would be those of chewing and swallowing and champing and regurgitation, the gasp of dying animals, the crash of tree trunks, the snap of stalks, the whirr of machinery turning things into other things, the ring of hammers, the screech of chisels, the crunch of bone on bone and mind on mind" (233). We remember this view, and the corresponding one that the bodily processes die without their spiritual illusions; it is a variation of the mad Saxby's in *The Chinese Love Pavilion* as well as the basis for Brent's admiration of his quarrel with God and for Brent's and Scott's view of his stature. The ontological void is what leads people like Cranston to substitute consumption for devotion or, like Daintree, to remain isolated and inwardly raging.

What Conway can offer Daintree (who would probably angrily refuse it) is what Sister Ludmila would in the *Quartet* offer to her destitute dying: to be on hand "should he want as he died some flicker of warmth from a fire other than the one he brought into the world himself" (232). Daintree through Cranston is indirectly responsible for saving his life. But Conway finds meaning in going to stay with Daintree in part because of what Daintree symbolizes, a union of the idealistic and the natural, an integration of spirit and body which Conway once found in his experience of the Kinwar tiger.

Images used in connection with Daintree are often natural and animal, suggesting largeness or great capacity. His face is that of "a lion too old and fierce to kill efficiently . . . His body transforms liquor into pure energy" (171). He is "a huge bear of a man" (149), and Cranston's dedication to medicine is dwarfed by his. He reminds Conway of "the bearing home of the Kinwar tiger" when he is borne drunken and unconscious on his palanquin, "one of his arms hanging loose, his white-maned head lolling" (169). The tiger, representative of natural life and vitality, has something in common with Daintree's large-spirited creativity. The young Daintree, then, is the ultimate representative of the natural, a relatively unrepressed representative of the individual as body ego. Since to be a truly dedicated doctor in this novel is to feel alive, he is also representative of the idealistic.

This union of the idealistic and the natural is of great importance to Scott and will be encountered again in *The Raj Quartet*, where the emphasis of the novels will be changed from the inability of the idealistic man or woman to find a meaningful occupation to the crucifixion of such people in pursuit of what they know to be the right. The theme is already present in a minor key in *The Birds of Paradise*, as Daintree was once broken by the Japanese for his rage over their barbarism. In the face of the lack of meaning at the heart of things, the same theme that Melville wrote about in his unsuccessful novel *Pierre*, those who survive and have their way are the strong rather than the just, those of superficial values rather than those who serve mankind, those who toe the line and consume rather than those who pursue altruistic goals and fight for their ideals, those who ride with the wind rather than those who ride

against it. And Pig Eye and the killing of the Kinwar tiger are examples of an incongruity between the way things are and the way
they should be. The individual's purpose, for Conway and Scott, is
natural and elemental, like the tiger's; it is also idealistic like
Cranston's and Daintree's and even, Conway comes to believe, his
father's. There is something noble, in the view of the novel, in elemental, powerless rage—as a form of protest against the lack of correspondence between the ideal and the real worlds.

The character of William's father, Sir Robert Conway, extends the
protest to the political sphere. Although a cold, rigid man, nick-
named Old Very Light (105), after World War II flares for his way in
any confrontation of freezing all parties into defensive position,
Sir Robert has in common with the large-spirited Daintree a determination to fight for an ideal even though he cannot win. Beginning
with Book Three, which is concerned in part with British abandonment of the princes, there is a corresponding diminishment of the
elder Conway. His portrait at this point provides one of Scott's first
portraits of the diminishment of the British in India: "For the icy
splendour had gone. He seemed to me to be diminished by his surroundings, by his knighthood which somehow squeezed him in between its Sir and its KCIE: by a manner towards him of Aunt Sarah's
which occasionally looked like indifference" (157).

When William and his father play chess one night, Scott introduces an extended image, a technique which would become common in *The Raj Quartet*, of the two-handedness of British policy toward the Indian states and democratic India. William's black pieces
are the Indian politicians of British India. Losing, his father is

> King's knight, Rajah's knight, impotent, beaten, but stubborn as
> hell. . . . Dingy Row's son had said . . . that the crown would stand by
> them . . . Wavell would see to it. So would men like my father.
>   But Wavell wouldn't be able to see to it. Neither would men like Fa-
> ther. They were pawns dressed up as knights. Logic demanded . . . that
> at last our strange dichotomy of principle should be exposed, that in the
> end the King-Emperor's crown should be revealed as sitting . . . crooked
> on his head. (160)

The British, as we shall see dramatized at great length in *The Raj
Quartet*, will abandon the princes while keeping the appearance of
principle. The elder Conway, enraged by this betrayal, had been responsible for Dingy Row's delay in signing the first agreement of accession and the consequent worsening of the conditions for
Gopalakand. At first William thinks his father played the fool by
making a public spectacle of himself, interrupting a private meeting

of the maharajah and members of the Political Department and threatening to destroy the preliminary documents which he called "instruments of a blackguardedly [sic] policy of intended seizure and forfeiture masquerading as agreements between free parties" (179). (By speaking, the elder Conway shattered the illusion that the princes were free to choose.) William, however, comes to have a more beneficent view of his father's action at the end of the novel.

As a writer, Scott is in search of fundamental truths about humanity. He is concerned in *The Birds of Paradise* not only with the lack of correspondence between the ideal and the real but with the limitations of memory and perception. Conway cannot be certain whether some of his memories are of real or imagined events, and this sense of ambivalence pervades the text. Signifying Scott's greater concern with internal rather than external realities, the titles of the four books refer to states of mind. The image of "The Wheeling Horsemen," the name of a vision Conway had of riding across the *maidan* to save his childhood sweetheart from the horsemen who were surrounding her, bears a relation to the central image of *The Raj Quartet*—that of a girl running who has been hurt in some way. He sees dimly in the distance a group of riders:

> Their horses seemed to be wheeling round and round as though in their midst there was something that had been hurt or someone who had been taken prisoner. I thought I saw a speck of white.
> It's Dora, I yelled. They've got Dora [and he speeds to her rescue].
> I never told her . . . because I couldn't be sure that it ever happened even as a game of pretend. And yet, "It's Dora, they've got Dora," and "I'm coming, Dora, I'm coming to save you," are words I must have spoken for they ring more truly to my man's ear in my boy's voice than any of the words I recall from boyhood. (69–70)

The image is fully representative of his attitude toward Dora, toward a sexual object that has awakened him; and since the image is probably imagined, it puts his childhood where Scott wants the past—in the blurred area between reality and fantasy, which is often how past events are remembered in a world where desires of the heart play a significant part in perception. In exploring differing perceptions and memories, Conway is "reminded . . . of the relativity of truth" (171). In superimposing childhood on adult past and past on present, the novel explores how truth is colored by one's state of mind and previous experience: "What I can say I know about the State of Tradura between 1924 and 1929 I know from such a variety of sources (from which my own imaginative deductions aren't excluded) that it's impossible to remember accurately who told me what or when or why. To that extent my Tradura is and was, per-haps, illusory" (39–40). And again, "My picture of Daintree is differ-ent from Cranston's picture of him. When I say Cranston's picture I mean, of course, my picture of Cranston's picture. It is hopeless trying to get at what we call the truth, but I had to ask myself the question. . . . The answer is that I've been trying to tell the truth about people as I thought they were and about myself as I thought I was" (173).

The merging of "the mind's eye and the real eye" (173) prevents the recollection of objective truth and is appropriate for the dreamy quality of the prose. But reality and fantasy merge in the world of art, and the following passage is reminiscent of Wordsworth's view of poetry as taking its "origin from emotion recollected in tran-quillity." The merging of "the mind's eye and the real eye" creates not real reality but a "reality of significance . . . where the drama of dull days lies. The arms of a day as you live it are not made for lying in, being hard and angular. Later you can lie in them, and the day is then transformed. You go back to it forewarned, wiser than it. Words that had never entered your head when the sun set on it now give it a substance it never had. You can also pick an old day up, like a shell, press it to your ear and hear the sound of the sea" (173).

Aside from being a novel of nostalgia and disillusionment, then, *The Birds of Paradise* is a book about artistic process, which appro-priately contrasts the random experience of the world to the selected experience of art:

> When I sit here writing these things down the days of my life in retro-spect seem to acquire a gravity that was mostly absent from the days themselves; Manoba broods beyond the window, responding to the rhythmic pulse-beats of my recollections; until I pause. Things get crossed out then, re-written in a different way, or I push the papers to one side, light up, pour a drink and, depending on the time of day, sit relaxed, eye the bed and perhaps think of Kandy, or go out into the clear-ing to talk to Melba or down the track to see Griffin or play cricket with his boy. Manoba stops brooding then; and the day is neither grave nor dignified but haphazard as always, a maze of distractions for body and mind. (182)

The drawing and redrawing of significant images of the past in an attempt to recapture the past as it was, Conway's stated aim in this novel, has much in common with the casting and recasting of im-ages that are also a blend of "the mind's eye and the real eye" in an attempt to find those that are artistically true.

Take the case of his father, the puzzle of whose behavior Conway had been unable to unlock. He wonders whether his father had been fond of him despite a cold mask of perfect form, whether he had "mistaken an acute shyness, total inability to show affection for indifference" (148). He does not know whether the memory of his father sitting by his mother's deathbed is "a picture of a man overcome in his stoic way by a grief deeper than I have ever known or . . . of a man using the time to memorise some instrument of policy lately come from Delhi" (158). Although he alternates between a view of his father as empty and hard-hearted and another as noble and idealistic, we come to believe with him at the end of the novel that however cold a man he was and remote in his relations with his son, however foolish in terms of practical affairs, given his denouncement of British pretence, he had held a noble aspiration. Although the cause of much of his specific behavior is left in shadow, one is left with an impression of truth of character that incorporates the ambivalence. Artistically Scott comes to see the "relativity of truth" (171) but, while dealing within this relativity and acknowledging that anything can be questioned, does not suggest either a lack of values on his part or the impossibility of believing anything at all.

By the end of the novel, Conway has spelled out why he is himself a profoundly disillusioned man. Without "a job that could be offered up like a sacrifice" (149), Conway, like Daintree, lacks a sense of importance to himself, and he ends his account with a moving statement of the bond between his father and himself—"[I] bitterly regret that not once in my life did I sit with him and let him feel that I understood how vulnerable is the illusion a man has of his own importance, not of his importance to others, but of his importance to himself, and how to speak of what drives him to sustain the illusion, of the means he finds to drive himself, of the dark that falls on him when the illusion is gone, is virtually impossible" (234–235). Yet his desire for such a life of high purpose was based on an illusion of the greatness of his father and of his own role as his father's heir: "It was the illusion of Father that I loved, the concept of him as an embodiment of what I was to be" (111). Like his father and like Hari Kumar in another way, William is exiled from "the prison" (83) of his Indian childhood, the world of his dreams. To free himself from that prison, to separate the reality from the dream, he writes the novel and finds that he is unable to do it, rather nostalgically recapturing the world of his dreams.

But the birds of paradise are only seen in the real world dead, stuffed, and in cages. Their use as symbol, an extension of the ephemeral Chinese love pavilion, is extensively and successfully developed. They are identified explicitly by Krishi as symbols of the

British Raj or, alternatively, as the Indian princes, implying an emptiness and unreality to their glory. There is a tawdriness and artificiality to the image of birds stuffed in a cage that has to do with the artificial preservation of illusion. They are the first of Scott's images of the dead Raj that needs to be blown away, and the boy Krishi wants to shoot them down. The British ideal of service is shown to be false in practical affairs as the British cut their losses and abandon the princes. But the symbolic meaning of these birds, whom no one has seen alive, who "live on celestial dew . . . and . . . could only be obtained when they fell dead upon the earth,"[8] is much broader— they are ideals of whatever kind which cannot survive in an imperfect world and die before they are actualized. Because people need to keep the illusion of their ideals, however, the birds are kept and stuffed. They are in a cage because illusion is a prison of a kind, and there is no sign of decay because ideals are not actualized but continue to exist as ideals.

The Latin name given to the greater bird of paradise is *Paradisaea apoda*, meaning "footless bird of paradise." Their footlessness is supposed to be proof of their supernatural existence. In fact, the natives of Aru kill them and cut off their legs for the commercial value of having them appear to be creatures of heaven, half believing themselves in the myths they have created. No one on the island, including Daintree, will quite admit the living birds are gone, reflecting the need to believe in illusions, the ideals, not merely the reality of human existence.

A human need for ideals is perhaps responsible for the suffering that they cause. Scott's imagery demonstrates attack by one's ideals, in effect suffering for one's ideals. That is the point of the child Dora's imagined "attack by the swooping, screaming birds" in the cage, reminiscent of the predatory birds of Brent's dream coming for Teena when Saxby intends to kill her in *The Chinese Love Pavilion*. In *The Birds of Paradise*, the emphasis is on disillusion and a diminished sense of one's own importance. Despite Saxby's search for his five souls and Conway's desire for evidence of "the reality behind the illusion" (170), both novels suggest that ideals are merely concepts of the mind with no corresponding external reality ("In reality there was no wind actually to ride into other than a fantasy wind across an open space and a fantasy wind of wings beating in a cage, the wings of birds whose legs were cut off to prove to fools there was such a place as paradise" [224]).

In recording the story, Conway has aimed to reenter the past, subconsciously to recapture past childhood happiness, consciously (by recapturing its truth, by separating reality from its illusion) to destroy the hold that yearning for an illusory ideal has over him. But he learns that he "hadn't killed the past by going back to Jundapur. I hadn't buried my dead. The dead weren't dead. Everything had grown directly out of the past, undeviatingly; you could squint from the rather blowsy flower down the stem and see the living root: a root which had shaped me to want to ride against the wind but also shaped me to drift with it" (224). In *The Raj Quartet* Scott would project an unrealizable ideal into historical terms, demonstrating on a political level the shaping force of the past.

Scott uses a superimposition of time and space to demonstrate this inescapable force. We see the life of Conway from early childhood through mature adulthood, and the Indian states of Tradura, Jundapur, Gopalakand, and prison camp in Malaya from the island of Manoba. The novel contains a remarkable recapturing of the feeling of childhood and of the growth of perception from early childhood to adulthood. When he exited the world of childish illusion and entered the world of adult reality, he says, "I . . . felt myself grow smaller in a world that grew bigger, so too I felt my father grow smaller, saw him in my mind's eye shrink into the actual mould of being a human being, the bottle from which as a child I had caused him to rise like a genie" (111). Past becomes present, and texture is enriched by the superimposition of childhood on present selves, of ideals on actualities. In attempting to recapture truth, or reality, as it is, in dramatizing the impossibility of totally separating reality from its illusion and escaping from one's past, Scott achieves a remarkable verisimilitude.

4. The Middle Novels II

The Bender

The Bender (1963)[1] has the same gently ironic tone that produced the mocking play on William Conway's lost aspirations in the parrot Melba of Paraguay as the only living bird of paradise. Like William, George Lisle-Spruce drifts and is unhappy about it, although drifting is differently defined. George has about him the sadness not so much of failed aspirations as of someone who never entered life's mainstream. Although the novel is no match for its predecessor or successor and George is something of a comic, picaresque hero,[2] the underlying message is one of seriousness and sadness, and the character of George Spruce lives. In this novel, as in *The Corrida at San Feliu*, Scott exposes the egoistic and egotistic character of human motivation and questions the ability of men and women to love selflessly.

Most of the other characters act as foils to George, who has had a sad life. He is kind, caring, amiable, good-natured, respectful of authority, sponging where necessary yet afraid of imposing, indecisive and impulsive in action. He has a calm, inquisitive manner, buries his anxieties in alcoholic dependence, is always in some kind of trouble, and has the kind of face, we are told by the third-person omniscient narrator who both observes George and writes from his point of view, that "had ceased to inspire confidence of the right sort, even in bars" (14). He consumes far too much gin and "has let himself run to seed" for some reason no one understands. Like Ian Canning, he sees himself with "detachment, some amusement and a certain despondency" (MC 11). He is critical of himself and leads an existence in which a successful borrowing from the bank of ten pounds (which disappears in drink by the end of the night and the novel) is enough to make him feel light-headed. His genuinely caring wife Alice has left him and married a wealthy businessman who has rebuilt her confidence and is better able to care for her. Before she left him, George had lost the ability to talk to Alice anymore because, like Tusker Smalley in *Staying On*, he felt that he had let his wife down.

George has two brothers, both younger—Timothy, a dull, solid, successful accountant in the process of being wooed away from his elderly partner, Wallingford, at an enormous increase in salary despite qualms of conscience, and baby brother Guy, a hustling, up-and-coming playwright exuding pure, selfish, masculine energy. George is not a success; on the contrary, he is the kind of person who hangs on to as much dignity as he can muster in the humiliating circumstances into which he is forever getting himself. He considers that several factors have caused his ruin: his small inheritance from his distant cousin, Sir ("Uncle") Roderick Butterfield, which deprived him of the motivation to find meaningful work; a case of adolescent mumps, which left him sterile; and a sense of "basic innocence," which leads him to expect the best of other people and himself and which "degenerates into conscience and a sense of [moral] obligation" so strong that he cannot "see . . . clearly what rights are [his]" (163). His inability to have children means that Tim's child, Gillian, upon George's death, will inherit the ten-thousand-pound principal that is yielding depreciated interest on which he is now barely managing to live. The plot centers on the fact that Tim is demanding of him repayment on a ten-year-old loan of two hundred pounds that he cannot repay. (The loan had kept George out of prison when it was discovered that he had secretly borrowed money from the firm employing him in order to repay pressing debts.)

There are not many options open to George. He thinks of asking Roderick's widow, "Aunt" Clara, for the money but cannot bring himself to do this, probably because he senses she would refuse. He considers and rejects various "chi-chi" (87) jobs obtained through Lady Clara's connections, one of which turns out comically to be driving high-class prostitutes to their rendezvous. In the end, he goes on a bender and chooses suicide, having decided that he is worth more to his niece dead than alive. His drunken, bumbling attempt to borrow a car for the effort is thwarted by two patrolmen who send him on his way to Tim's house, where Gillian has nearly drowned in trying to bring on a spontaneous abortion by drinking gin in a hot tub. Tim, blaming the attempt on Gillian's interview with George, tells him he will forgive the loan and even give him an additional fifty-five pounds if he never sees his niece again. But George genuinely cares about Gillian, who is also his goddaughter, and refuses to be bought. This wins the respect and affection of his sister-in-law, Sarah (who had previously seen him as "the wastrel" [79]). He is taken into the family and invited to go with Gillian to Wales to await the birth of the baby. The novel ends when he hangs up the phone after talking to Sarah to find that "the happiness that did not have to be pursued had suddenly been encountered" (220). The man who cannot talk meaningfully anymore except to strangers or into the telephone (182) has managed to communicate to his brother in a face-to-face interview (albeit in retrospect) his concern and affection for his brother's daughter.

The action of the novel takes place within forty-eight hours, double the time of James Joyce's *Ulysses*, and the movement is from aimlessness to acceptance, from a problem to its solution. This drinking spree and the novel end in the love for which George has been searching. Egoism (individual self-interest as the actual motive of human behavior) and egotism (an exaggerated sense of self-importance) are the novel's underlying concerns. So Tim in the end does what is in his own best interest at the expense of Wallingford's ease in retirement, just as he had kept George out of prison at least in part because he wanted to avoid the disgrace to the family. Aunt Ada wonders whether the negative impressions she had of her father as a child were not mainly because he appeared to love her sister Violet more than herself.

George considers himself and Stendhal egotists: "Writing journals, memoirs [Stendhal] and ringing people up on the telephone [George] were the marks of egotism, the only real outlets the true egotist had" (35). "You could say all that you had to say about yourself (which was the only reason for what was called conversation) on postcards and the telephone; and in memoirs you left behind when you died" (35). Yet George strikes us as selfless to the point of absurdity, at the opposite end of the spectrum from the novel's two unconscionable extrovert egotists/egoists, both sketched in caricature for comic effect, Lady Clara Butterfield and Guy Spruce. Lady Clara (a prototype of the gross proprietor of Smith's Hotel, Lila Bhoolabhoy, in *Staying On*) is a butcher's daughter who has risen through her father's money and an aristocratic marriage to what she imagines is social prominence; she admires Guy as a possessor of the "Pure Power" (33) she reverently intones into her tape recorder. She has no admiration to spare these days for George, whom she intended to be "a charmer" (54) if not "a force" (158) but who has turned out to be "a pudding" (158). George's lack of masculine force is indicated by his macho brother, Guy, who considers him dead from the neck down (and his brother Tim dead from the neck up) and by his sterility.

Lady Clara, who takes it upon herself to show young people that there is no authority higher than their own ambitions, finds George a disappointment. "You can't get it out of your head that there is some kind of higher authority" (156), she tells him, and "There is no such thing, George, as the utterly altruistic action" (155). George is the only character in the novel who feels impelled toward utter self-lessness and impulsive action, despising himself for perfectly natural feelings that have to do with self-love and self-interest. As he says into Aunt Clara's tape recorder (the message is not recorded because he has neglected to turn on the microphone): "I want to be loved for what I like to think I am instead of despised for what I really am. So perhaps by basic innocence I really mean the basic expectations of a louse who looked after his brother not because he liked his brother but because he hoped that looking after his brother would make his mum, who liked his brother better, like him too or even instead" (164). George will accept in himself only selfless love because he believes that only such love will win him love. Selfless love leads to self-sacrifice, and George is absurdly, comically willing to kill himself so that his niece can collect her inheritance.

At the heart of George's difficulty in expressing a desire for what he wants, or even, perhaps, knowing what he wants, was his relationship with a nasty, critical, socially pretentious mother, frightening to a young child and reminiscent of Marion Hurst and her destructive influence on her son Edward in *A Male Child*. In an incident revealing of this relationship, George's aunt, Ada Lisle, remembers on her deathbed a lovely new hat with cherries on it that she had bought with money her brother-in-law had given her for her birthday. Little George, who admired the cherries, asked:

Are they real, Auntie Ada? . . . Vi [his mother] slapped his hand before he could even get near them. I thought he was going to cry, but he never cried. He kept looking at the cherries all through tea. Vi wouldn't let me take my hat off even though the pin was killing me because it wasn't done in the best society to come to tea and not keep your hat on. You've forgotten everything our father taught us, Ada, she said, and I said, That's right, Vi, I never touch a drop. That was the time George said, Was grandpa an awful old soak? and Vi buttoned her mouth up and got that look that always frightened me because I thought the devil had got into her. (39)

Despite the novel's positive ending, one senses that the negative self-image and lack of self-confidence that George exhibits through-out the novel will ensure the continuation of his painful search for love and acceptance. As the reader is reminded several times by the interposed deathbed memories of Aunt Ada, his mother made no se-cret of the fact that she preferred Tim. George takes after his father, and it would appear from her sister's description that Vi took out her aggressions on her husband as well; painting pictures instead of earning good money, he was unable to gratify her fantasies of social advancement. George was brought up by his mother to desire in-tensely a world that was closed to him, and he describes the family's "sucking up" to their rich relations. The passage below poignantly portrays a small child on the outside, peering into a world his family, despite their social pretensions, lacks the means to enjoy. These feelings of deprivation were reinforced when he was sent by Uncle Roderick to a prestigious private school but had no chance of attend-ing the university because no one was either willing or able to pay for it. He would have liked to have planted tea or rubber, or mined tin, as was Roderick's original plan for him, but Clara stopped that, intending him to charm himself into the society of influential people. So strong was George's desire for the world that had been de-nied him that, as he tells Aunt Clara's tape recorder, he suffered a childhood confusion of reality and illusion. To his perception, then, it was almost as though the wished-for world of workable social con-nections were the real world:

> "I was brought up . . . not to accept my environment. There were these people next door called Proctor and if it hadn't been for Mr. Proctor and his bicycle I might have come into the world with no doctor and quite on my own in an air-raid, but as I see it I was always taught to believe that in one sense the Proctors weren't there at all because the Spruces, that's us, the Spruces in this same sense lived in a totally different world, a world of titles and connections and privileges that existed even if they did not actually work, for us, I mean for the Spruces, so that this totally different, this totally illusory world was the real world and the world of Mr. Proctor and the terraced villas and the whining voices and the swank and the bad taste and the loud laughter at night when some-body's door opposite opened to let out neighbours was the illusory, un-real, not there world." (176)

This passage might represent as well Scott's childhood view of the world, providing us with a key to his fascination with the juxtaposi-tion of reality and illusion. Although George Spruce is not Paul

Scott, they would appear to have much in common.[3] For our purposes here, it is enough to look at the characteristics of the novelist that George demonstrates. The omniscient, third-person narrator shares with him an acute sensitivity to the physical world, a preternatural awareness, and a delightful, comic use of metaphor, so extraordinary that George asks himself at one point: "Why should I be pursued by all this symbolism?" (27). The delicacy and sharpness of George's perception is matched only by his habit of metaphorical thought whereby language of great seriousness is attached to the commonplace. The confessional, for example, in George's view is "that left-luggage department to which the travellers never return except to bring more bags" (25). (The narrator, using the same light, ironic tone, delightfully describes the freshly bathed feet of old Lady Butterfield as "nestling into a goatskin rug like two lobsters side by side in Neptune's beard" [34]). Or, being taken off hold by his brother's secretary as George is telephoning from the hall of his rooming house, George "felt like an archaeologist who, with patience alone, had unearthed an old civilization" (26). The delicacy of his blocked sensibility is to be contrasted to the heavy expressionism of Guy, in many ways his inverse, who is rewarded for badgering the commonplace to create meaning in his plays à la Tennessee Williams or Paddy Chayevsky. This sensitivity goes along with the human perception that enables him to see that Gillian, for all her adolescent cynical indifference, has not imagined what it will be like to see and then give up her baby. It is George who makes her more aware of her own feelings, resulting in her near-fatal attempt to abort the pregnancy. And it is George who understands, finally, that Aunt Clara, despite her Thursday soirees, is in fact a lonely old woman.

The writer in George, as it were, is evident when he hears, accidentally at first, Lady Butterfield's stream-of-consciousness tape recording:

> George thought of his own handsome ears, what he looked like in a bathing suit, the poor prospects for a man who wasn't a force, the Sungei Labong Five per cents, his narrow escape from the Marble Arch, the disappointment Guy was in for, the experience you might have of cows, and pure power in roughly that order. And when he had thought of them in that order, and then in another, and then all jumbled up, he thought of them as a totality and from that totality there emerged the kind of thought that was really an image without words, and sad in its way: the image of an old lady talking to a Grundig because there was no one else to talk to, even on Thursdays. (167–168)

The transformation of this jumble of images into an image that pierces the very essence of the character sounds very much like the intuitive creative process of a novelist. In Scott's next novel, *The Corrida at San Feliu*, he would demonstrate that process in great detail, and in *The Raj Quartet* he would again allow the reader the satisfaction of arriving at a complex truth through a totality of impression.

The Corrida at San Feliu

The Corrida at San Feliu (1964) is a marvelously inventive book of which Scott was quite proud.[4] It is an extraordinary expression of the symbiotic nature of reality and illusion, a novel about creative process that demonstrates the subtle relationship between the events of a writer's life and those of his imagination.

The book begins ("Edward Thornhill, a Preface") with a reference to the death of Thornhill and his wife, Myra, when their car was washed away during torrential rains in Catalonia. Despite warnings of the dangers of flooding from his publisher in Barcelona, Thornhill was trying to get to their villa on the Costa Brava, probably to ensure the safety of his manuscripts. After his death, the lengthy autobiographical manuscript, "The Plaza de Toros," is discovered in his library, along with an allegorical sketch ("The Leopard Mountain"), a disguised autobiographical piece in the third person ("The First Betrayal"), and the short beginnings of his first and second attempts ("The Arrival in Playa de Faro" and "The Arrival in Mahwar") at writing a novel about "two people who turned up somewhere in disgrace."[5] *The Corrida at San Feliu* comprises these five parts, ending with 'The Plaza de Toros,' which comprises two-thirds of the novel and provides a description of Thornhill's relationship with Myra, his discovery of her infidelity, and his subsequent visit to the corrida. In closely relating Thornhill's developing fictional episodes to the events of his own life, "The Plaza de Toros" also provides an explanation of his creative process. The preface is written by a close personal and business associate in publishing[6] who assures us that "the novel [Thornhill] planned was certainly never written, but the preliminary stories, completed or scarcely begun, and 'The Plaza de Toros'—a personal investigation into his obsession with the incapacity of men and women to love unselfishly . . . may be reckoned to stand in its stead" (9). The publishers have decided that these papers, conceived separately, are yet "complementary and interdependent" (9) and should be published together. Scott's use of the novel as solvable puzzle, perfected in *The Jewel in the Crown*, is demonstrated

here. The question planted in the preface is whether Thornhill committed suicide, taking his wife along with him.

Thornhill, the orphaned son of medical missionaries, grew up
with his grandfather, radical, atheist, anticolonialist, and educational and medical publisher, and his Uncle James, who was jealous
of him and afraid that he might get some of the Thornhill money.[7]
Grandfather died when Edward was representing the firm overseas
(as did the young man in "The First Betrayal"), and Edward resigned
on his return, complying with Uncle James's desires. From James,
"the kind of man who couldn't bear the thought of anything belonging to anyone else" (12), Thornhill developed in "The Leopard
Mountain" the character of Saunders, the scrap merchant who owned
or held in mortgage most of the good farmland in the valley where
he lived. Saunders decides to kill a real or imaginary leopard that is
supposed to be lording it over the surrounding wilderness, because
"a leopard, real or imaginary, had no business owning anything, even
a wilderness" (20). To hunt the leopard, he takes the two wheels left
on the truck, the only possession of his scrap manager, Thompson,
on whose farm he had foreclosed. Thompson is a homely, hardwork-
ing, simple, honest man of whom everyone takes advantage. When
Saunders deliberately takes his friend's wheels, Thompson realizes
how he has been taken in by everybody, including himself, and that
underneath his good-heartedness he wanted material possessions as
badly as anyone else.

So Thompson forges Saunders's name, rents a truck and supplies,
and follows him to the mountain. He wants to kill the leopard before Saunders can do it. But his unconscious has other intentions,
which the alert reader may detect in such sentences as "When he
reached the spot [of Saunders's truck] he thought that the truck had
that bleak appearance of a possession its owner would never return
to" (30). Glimpsing what he thinks is Saunders, Thompson believes
Saunders is in mortal danger and searches the thicket for the leopard. Seeing a movement in the bushes and imagining that he sees the
leopard's mask, he fires, killing Saunders. Discovering what he has
done, he laughs perversely, without really knowing why he is laugh-
ing. The story is Hawthornesque, again reminiscent of "Roger Malvin's Burial" in its use of controlling unconscious motivation.

We meet the two people in disgrace in India in "The First Betrayal," a sketch which, like "The Leopard Mountain," was written
after the two aborted attempts at the novel which follow them and
before the autobiographical "Plaza de Toros." (The sketches probably represent Thornhill's attempts to find his true subject.) Bruce
and Thelma Craddock, he the artist forever sketching and painting,

she the bored accompanying wife, are snubbed by Mrs. Clipsby-Smith for having "committed some awful breach of the rules and regs" and have, in her husband's opinion, "come all this way to Darshansingh to hide their faces" (55). Thelma and Bruce are incidental to the sketch, which is concerned with the desire of a young man (from whose point of view the story is told) for Mrs. Clipsby-Smith's daughter, Leslie. This desire appears to be based on her contempt for him (which begins when he almost runs into her and then falls off his horse) together with his pity for her obvious unhappiness. When he succeeds in awakening her and realizes her innocence, he loses interest. The young man whose name is withheld is Thornhill as a young man in India; the young woman is a girl he had actually met there in 1925.

The sketch, as the reader discovers in "The Plaza de Toros," represents the conscience-stricken Thornhill's first betrayal; the second is his inability to prevent the suicide of his first wife, Mitzi, whom he had married out of pity (he believes she needed the emotional stability love would have provided). The third and most significant is the stealing of his second wife, Myra, from James's good-natured son, John, who was killed in a drunken driving accident shortly thereafter. He feels the most remorse for this, and a sense of retribution, for the situation is reversed and now Myra is betraying him by having an affair with a young man known to us only by Thornhill's term for him, "the godling."

"The Arrival in Playa de Faro" is not quite seven pages long. Thelma and Bruce Craddock, here representative of Myra and John had the future been theirs, turn up at Playa de Faro, a beautiful, lazy setting on the Mediterranean coast. Bruce Craddock is attractive to many women, Thelma is beautiful, and they are devoted to each other. Since Myra and John were denied a future, Thornhill has the constant public smiles of Bruce and Thelma fade when they look up at their beautiful villa (69). In "The Plaza de Toros," Thornhill writes that he abandoned this first attempt at his novel because it was not turning out to be a story about two people who turn up in disgrace: "In a place like Playa de Faro, Bruce and Thelma weren't capable of supporting the penitential load I tried to put on them. They kept wanting to shrug their shoulders, go out and around and have a good time" (77). Because the setting was inappropriate to the characters, the conclusion to which he was leading them did not "fit in with the original picture of them" (78), suggesting that the image is of prime importance for Thornhill, as it was for Scott. The setting, intuited as part of the story, must match the image as originally conceived.

So Thornhill tried a very different, more successful setting. In "The Arrival in Mahwar," the lovely Playa de Faro has turned into Mahwar and "this terrible place" (70), the Panther House. The Panther House has a haunted atmosphere somewhat reminiscent of the Bibighar Gardens in *The Raj Quartet* and a depressing history (a panther, deprived of her cubs, steals a child to raise). The shift is matched by such details as the changing of Thelma's hair from gorgeous tortoiseshell in the previous sketch to "brown, lustreless," bleached at the ends (70). Thelma is plain instead of attractive and knows that Bruce finds her old and ugly. The mood created in these details suits the desperation of people who turn up in disgrace and reflects Thornhill's feelings about stealing his betrothed from his cousin, John. In this version, it is not Bruce but Ned Pearson who represents John. He is married to Leslie and, disgraced, kills himself when his affair with Thelma becomes known. (This section was written before "The First Betrayal," as though the image of unhappy Leslie, brought up as a boy, led Thornhill to tell her story.)

Fiction for Thornhill has its origin in fact. Although Thornhill fictionalizes his accounts "to create a correspondence of reality that won't cause them pain" (74), he bases his characters on people he has known. The details are often different, but the emotional truth remains the same. Craddock's biography, described in "The Plaza de Toros," is similar to Thornhill's, although Craddock is a civil servant in India righting wrongs. Thornhill and his character Craddock are both artists: Thornhill a writer, Craddock a painter. Both marry women out of pity rather than love and their wives subsequently kill themselves. Both Leela, the fictional half-Indian princess kept in her English grandmother's house as protection from a world that disapproves of mixed blood, and Mitzi, the half-Jewish girl who has lost her family in the Nazi holocaust, cannot face the harshness of the real world. Myra and fictional Thelma, both second wives and victims of unhappy childhoods, marry men too old for them before they are awake to their own sexuality; each feels she is living a dead life with an artist-husband who has taken her from a previous engagement, and each has an extramarital affair with a younger man. "[Myra] was Thelma with her eyes closed, imagining the heat. . . . Even in repose her body was disciplined to conform to certain standards of conscious grace; but strip her of that grace and of her beauty and she was Thelma" (167).

But it is not an exact correspondence; sometimes there is an inversion or a duplication. Bruce is more in control of the fictional relationship, whereas Thornhill is actually more dependent on Myra. He puts fictional Ned (who must also represent the godling) in the wrong by having him betray his wife, Leslie, and also, by his suicide, his lover, Thelma. And the relationship between Ned and Thelma was, oddly enough, something like the relationship in "The First Betrayal" between young Thornhill fictionalized and young Leslie. One impression in a writer's life can lead to multiple characterizations: "Lesley is for ever a child to me, one who was touched and woken before she knew what touching was, what waking meant. Like that, she is an embodiment not of her own innocence, but of everyone's, which is why she turns up in so many different disguises, not only as the memory of a girl I knew years ago in India, but also as Ned Pearson's wife, as Thelma Craddock, with her mother in Kashmir, as an unknown girl standing on the beach at Playa de Faro, gazing at the sea; and also in that picture of Myra as a child, travelling as Thelma did between one parent and another, looking to be loved" (166).

Part Two, the autobiographical "Plaza de Toros," was written quickly, at Playa de Faro, after Thornhill's discovery of his true subject; it was he and Myra "who had turned up in disgrace." Thornhill's visit to the corrida, a place he had always sought to avoid, came immediately after he had despairingly confirmed his wife's affair, intuited from distant, voyeuristic observation through binoculars, with the godling. "Pickled in liquour" and "ruined by curiosity" (102), he had watched them closely on the beach, day after day, imagining their conversation in great detail, letting the tension build (as Craddock did when Thelma was unfaithful) instead of ending the relationship, as he knows he could by questioning Myra. Like Craddock, he has "a ramrod core . . . that would sooner break than bend" (166) and takes an unconscious masochistic pleasure in silence.

He has an uncanny intuitive sense, an ability to see the unseen, much like Marion Hurst's in *A Male Child:* "When I was born . . . something monstrous attended the lying-in, cursed me with the inability to see only what is there physically to be seen and left me with one of its own dark offspring" (94). The dark offspring, García Lorca's Duende, (meaning "imp, ghost, goblin" [79]), is the creative spirit, perverse like Poe's and deformed:

> [In Spain,] whatever type of work or performance it is it counts for nothing unless the Duende [who is inside] is heard.
> I think of my own Duende as a little black hunchback who draws pictures on the walls of his dungeon. When I find the pictures moving he shrieks with laughter. When I find them comic I hear him weeping in the straw. There's a chain on his left leg and there's one part of the dungeon wall he can't get at to draw pictures on. I shout at him to break the chain. He curses me and tells me to break it myself. We both bleed from

the strain. The book I would write is the picture he would draw on that part of the wall. You wouldn't recognize them as the same, but he's got to. If he does the chain is broken and he leaps across the page too quickly for you to see anything but his shadow. He draws his pictures and I write my words. Then you feel him.

To the Duende the physical world is bare, ugly, beautiful. He is naked, disarmed, crippled; aching with the pain of his imprisonment and his deformity. What is inanimate in the world—trees, hills, mountains— they kill him with their tranquillity. At night the Universe looks intolerable to him, unbearably indifferent. There's nothing, nothing he can do to molest or change or halt it. What he paints or draws or sculpts or writes is done with this knowledge, but only to make his life bearable.

But it is only paint, only wounds, only thought, only imagining. It is an artifice, a malformation, a malpractice, a mask, a joke, a game. If he's lucky some of his games are good enough to be handed on as proof of what can be done when you play the game hard enough, well enough. (79–80)

I have quoted at length from this passage because it is so descriptive of Thornhill's creative process. It is especially important because the idea of the chained, crippled Duende is critical to a conception of art as the result of a psychological wound or imprisonment. Thornhill's Duende enables him to practice his art, an art whose value he questions even as he is compelled to perform it. He is described by his business associate as a man undergoing an "agonizing reappraisal" (17). He imagines Myra saying to the godling: "He needs me. It used to be I in a curious way who needed him. . . . Now I only need not to hurt him. At the moment, everything and anything can hurt him. He's afraid of dying, of being old. He's put everything into his work. He's drained himself. He wonders what it's been worth, what it adds up to" (119). His sense of guilt at having stolen Myra from John is exacerbated by the difficulties in their relationship and by his suspicions of her infidelity. One problem is that he spends so much time living in his imagination, looking right through his wife, not speaking to her "as if [he is] saying it all in [his] mind to someone in [his] book" (123). And like the wife of David Chalmers, the publisher's reader in "Mango Rain," Myra remembers that he used to show his work to her and ask her opinion but no longer does (125).

Thornhill's lack of vitality is expressed in the emphasis on his age (sixty) as compared to Myra's youth (forty). Despite his devotion to his art and compulsion to practice it, Thornhill feels that art is dead because it is merely an illusion.[8] Echoing his own thoughts, he has Thelma think: "I sit like a ghost in the dead fields and Bruce sits like another ghost with his easel and his paints attempting illusions of life. He does not know that what he paints is dead. He sits under his black umbrella shading himself from a heat and a glare that do not exist except in his mind where they exist as he remembers them from the time before the sun died" (124). The wound which permits the practice of Craddock's and Thornhill's art also limits the living of their neurotic lives to the metaphorical shade rather than the sun, where the godling who is so attractive to Myra spends his time. If art is in one sense dead for them, it is because it exists too much in the head; there is an intuitive recognition here of life as body ego when Thelma adds: "But all that exists outside of us is Ned's body. It generates heat in me from the grave" (124). From the early novels, we have seen that a basic quest of Scott characters has been to live fully, often expressed as performing hard physical labor rather than doing paperwork, and we are not altogether surprised that Thornhill finds it "better to have built one strong bridge or ploughed one straight furrow than to have scribbled away for years trying to create order out of chaos" (102–103).

Significantly, the man who sells him a ticket to the corrida is a hunchback, symbolically his creative genius that he also recognizes as the voice of truth, the voice that must find the connection between reality and its appearance. The Duende will make him see in the tableaux of the corrida connections with life and with art. The reader sees them also, for the primary image of Thornhill's autobiographical manuscript, "The Plaza de Toros," is also central to *The Corrida at San Feliu*. Figurative descriptions of the cornered bull are lengthy, complex, and occasionally overstated. But mainly the novel's extended comparisons work well. Often the bull, Thornhill is occasionally the torrero, or the horses who cannot scream when the bull's horn finds their bellies because their throats have been cut. The central image of the corrida presents a paradigm ("It would not have been difficult to have seen in the pattern of the corrida the whole pattern of a single human life" [203]). This paradigm fits the various events of his life, the lives of those close to him, and also the lives of his characters. It is an "allegorical fantasy in which the bull is a young man . . . and the arena is that little bit of the big wide world God tells him he can have for himself if he works hard at it and is able to teach every other marauding bastard to keep his hands off it" (203). The art of one man clothes the same themes in many guises; as we saw in "The Leopard Mountain," life is a losing struggle for power and possession, love a mere staunching of wounds.

Thornhill goes to the corrida wondering whether he can really watch an animal being baited in the course of a public entertainment and comes away finding that, as the bull's life is not his own, he does not really care. Men and women are unable to love selflessly, he concludes, as he sits "waiting for the personal revelation of what he really means when he says, as he has said so often, so glibly, for nearly sixty years: I love, I care, let justice be done, teach us to forgive, hoping that . . . today, through the medium of this art . . . there will be a glimpse of the reality behind the illusion that man can care for someone other than himself" (213). In thoughts that appear to be disembodied, he concludes unhappily that whatever men and women do they do for themselves. Myra will return to him not for his sake but because she is more comfortable with their lifestyle. "We are all members of the same disgraced species," he thinks. "The man in that seat down there who covered his eyes when the first pic went in covered them for his own sake, not for the bull's. . . . Is there a cruel action in the world that any of us will resist if we don't perceive in it, however distantly, a threat to ourselves or to our self-respect? Is there a cause in the world we will support unless by supporting it we feel ourselves individually uplifted?" (213).

What leads him to such questions is difficulties with self-love and a dissociation from his own feelings. Like so many of Scott's early protagonists (Jim Taylor in *Johnnie Sahib*, Joe MacKendrick in *The Alien Sky*, Ian Canning in *A Male Child*), Thornhill's Bruce Craddock feels an inner emptiness: "If I look back on my history isn't it a tale of emptiness I have tried to fill but never succeeded in filling?" (154). The sense of emptiness, we might have concluded from *The Bender*, was based on a fundamental repression, an insistent substitution of what one should do for what one desires to do, not necessarily in behavior, which must always fall short, but in sensibility, leading to dependence and a strong sense of guilt. What makes Thornhill fear "the terrible void and the deep blue darkness of endless frightening space" (202), which he then fills with his art, is a loss of self projected onto the world. Thornhill is a man plagued by guilt, tormented like Craddock, by memories of those he feels he has betrayed. Something of his psychological makeup is evident in his first novel, *The Dark Mission*, where Biddle, a middle-aged English missionary in Africa, suffers from dreams of racial guilt. Not until he receives external punishment for certain crimes subsequently committed is Biddle freed from the self-punishing creations of his tormenting superego.

Thornhill is preoccupied with his discovery at the corrida, then, because self is repressed. The return of the repressed—the unconscious insistence on what he considers the ugly element of self in his various selfless motivations—is what makes Thornhill's (and

Craddock's) Duende perverse. He laughs at what Thornhill thinks serious and cries at what he thinks funny. Biddle's Duende must have been responsible for his seeing black rather than white saints. The Duende, combining elements of the id and superego, is there to question motivation, whether Craddock's or Thornhill's. The Duende must have been in the garden, Thornhill concludes, when Thornhill asked Myra to marry him. He laughs when Edward takes Myra from John, a man nearer her own age, as though to say he had gotten even with the wrong man, John instead of his greedy father, James. The Duende must have been there when Thornhill wanted to laugh at Uncle James's grave without understanding the reason; through John's death he is to inherit some of James's money.

We have seen that the Duende is the source of Thornhill's creativity. As the element of the controlling unconscious, the element that Thornhill considers truth (he teaches him, for example, that "good and evil grew side by side" [94]), the Duende represents a truth that, unknown to Thornhill, balances the purity and dispassion of Thornhill's conscious motives by its exaggerated negation. (He married Mitzi and Craddock married Leela out of pity and a sense of justice rather than love.) This relationship is also evident in Craddock's paintings, where art is again described as a game, a kind of perverse game the artist is compelled to perform: "Only in this little game with canvas and easel has the monstrosity [his Duende] been kept quiet, but now even in this he has begun to show his venom. The hills he makes me paint are not beautiful like the Mahwari Hills. They are tortured, molten, full of purple lava and shadows and poisonous vegetation. Looking at my canvas I can smell the rankness. The colours are bitter, deadly. They consume the canvas in blue green and purple flames and in the flames I see the faces of those I have loved and those I have betrayed" (142). However, once Thornhill admits his presence, admits the inability of people to love selflessly, he believes that his Duende no longer has the same power to torment him.

In acknowledging the resemblance between himself and Myra and Bruce and Thelma Craddock, Thornhill recognizes the merging of his life and his art. We see the same blending in "The Plaza de Toros" as we move without warning and without being sure of the dividing line from his matter-of-fact observations of Lesley searching for a swimsuit to the events of his imagination as Lesley takes off her swimsuit on the beach and sacrifices herself to her first sexual penetration. The five separate parts of the novel represent the same blending; taken together, they provide clues to whether or not Thornhill deliberately engineered his own and Myra's deaths. The business associate who wrote the preface tells us: "To those who knew him well, the image of him driving through rain and rockfall in an attempt to get back to the work that mattered much to him, even though he could call it publicly 'all play', is far more convincing than that of a man driving recklessly to end his own and his wife's lives. As a man, Edward Thornhill had no time for death by decree, and is unlikely to have signed his own death warrant" (18−19). And five weeks after the corrida, shortly before his death, he writes in his journal of the Duende who "will be with [him and Myra] a long time yet" (215), and speaks of the sense of opportunity, of his now being able to make discoveries, as Biddle could have made them once he was free of his plaguing dreams. Given the evidence, then, it is doubtful that he consciously courted death.

But having broached with his wife the subject of her faithlessness and having unwillingly confirmed her guilt, Thornhill is no longer the man he was. What he calls "the last day of his life" (173), the day of the bullfight, which takes place six weeks before his death, is his figurative way of saying this. Continuing the image of the corrida, he says: "If we come out of the querencia of our privacy [his silence] we are wounded and destroyed" (111). Numbed and "apparently incapable of movement" (206) at the corrida, he, like the bull, is aplomado, waiting for death "not with a desire for death but because it has worked itself to a standstill fighting for its life" (212). We cannot ignore the fact that Thornhill took unnecessary risks. He ignored strong warnings not to attempt the journey, drove at night, and missed the road sign warning of the closed bridge. The novel therefore leads us to conclude that the Duende, the power of Thornhill's punitive, creative unconscious, dictated the eternal union in death of Edward and Myra, a union that is the culmination of what he calls elsewhere, in connection with the slightly varying images of the corrida, "my own endless struggle to transmute the raw perpetual motion of life into the perfect immobility of art" (202). Art for Thornhill has a timeless quality somewhat reminiscent of Robert Browning's "Porphyria's Lover." This timelessness is first encountered in *The Birds of Paradise* in the images (such as Dora surrounded by horsemen) described as *transparent* and later perfected in *The Raj Quartet*. Thelma imagines such a union with Ned at the very end of the novel in a section of "The Plaza de Toros," written shortly before the flood that took the lives of the Thornhills: "What I was, and what Ned was, has passed from this dimension of space and time to another. . . . I let him draw me down on to the bruised grass. He enters the wound he has opened. With my hands I feel his back burning in the sun. And like this we are turned suddenly to stone, because here a union, an awful wholeness has been achieved between man and nature; and so we lie for ever in carved cohabitation, in the dark and in the light, in the rains, through all the seasons of the year, immortally joined" (221).

We have been subtly, carefully prepared for the controlling influence of unconscious motivation in the story of "The Leopard Mountain" and in various details in the lives of Thornhill and Craddock, such as the accidental deaths of their defeated rivals shortly after losing their betrotheds. The conclusion is not spelled out in the novel but is part of the puzzle that must be pieced together, a question considerably more difficult for the reader to solve than that of what happened to Daphne Manners in *The Jewel in the Crown*.

Because Thornhill aspires to unrealistic ideals, he is driven by unconscious forces to deny his own picture of himself: "Craddock . . . was the man my hunchback made me see when I looked into [the mirror] at my own reflection: the naked construction of bone under the dissembling flesh; the whole skeletal structure of the inner silence that would be left if layer by layer my pretensions to articulate compassion for human frailty were peeled away" (167). It seems likely that Scott created a series of recessive portraits. If Craddock is the picture the Duende makes Thornhill see in the mirror, then Thornhill must be a picture of himself that Paul Scott saw in the mirror.[9] This portrait would not be strictly accurate but slanted toward the negative, even as Thornhill questions "what hunchbacked need made me portray Myra in the character of Thelma as ugly and unfulfilled, and myself as a man apparently devoid of feeling" (156). There is some reason to support the view that in *The Corrida at San Feliu* Scott has described the nature of his creative process and his related emotional suffering. Having had Thornhill conclude that human beings are unable to love unselfishly, Scott would be free in *The Raj Quartet* to make a sublime statement about selfless love.

5. Origins of *The Raj Quartet*

T. S. Eliot wrote in "East Coker" that "one has only learnt to get the better of words / For the thing one no longer has to say, or the way in which / One is no longer disposed to say it. And so each venture / Is a new beginning, a raid on the inarticulate." Paul Scott liked to quote this passage (IPF 131), for he considered words a very imperfect approximation of the images that peopled his mind. Scott claimed that he "would give almost anything not to have to [write]. How much better if you could become a sort of piped music, if readers could plug into you and receive their images direct" (MM 84). Nonetheless, his photographic memory gave him an advantage as a novelist; his books are intensely visual. In "The Form and Function of the Novel" he indicates his "inclination to think in images, from which ideas can be intuited" (16). Writing was "a discovery" (AW 38), a chance to uncover the meaning of his images.

A novel, for Scott, is an exploration of a series of images derived from a single image, "everything . . . flow[ing] from it and back into it . . . like [the part] played by . . . the irritant in an oyster around which the pearl forms" (FF 8). He saw the novel as "really *one* image . . . and . . . the problem is not so much one of relating different images to each other but of digging into the central image to try to extract all its possible components and then—and only then—trying to relate them back in what will be a logical order" (AA 116). The process is an organic one, as Scott illustrated in detail in *The Corrida at San Feliu*. His images develop around what he calls his "prime mystery" (MM 82). The world he first forms out of and around that original visual image is "audible . . . but . . . shapeless and incoherent" (FF 10). The process itself, then, is responsible for the sense of totality, complexity, and density so characteristic of *The Raj Quartet*. When he shaped the novel, "ordering [the] chaos" of his imagination, he deleted people and events in the process; the extent of his fantasy remained far greater than what was contained in the finished product.[1]

What is the image that holds this central significance in *The Raj Quartet?* In "Method: The Mystery and the Mechanics," Scott describes its origin in the aftermath of his 1964 stay in Thimmapuram. He had just come from Calcutta, where he had encountered an anglicized Indian having an affair with a young white woman. For ten days he lived in the home of his ex-havildar in the Indian army, B. V. V. Narayana Doss (Narayanji), the village council head, who, in his account, had the only house—the others were mud huts (ES 133).[2] He would later use the experience as a model for District Commissioner White's overnight village stay in *The Jewel in the Crown.* Conditions were extremely primitive by Western standards, and Scott suffered severe culture shock. In the essay "India: A Post-Forsterian View," written after he had had some time to distance himself, Scott described the experience:

In India this last time, for ten days, which I was assured beforehand was nine days too long, I lived in an Indian village, twenty miles from anywhere—no telephone, no doctor, and—as the young ladies in the coffee rooms would say, no toilet. I performed what these same ladies would describe as my daily duty . . . in the fields. I performed it more often than was customary because within a few days the entereovioform did not have the advertised effect. I submitted on every return to the compound to a ritual washing of the feet by a daughter of the house, and to the morning ritual of being shaved with a cut-throat, hot water, and no soap—shaved from forehead to neck, including eyelids . . . before a crowd of onlookers. . . . And after a while I started giving orders and when crossed, raised my voice. Upon my Fielding face I felt, superimposing itself, my Sahib's face. Irrational fears had entered. . . . If there had been an English club down the road I would have yelled *Koi Hai* and gone there by bullock cart. Instead I went . . . to the Hindu temple and . . . came away convinced from the bitter taste on my lips that I had been involved in a purification ritual that included drinking cow's urine. I emerged marked on the forehead. Like Cain . . . [yet] on the blessed day of departure, I understood well enough that I'd been in nothing more terrifying than the presence of human curiosity, human affection, and particular human customs. . . .

Idleness, illness, primitive conditions, fear of the strange and alien, ready acceptance of tin-god attributes, until I experienced them in one implacable combination, I did not truly understand in my flesh and bones, the rock on which Turtonism is founded, . . . the secure nature of the stout encircling wall which [the English] erected to protect themselves. I think perhaps most of them did not understand it either and still do not. At this level, Turtonism is an instinct, not a faith. . . . The

thick layer of Turtonism which I discovered in myself is what appals
me. (129–130)

The village experience affected him so profoundly that he wrote to
Jean Leroy of David Higham Associates that the experience had
taught him "more about the (cultural shock + fear = prejudice)
equation than 20 years of liberal thought, liberal assumptions (including 3 years of living in British India) ever did"[3] and that, for
once, he wanted to write about the experience itself rather than fic-
tionalize it. As a consequence of this experience, he is able to communicate the effect of psychological defenses on character and society with astonishing realism as well as convey the root of the
Westerner's fascination with the East.

After the village experience, Scott made tentative stabs at beginning a novel, the unfinished "Mango Rain." He had been interested
in the "out-of-season rain which comes in time to ripen the man-
goes. The fruit . . . was human love, the kind that crosses the barrier
between castes and creeds, black and white" (MM 81–82). He could
not get the novel started, however, because he had not got past his
own experience; there was no image. The image that finally came to
him one night, "as images always do, apparently by chance, unexpectedly," he used not for "Mango Rain" but for the central image of
The Jewel in the Crown. As antecedents of *The Raj Quartet* he identifies "the trauma of the Indian village experiences, the desire to get
away, to run, the knowledge of the dangers that exist when you attempt to cross bridges, the whole feeling of the British in India, and
the feeling of India itself—a vast, flat territory, strangely forbidding,
somehow incalculable, ugly, beautiful. And there she was, my prime
mystery, a girl in the dark, running, exhausted, hurt in some way, yet
strangely of good heart—tough, resonant. Her face and figure a sense
rather than an observed condition. But she runs" (MM 82). He did
not yet know from what she was running or to where. But once he
had the image, he could mine and exploit it. To place the image in
time and place, he then "bombarded" it with facts and waited for
them to stick: "That English girl in Calcutta in 1964—nothing could
ever have made her run—not there, not then. The girl in the image
was running, you might say, from that village I stayed at. The village
that had already been translated in my mind into a symbolic experience of confrontation between East and West. The last great confrontation between East and West in India was in 1942." (MM 85).[4]

To develop Edwina Crane, he says, he created a variation of the
original image with differing but complementary qualities. The
character was inspired by Marcella Sherwood, an English missionary

dragged from her bicycle and left for dead in the riots of 1919, but it is Daphne's bicycle which ends up in the hands of the police. Miss Crane was not alive for Scott until (with the help of his Duende) he saw her removing from the wall of her bungalow for his Quit India policy the picture of her one-time hero, Mohandas Gandhi: "Well, there she was, a half-baked elderly English liberal making a half-baked gesture. And the image of the picture being removed created another of a picture that stayed up—an old engraving showing Queen Victoria receiving tribute from representatives of her Indian empire. The title of the picture was 'The Jewel in Her Crown.' The whole history of my missionary was suddenly revealed by her possession of these pictures, her history, and her attitudes, her good intentions, her liberal instincts, her failure emotionally to cross the bridge between East and West. The book suddenly could begin *behind* the image of a girl who *had* crossed the bridge between East and West" (MM 88). At the height of the 1942 riots, Miss Crane is traveling with an Indian colleague who is killed protecting her. She insists on holding his hand:

> It is negative, useless, stupid, but—in its context, *right*—the novel is away. Going in through the back of the original image has begun to unlock its mysteries, and in this particular case . . . *by leading up to the climax of the riots it has suggested that the form the novel will take is that of approach*, through different eyes, through different histories, from different vantage points in time—to a central point of reference, which is exemplified in the original image—the action of that image and the implicit emotional context of that image.
>
> Yes, truly, Miss Manners is in love with her Indian—and he with her, and she would not limit the expression of it to holding his hand when he is dead. They could not, of course, have chosen a worse time, a worse place, to be in love with each other. It was my job to explore the reactions of many different people to that time and those circumstances. The image had exploded in all its complexity; it was my job, somehow, to recontain it. Once I had seen what it was, it was a comparatively easy book to write. (MM 89)

The Raj Quartet must be seen, then, as an explication of a single image that creates, by association, multiple images. The novelist must communicate these images. In doing so, Scott says, he will be communicating the inner significance that created them in the first place.

Scott liked to stress "the dramatic quality of the novel and the tension at its heart."[5] When he wrote creatively, he began with an image of "two human beings in a situation. Out of that image comes the tension, and out of the tension comes the characterisation, and out of that comes the structure, and finally out of that comes the words."[6] Beyond the image of a girl running, one of the early images of *The Jewel in the Crown* in Scott's imagination must have been the confrontation at Sister Ludmila's Sanctuary between British Superintendent of Police Ronald Merrick, who is of working-class origin, and the anglicized Hari Kumar of upper-class English background. The passage below is suggestive of how the novel is created by an explication of dramatic tableaux:

> So we . . . follow[ed] a few yards behind Mr. Merrick, so that we heard the first words, the first words in the affair that led to Bibighar. As we approached. Merrick. A clear voice. As if speaking to a servant. That tone. That language. The Englishman's Urdu. *Tumara nām kya hai?* What's your name? Using the familiar *tum* instead of the polite form. . . .
> "What?" he said. And spoke for the first time in my hearing. *In perfect English. Better accented than Merrick's.* "I'm afraid I don't speak Indian." That face. Dark. And handsome. Even in the western way, handsome, far handsomer than Merrick. . . . "Come," I said, "come to the office," and made to lead the way but already the Bibighar affair had gone too far. In those few seconds it had begun and could not be stopped because of what Mr. Merrick was and what young Kumar was. . . .
> "A statement. I come with you under protest."
> And all the time in those accents so much more English even than Merrick's. And in Merrick's book this counted against him. For in Merrick's voice there was a different tone, a tone regulated by care and ambition rather than by upbringing. It was an enigma! Fascinating! Especially to me, a foreigner who had . . . heard [an] Englishman often rail against the sharp clipped-spoken accents of privilege and power. And here, in spite of the reversal implied by the colours of the skin, the old resentments were still at work, still further complicating the conflict. (J 143–145)

The narrative of *The Raj Quartet,* particularly of *The Jewel in the Crown,* might be seen as a working out of the elemental race-class conflict inherent in this image. The conflict is represented in the confrontation of these two characters, an instance of Scott's fondness for reversal and polarity. It is not surprising, then, to find an implicit criticism of the class system as well as of racial prejudice woven into the texture of *The Raj Quartet* at all levels of society, Indian and English. To choose at random some examples, there is Duleep Kumar's ambition (born of his own career frustrations) to turn his son into an Englishman; Hari's losing caste for crossing the

black water; the Mayapore cantonment ladies' condescension to
Miss Crane, speaking to her "in tones that would have suggested to a
stranger that Miss Crane was only a mission school teacher and as
many rungs below them as it was socially possible to be and still be
recognized" (J 29); Lady Chatterjee's being thrown out of the English
hospital when she goes to visit Englishwoman Crane. Ram Dass,
Lili's houseboy at the MacGregor House, obtained his position on
the gardener Bhalu's recommendation but "has since had little to do
with the gardener because Bhalu's position is so inferior to his own.
He will not admit a family connexion. . . . The cook despises them
both. He has cooked for a maharanee in his time" (J 94). Seen together, there is surely an element of the ludicrous in these class and
race distinctions, ironically revealing of human nature and indicative of Scott's splendid control over his material.

To recapitulate, then, Scott in his novels is communicating the
significance of his images, formed from association and born of a
single image. To communicate his images, he must shape them:
"The writer takes human reality apart in his mind and reassembl[es]
it in a way that will expose it" (FF 26). Scott reassembled the pieces
of *The Raj Quartet* to expose his characters and emphasize his dramatic climaxes—images charged with moral and psychological significance are drawn in tableau and restated from different vantage
points, creating a truth of total effect. The "cross-indexing of detail"
does not, as one critic puts it, "shrink our image of the literary world
of the *Quartet.*"[7] On the contrary, repetition with variation gives
Scott's images the validity of the familiar in so large an enterprise,
intensifies them, and expands them as symbol.

Although all matters of technique and characterization are subordinated to the primacy of the image, there are other matters that
bear mentioning in a discussion of the origins of *The Raj Quartet.*
Scott's return to India in 1964 allowed him to remember and relive
the India he had lived through between 1943 and 1946 with the
benefit of his mature sensibility and by now considerable knowledge
of Indian history. The part played by his widowed, Rajput hostess
and dedicatee, Dorothy Ganapathy, in the creation of *The Jewel in
the Crown* cannot be overestimated. Her name is pronounced Gan-
pati, identifying her with the god of good fortune, wisdom, and
learning who is the guardian of writers. The identification was not
lost on Scott, who adopted the Ganesha of Hindu myth as his colophon. It was very important to him that Dorothy Ganapathy like
"her" book. He shared the exhilarating reviews with her, carefully
typing them out for her to read, and wrote that he had established
with her "a most valued friendship which I have done my best to

celebrate in this novel." He even credits her with enabling him to write the novel: "Without that initial welcome from you, what would I have made of my sentimental journey back to India?" The letters indicate a sentimental, even mystical attachment.[8] Scott may have seen her as Mother India. The warmth of the reception she gave him, the nurturing atmosphere she undoubtedly provided, not to mention the close friends to whom she introduced him,[9] these elements, taken together with his village experience, which shook him to the depths of his being, are probably responsible for the strengthening of his sense of self and for the consequent shape of *The Raj Quartet,* centered as it is on the image of a girl running, hurt in some way, yet strong, enduring. This image reflects the *Quartet*'s strongly positive, life-affirming values, which stand in sharp contrast to the sense of emptiness expressed by the protagonists of so many of the early novels.

The writing of his fiction was the blending of reality and fantasy that intrigued Scott and that marks his novels: "The riots are real. The historical and political scene is factual. The dramatic situation of the criminal assault, the arrests, the treatment of the prisoners, is imaginary, but it is based very broadly on fact" (MM 77). Although he could not easily think of himself as himself, Scott to a limited extent saw himself as the Stranger ("Such hospitality as I had from you, such kindness to the Stranger in the novel, is never forgotten, never presumed upon"[10]), trying to puzzle out what went wrong in the British-Indian relationship, with the help of Dorothy Ganapathy (who must have inspired Lili Chatterjee). He modified the characters of the mixed couple he had met in Calcutta, shifting them back into a time of great stress to add dramatic interest. He used his own experiences, particularly what he had learned about the strength of the communal response from his stay in Thimmapuram. His village experience appears again and again, as Daphne's visit to the Vaishnavite Temple and "her suspicion that she had drunk cow urine"; as young Robin White's being shaved without soap in the village, fearful of being blinded by a slip of the barber's hand but later finding a flower on his saddle; as Miss Crane's self-consciousness and embarrassment at finding a chair set out for her in the middle of the road. He taught the village children some English words, just as Miss Crane's children were taught some English from the picture of Queen Victoria on her throne. He saw the leper who appears sporadically in *The Jewel in the Crown;* and the Chillianwallah Bazaar, which repelled poor Hari Kumar when he was forced to return from England to live there with his Aunt Shalini, was a meat market where Scott saw purchased "meat already bombed by a million flies."[11] In *A*

Division of the Spoils, he makes use of Dorothy Ganapathy's flat (with the view across the Oval), projected upstairs.[12]

Scott appears to have shared with Nathaniel Hawthorne an intensity of imagination which made the world of the mind more real than the physical world[13]: "Dorothy, my dear, I was touched by your description of your party on the 16th. I expect I knew quite a number of the people there, and having heard about how they all stood up when you gave the toast I feel almost as if I had been there. Distance, time, separation: these are mere illusions of the physical world. One is joined, more deeply, in the mind and in the heart. If the food disappeared very quickly from the table you can assume that I was there, too, eating my portion, a grateful but invisible ghost." Yet the realization of his deepest desires seemed like dreams to him, as he wrote to Narayanji: "Sometimes I wake up in the morning and think that it is a dream that I am coming back to India for a visit."[14] It is not surprising, then, to learn that Scott, like Edward Thornhill in *The Corrida at San Feliu*, spent a good deal of time living in his imagination, exploring the significance of his prime image: "Almost every one of your waking hours is spent considering it, exploring it. You can carry on a conversation and still be thinking of it."[15] During the time he wrote the *Quartet*, he did as little reading as possible of other people's fiction about India; he did not want to confuse their picture of India with his own.[16]

In order to write the novels, Scott had first to recreate the entire society in his mind. Part of the fascination for him must have been to work out how the society functioned. His historical reading enabled him to complete his detailed picture, a total re-creation. Scott was at great pains to write the story as it might have happened, to be accurate down to the last detail. He read about the history of British India for more than fifteen years before he began writing *The Jewel in the Crown*. So involved did he become with the lives he read about that he used to dream about them.[17] Yet he needed to fill in certain gaps in his detailed knowledge and assure himself that specific instances of what he imagined about the way the society worked were accurate. He would write to the India Office Library to research some of his information, or his English contacts might try to obtain the pamphlet "Duties in Aid of the Civil Power" because he wanted to "get . . . right the details and drill of co-operation between the civil and the military." Or, because he wanted Ronald Merrick to get a DSO from the viceroy, he asked M. M. Kaye to find out from her husband, a general in the Indian army, whether a viceroy would ever award a DSO to a junior officer or whether he dealt only with civil honors.[18] He wrote to Dorothy Ganapathy many times, asking her, for example, to consult with the judges and lawyers she knew to doublecheck on whether it was section 144 of the Criminal Code that "enabled district authorities to lock someone up (without trial) if they were thought to be harmful to the District (as distinct from harmful to nation when the Defence of India Rule was invoked)." He needed to understand the law and the situations into which he was placing his characters:

> If it is not a long section I'd be quite interested to see the wording—but mainly I would like to know this: that given, say, a man locked up under this section of the code, during say the troubles of 1942—locked up not as a *proved* subversive or rioter but as a suspected subversive, without trial—how long might one imagine his detention lasting? In the case of well known people who got put in jug under Defence of India Rule the place of detention was often kept secret. Would the same apply to a small-fry, detained by the local authority under section 144? If not, would just his family know which prison he was in? And what kind of imprisonment would such a man undergo? Rigorous imprisonment? What did this actually entail as regards work or labour?"[19]

For questions on Indian music, he consulted singer Dipali Nag, his Calcutta hostess, who found and translated the raga used in *The Jewel in the Crown*. (He imagines Parvati, the child of Daphne Manners and Hari Kumar, as a pupil of hers.)

Scott builds his own world in India—the same one that frequently exists in more than one novel and has some basis in the world, remembered or historical. He was fond of using some of the same places and even some of the same characters through the novels. Thus, Smith's Hotel (based on Greens, a small hotel remembered from Officers Training School in Belgaum)[20] is found in Marapore in *The Alien Sky*, mentioned briefly in *The Raj Quartet*, and used for most of the Pankot setting for *Staying On*. Marapore, a city in *Johnnie Sahib* and *The Alien Sky*, becomes Mayapore (appropriately, the city of illusion[21]) in *The Raj Quartet*. (Mayapore was a generic city, "an amalgam."[22]) Bibighar, the center of the tragic love of Daphne and Hari, was inspired by "that other Bibighar at Cawnpore" (J 146). During the Sepoy Mutiny, British women and children were kept in the Bibighar, the House of the Women, and then murdered by men of the Nana Sahib before they could be rescued. Brigadier-General Reid, who fired on civilians during the 1942 riots in *The Jewel in the Crown*, was inspired by Brigadier-General Dyer and the 1919 massacre at Jallianwallah Bagh, also memorialized in dowager Mabel Layton's nightmares of "Gillian Waller" in *The Towers of Silence*. Scott liked not only to transform actual historical places, characters, and events; he also was fond of giving places that played a significant role in his fiction tragic histories that would be repeated in another form in the main body of the text. (We have already seen how the history of the Chinese love pavilion, where men lost their heads, was played out when Tom Brent's beloved Teena Chang lost her life there.) This predilection is evident in *The Raj Quartet* in the embroidered tales of Bibighar, the palace of a prince whose love for a singer was never consummated, a place later destroyed by a fanatical Scotsman, MacGregor, before he lost his own life in the Sepoy Mutiny.

Minor characters would sometimes catch Scott's interest, or a character who played a major role in one novel would again appear briefly in another.[23] Tusker and Lucy Smalley, minor characters in *The Towers of Silence*, are the protagonists of *Staying On*. Sir Robert Conway, who plays a key role in *The Birds of Paradise*, reappears in *A Division of the Spoils*, again as a Resident advising a maharajah to delay signing the Instruments of Accession until the lapse of paramountcy. Occasionally the same type of character is found in more than one novel. The spiritually dead Colonel Manville in *The Mark of the Warrior* has much in common with Adjutant Kevin Coley in *The Raj Quartet*. And Major Reid of *The Chinese Love Pavilion* is a predecessor of the more empathetic Brigadier-General Reid of *The Raj Quartet*, both trigger-happy military men unable to understand why they are being punished. An important principle of Scott's was to make his antagonists sympathetic. ("Reverse! . . . The moment of reversal is when the antagonist becomes the protagonist."[24]) Despite the fact that he loathed the type, he saw the necessity of making Brigadier-General Reid courageous in the face of his wife's death from cancer and his son's detention in a prisoner-of-war camp in Japan.

Scott was fond of modeling his characters on real people. He once wrote, "I suppose every character has a flicker in him or her, either of myself or of people I've met, briefly, or known fairly well, or all of them. . . . No character is entirely out of the imagination, and yet none is anything but imaginary."[25] He altered their personalities and placed them in situations of stress where they would be caught between conflicting social forces and have the limits of their psychological strength tested. He once said that his daughters provided the inspiration for the Layton sisters and that Roland Gant's prisoner-of-war experience was the model for Colonel Layton's.[26] He used the story of Brigadier-General Dyer and the Amritsar massacre of 1919 to create Brigadier-General Reid and the Mayapore riots, and Mother Teresa to create Sister Ludmila. Sir Conrad Corfield, once head of the Political Department of the government of India, probably played a part in the creation of British Resident Sir Robert Conway; and Chadravarti Rajagopalachari's quarrel with Congress may have been used to create Congress Party politician Mohammed Ali Kasim.[27]

When Paul Scott began *The Jewel in the Crown*, he had no idea that the novel would grow into four parts and an epilogue of modern India. Whereas the Quit India rebellion of 1942 provided the background for the first novel, the succeeding years leading to partition provided the setting for the following three. His overall object, he wrote to Dorothy Ganapathy, was to examine the effects of the whole British connection. In so doing, Scott used facts for an imaginative act that transcends time and space. He was attempting not a documentary novel or a novel of fact such as Truman Capote might have written but an imaginative re-creation, a blending of fact and fiction to create a deeper meaning of history.

Once his Duende provided the image of the girl running, the Defence of India laws gave him a historical focal point onto which he could project the story and values he saw implicit in this image. In examining the effect of the Defence of India laws, his aim was no less than the re-creation of an entire society. Appropriately, *The Jewel in the Crown* begins with a landscape and ends with an aerial view, creating the sense of a total vision. In one sense the novels are about detective-narrator Scott discovering the story and values implicit in the unifying image of the girl running. The truth he seeks is at once moral, historical, social-racial, psychological, and metaphysical—a totality even as the total picture of the society it describes.

6. Overview of *The Raj Quartet*

The Raj Quartet embodies a criticism of the repressive Defense of India laws, which could imprison on suspicion of sedition, and takes as its historical starting point the arrest of Congress Party leaders on August 9, 1942, for voting support of Mohandas Gandhi's exhortation to the British, in the midst of war with Japan, to "Quit India, and leave her to God or to anarchy." The rioting which followed the arrests leads in *The Jewel in the Crown* to the roadside attack on the devoted Edwina Crane, supervisor of Protestant schools in the Mayapore district, the murder of her companion, Mr. Chaudhuri, resident teacher at the school in Dibrapur, and the gang rape of Daphne Manners, the unconventional English niece of Lady Ethel Manners, in the Bibighar Gardens immediately after she and Hari Kumar (formerly Harry Coomer), an English public-school-bred Indian, have made love. Hari is arrested as a suspect, and although Daphne refuses to cooperate with the authorities, the Defense of India laws provide District Superintendent of Police Ronald Merrick with a handy device for incarcerating indefinitely his rival for her affection.

In *The Day of the Scorpion*, set in the provincial capital of Ranpur, the laws' injustice is again portrayed in the arrest and imprisonment of Congress Party leader Mohammed Ali Kasim, a man of uncompromising principles who favors Indian independence and unity and whose elder son, Sayed, commissioned into the king's army, turns traitor and joins the Japanese-led Indian National Army chiefly be-

This chapter is a revised version of an article that was previously published as "Paul Scott's India: *The Raj Quartet*," *Critique* 20 (1978): 100–110. Copyright © 1978, Heldref Publication, 4100 Albemarle St., NW, Washington, D.C. 20016. Reprinted by permission of the Helen Dwight Reid Educational Foundation. (The plot summary incorporated here does not appear in the published article.)

cause the British have arrested his father. The novel minimally continues the story of Hari Kumar. When interviewed at the Kandipat
jail by the governor's aide, Captain Nigel Rowan, Kumar learns that
Daphne has died in childbirth and describes Merrick's sadistic and
sexual abuse. The third and dominant strand of the novel begins the
story of the Laytons, a military family living in the hill station of
Pankot. Responsible Sarah Layton is in many ways a replacement for
Daphne Manners, and her popular, unstable sister, Susan, marries
Muzzy Guide officer Teddie Bingham at the palace of Kasim's kinsman, the nawab of Mirat. Captain Ronald Merrick, who has now
joined the Indian army, is best man. Teddie is soon killed in battle
and Merrick is badly wounded trying to save him. A pregnant Susan
goes mad.

The highly symbolic *Towers of Silence* adds very little to the plot
but deals symbolically with the history of Britain in India and the
British illusion of principle. The lens of the camera hones in on the
British military community in Pankot, particularly on the figure of
the retired missionary of the Bishop Barnard Schools, Barbara Batchelor. Structurally a description of Barbie's history and her decline
into madness, the book circles back to incidents dealt with earlier
and presents a close-up of Layton family life. Barbie has been taken
in as a companion to Sarah's grandmother, old Mabel Layton, which
puts her on the wrong side of Mabel's daughter-in-law, Mildred, wife
of Colonel John Layton, a prisoner of war. After Mabel dies, Mildred
takes possession of Rose Cottage and throws Barbie out. Meanwhile,
Susan, delivered of a baby boy, places him in the center of a circle of
kerosine which she lights in an unsuccessful attempt to "free" him.
Sarah, seduced in *The Day of the Scorpion* by a womanizing Captain
Clark, has an abortion. To her horror, Barbie discovers Mildred in an
adulterous relationship with Adjutant Kevin Coley. Barbie is in a serious accident shortly after meeting Merrick, who is on his way to
Simla to be decorated for bravery by the viceroy. She dies soon after,
mad and speechless, at the moment of the atom bomb blast in
Hiroshima.

A *Division of the Spoils* shows a tightly ironic, energetic prose
style which contrasts with the largo of the preceding movement.
The novel demonstrates the result of British alienation from India in
the 1947 division of the country, the sectarian train murder of Kasim's younger son, Ahmed, and the abandonment of Kumar to his
fate. Much of the story is a reconstruction by the narrator of the
Quartet from the point of view of a new character, Field Security
Sergeant Guy Perron, an upper-class student of British imperial history who has decided that the military ranks are a most interesting

place to study human behavior. He is passing the time in Kalyan, near Bombay, in anticipation of Operation Zipper, the invasion and liberation of Malaya, when he meets and is attracted by Sarah Layton, who is in Bombay to greet her father, still suffering from his experience as a prisoner of war. When Perron catches Colonel Ronald Merrick's eye, he is forced to transfer to Merrick's division in intelligence. After watching his sadistic and humiliating methods of interrogation, which lead to the death of an Indian National Army havildar from Layton's regiment, Perron, with the help of an influential aunt, has himself recalled.

Using devious and arcane methods, Merrick succeeds in getting into the files of Susan Layton's psychiatrist and marrying Susan, who has partially recovered and to whose class he aspires. So strong are Rowan's feelings of revulsion for Merrick that he consequently decides not to marry Susan's sister, distressing Sarah but making her courtship possible for Perron. Before Perron leaves for England, he and Sarah make love casually in the Moghul Room of the Old Summer Palace. Kasim has a private interview with Sayed, who is in Merrick's custody. During the interview he tries to brief him to say nothing critical of the British during his court-martial and is appalled that he cannot convince Sayed of the error of breaking his contract by joining the Indian National Army.

When Perron returns to India in June 1947, he learns of communal riots in Mirat and the death of Ronald Merrick, murdered finally by people who took advantage of his homosexual proclivities in revenge for the six Indians, including Kumar, who had been wrongfully imprisoned and tortured in the Bibighar affair. Although Governor Malcolm and Rowan are eventually successful in achieving Kumar's release, he is left as a "permanent loose end" (D 499), living in circumstances that once appalled him, tutoring students in English, and sadly resigned to the limitations of a life that once promised so much.

In the first sentence of *The Jewel in the Crown*, we are asked to imagine "a flat landscape, dark for the moment, but even so conveying to a girl running in the still deeper shadow cast by the wall of the Bibighar Gardens an idea of immensity, of distance, such as years before Miss Crane had been conscious of standing where a lane ended and cultivation began: a different landscape but also in the alluvial plain between the mountains of the north and the plateau of the south." The passage, which contains Scott's prime "mystery," foreshadows the tragedy of the English girl, Daphne Manners. It is followed immediately by a statement of Scott's subject which anticipates the analogic quality of the imagery by tying the personal to the historical and insisting that, on both levels, the concern of the novel is moral:

> This is the story of a rape, of the events that led up to it and followed it and of the place in which it happened. There are the action, the people, and the place; all of which are interrelated but in their totality incommunicable in isolation from the moral continuum of human affairs.
>
> In the Bibighar Gardens case there were several arrests and an investigation. There was no trial in the judicial sense. Since then people have said there was a trial of sorts going on. In fact, such people say, the affair that began on the evening of August 9, 1942, in Mayapore, ended with the spectacle of two nations in violent opposition, not for the first time nor as yet for the last because they were then still locked in an imperial embrace of such long standing and subtlety it was no longer possible for them to know whether they hated or loved each other, or what it was that held them together and seemed to have confused the image of their separate destinies. (9)

The passage suggests that an organizing key to *The Raj Quartet* is its sense of totality and complexity and hints at a connection between the rape and the relationship of England and India. These two levels of meaning, the personal and the historical, will be extended through the four novels.

The sense of complexity extends to genre, which eludes simple definition. Essentially *The Raj Quartet* is a *roman-fleuve*, like John Galsworthy's *Forsyte Saga*, which takes its structural unity from images, themes, and characters common to all four novels. It is also essentially a moral detective story, like Conrad's *Lord Jim*. The narrator is the detective who assembles his clues in the form of recurring images gleaned from interviews, depositions, and diaries, and presents his material frequently in re-creations, as though he is coming to his information at the same time as the reader.[1] Aside from the facts, what actually happened that fateful night of August 9, 1942, he seeks to discover the complex interplay of historical events, class and race forces, and elements in human psychology that share in the related tragedies. Additionally, *The Raj Quartet* is as much a philosophical tragedy as any of Thomas Hardy's novels and has something in common with the vast canvases of Tolstoy and the psychological novels of Henry James. But if Scott probes the depths of his characters with a sensitivity that is moral as well as social and psychological, he presents the physical world as well as the historical setting in vivid detail. In this he is the superior of

James, who tends to develop the inner world of his characters at the expense of their physical surroundings.

The novels must be seen, secondarily, as historical novels. They are not historical novels in the usual sense because "the author's deepest concern is with individual destinies caught in the collective destiny of a given period of violent upheaval"[2] and because Scott lived through the age he wrote about.[3] Yet his novels fulfill our expectations of the historical novel, concerned as they are with the legacy of the past, race and class discrimination, and conflicting nationalisms and ideologies. They are well suited to Sir Walter Scott's classic definition, as recorded in his prefaces and introductions to the Waverly novels: two cultures in conflict, one dying and the other struggling to be born, cause an upheaval into which fictional characters are introduced who move among historical figures and who participate in historical events, re-creating a personal and direct portrait of an age. Additionally, Scott shares the historical novelist's "strong temptation to try and produce an extensively complete totality."[4]

Scott's specific historical subject in *The Raj Quartet* is the failure of British imperialism, the turmoil the British created and were caught by in pre-independence India. The novels dramatize the debacle of division, not only of India and Pakistan, but, more centrally, the divorce of England from the Indian subcontinent in the years leading up to and including partition. Panoramic in scope and microscopic in detail, the books recreate the events, sights, sounds, and smells of British India in the 1940s. Scott presents a picture—politically, sociologically, and psychologically revealing—of how two nations came into tragic confrontation, and of how and why British rule ended in failure and a sense of diminished importance.

The narrator, in the course of his 1964 travels, takes the reader on at least five journeys: a historical-temporal one going back to events that occurred in the turbulent India of the 1940s; a spatial passage through the imaginary Mayapore, Mirat, Ranpur, and Pankot, in which the destinies of the characters are worked out; an ethical search for the villain behind the related tragedies of the abandonment and division of India as well as the separation and sufferings of an English girl and her English-bred Indian lover; a metaphysical quest for a resolution between the conflicting forces of love and death in the world; and a journey into the mind investigating psychological defenses and a mind-body dualism, symbolized in *The Jewel in the Crown* by the divided city of Mayapore. The journeys are interrelated, with complex unifying effect. Union is the aim: England and India, white and black, soul and body; but division and insularity are what finally remain of shattered political, sociological, and psychological ideals.

In his concern with British imperialism, Scott appears to have much in common with other writers of the colonial experience, but some striking differences in theme and tone heighten our perception of Scott's individuality. To contrast Scott with Kipling is to see each as a reflection of the opposing values of their times. Kipling, writing shortly after the heyday of imperialism, captures a sense of pride in British accomplishment, a faith in the success of the imperial purpose whose failure Scott laments. Kipling writes of the marriage of East and West, a union of unequal partners since he takes for granted a national and racial superiority. Scott's ideal twentieth-century marriage of East and West, on the other hand, is not imperialistic but egalitarian, symbolized in the tragically aborted union of Daphne Manners and Hari Kumar. Kumar represents the supposed imperial ideal, or Macaulay's brown-skinned Englishman come to life, to show how illusory were the good intentions of most Englishmen toward Indians, based on an implicit idea of superiority.

For Scott imperialism suggests the failure of an ideal and of an administrative structure that was, for all its flaws, essentially sound. The irony in Scott's vision of the Raj (one has the sense that its nineteenth-century grandeur was largely illusory) is restrained and subordinated to his sense of resigned sadness. Where Kipling imagines a British India of pride and legend, Scott mirrors his countrymen's lost moral purpose and self-definition. In *The Day of the Scorpion*, Officer Teddie Bingham, oblivious of his own safety on the World War II battlefield in Burma, stands up in his jeep to call for his regiment's Indian National Army deserters to return. His extraordinary act is, as an observer realizes, the stuff of a legend where Teddie might well have succeeded; but even if he did not, Teddie's death rewritten in Kipling's manner would be viewed as a noble sacrifice, something Private Mulvaney might marvel over and feel inspired by, as he does by the death of ol' Pommeloe, who lost her life from sunstroke while attending to her poor "bhoys" dying from the cholera. In *The Raj Quartet* the British community and probably his regiment as well see Teddie's demise as a pointless and unnecessary death caused by the courage of a delusive belief in a loyalty that no longer existed, if it ever had.

George Orwell's Swiftian bitterness and irony at the Raj's injustice is Scott's disillusionment and sad resignation. Scott's view appears the more rounded and objective, for Orwell's Raj has no positive features but is a caricature of evil. It is exploitative and suppressive, arrogant and arbitrary, like many of the characters in *Bur-*

mese Days. Little in Orwell counters what, from a psychoanalytic point of view, might be thought of as his anal-erotic resentment of the East. The East is almost exclusively a place of dirt and smell; the hero, Flory, has dirty bachelor's quarters and eats "pretentious and filthy meals."[5] The novel has no favorable image to oppose silly, superficial, ridiculously romantic Elizabeth's disgust with dirt and sensuality. Moreover, Orwell's protagonists tend to share a curious moral weakness. His heroes are often, like Flory, well meaning but weak and cowardly. Debauched and alienated, Flory lacks the courage to face the row with his smutty countryman, Ellis, that he feels would get his Burmese friend, Dr. Veraswami, into the club and make him inviolate from the calumny that is destroying his reputation; instead, Flory is prevailed upon to sign a letter which in effect calls his friend a nigger. The extent to which we are moved by his later suicide is, therefore, limited. Scott has a much more beneficent view of the best of human nature, and his heroes and heroines find meaning in extending themselves regardless of personal risk.

E. M. Forster provides an interesting comparison so long as we remember that, despite a certain similarity in concern with the Anglo-Indian relation, the philosophies and styles of the two writers are different, even sometimes antithetical. Scott shares with Forster a concern with aspects of the imperialistic relationship that prevent friendship or union between the two peoples. Scott, however, converts the central dramatic incident of *A Passage to India,* the attempted rape in the Marabar Caves of foolish Adela Quested, an imaginary event which at length succeeds in preventing the development of the friendship between Aziz and Fielding, into an actual rape of an English girl, which is similarly causative in preventing marriage with her Indian lover.

The dynamic Marabar symbolism, embodying the negative philosophy of *A Passage to India,* enjoys an emphatic role comparable to Scott's multilevel symbolism pointing to the frustration of union, but Forster's inability to transcend Marabar limits the philosophical appeal of his novel. The attempts at capturing joy and meaning in the "Temple" section of *A Passage to India* fall far short of the powerful conviction embodied in "Caves," where he expresses the same metaphysical and psychological doubts as to the meaning of existence that Helen's sister in *Howards End* finds in the goblins of Beethoven's *Fifth.* In *A Passage to India* a sense of inner emptiness is symbolically realized throughout the novel, in the "Boum" of the caves, the godlike vacuity of the nonthinking punkhah wallah, the sunrise whose supreme moment reveals nothingness, and the death of Mrs. Moore at sea, unredeemed from that dreadful state of un-belief in which Marabar has left her.

Despite the technical brilliance of the novel, one may feel some-what less than satisfied with the silly, tinny, Godbolean answer to the negativism of Marabar and unhappy with the weakness of For-ster's positive values. Scott has metaphysical doubts, too, but the psychological core of his masterpiece is solid; his philosophy is sad-dened rather than weakened by the ontological vacuum. While Scott finds illusory the belief that the forces of love will overwhelm those of destruction, he provides an answer to Marabar. Taking as his credo Eliot's lines in "East Coker," "We must be still and still mov-ing / Into another intensity / For a further union, a deeper commu-nion" (IPF 132), Scott insists on the absolute human value of crea-tive love.

Each of the characters embodying the values of *The Raj Quartet* attempts to cut across either social, political, or psychological bar-riers to achieve some form of union, usually with or for India and Indians; and each is betrayed by a combination of overwhelming forces. Tragically, the price of love or attempted union is often some form of diminution, but the characters rarely doubt the rightness or value of their goals and remain, in Daphne's words, "imprisoned but free, diminished by everything that loomed from outside, *but not diminished from the inside*" (J 405). Scott envisions a world of the "malign spirit," where only a few have the vision or the courage to act out of love or true principle, a quality which in any event often destroys its possessor. Since the authentic "hero" of these books of shifting central focus is not the English-bred Hari Kumar, as one would at first suppose, not "India, as she passes from one epoch to another,"[6] but creative, egalitarian love, the "villain" is not the Brit-ish policeman Ronald Merrick so much as the forces of insularity which victimize protagonists (human embodiments of love) and an-tagonists alike. Whether in politics or human relations, the enemies of love are self-interest and barriers to communication, insular forces apparent in "the white robot," the system of the British Raj that destroyed the union of Hari Kumar and Daphne Manners, and in the psychological defenses against inner fears and desires.

Parochial forces are the crushing enemies that are often and mem-orably symbolized in Scott's novels. Like the recurrent image of the scorpion, which appears to sting itself to death when encircled by fire but is actually burned by the heat, the British Raj and the human condition are surrounded by indifferent and destructive forces. Such insular myopia in times of great emergency led General Dyer at

Amritsar in 1919 (or Scott's fictional Brigadier-General Reid in Maya-pore in 1942) to shoot into an unarmed crowd; just as it led a fic-tional British policeman, irrationally convinced of an innocent man's guilt, to incarcerate and torture him. These insularities are re-sponsible, in Scott's view, for the general tragic failure of the British in India, the thwarted, "abortive human intention" (J 208) to bring order, unity, and peaceful, prosperous self-government to a country whose people suffered as much from some of their own superstitions and religious practices (as in *suttee*, the Hindu practice of burning widows on their husbands' funeral pyres) as from poverty, humilia-tion, and death inflicted on them by autocratic despots, greedy *ze-mindars* (landlords), and warring factions. Narrow detached inter-ests were responsible for the imperceptive British policy and Indian overreactions that led to the destruction of an admirable moral and political ideal. Scott's Indian lawyer, Srinivasan, translates T. S. Eliot's "Between the Idea and the Act/Falls the Shadow" into politi-cal terms when he observes that "there is always an unmapped area of dangerous fallibility between a policy and its pursuit" (J 199–200).

By the end of *A Division of the Spoils*, Scott shows clearly that the most admirable aspirations of the British for India were based on illusions. As a diminished Hari Kumar once wrote for the *Ranpur Gazette:* "I walk home, thinking of another place, of seemingly long endless summers and the shade of different kinds of trees, and then of winters when the branches of the trees were so bare, that recalling them now, it seems inconceivable to me that I looked at them and did not think of the summer just gone, and the spring soon to come, as illusions; as dreams, never fulfilled, never to be fulfilled" (D 597–598).

Scott's view of British history in India is close enough to that of reputable historians to suggest that *The Raj Quartet*'s portrayal of the scene and of British policy errors could be taken as an objective historical view, one that, in historian Max Beloff's view, revitalizes history by making historical events "more directly intelligible than these events might otherwise be to us."[7] This judgment reflects the fact that Scott's ideal is broadly humanist as well as historical; his convincing re-creation of the bewilderment, frustration, and failure of the British living in India in the 1940s is a dramatization of the whole experience of the Raj and persuades not so much by rational argument as by feelings and intuitive insights. The historical dimen-sion is critical,[8] but *The Raj Quartet*, like any fiction, is a metaphor for an author's view of life,[9] and its history is subordinated to other components.

To criticize Scott for "a muted celebration of a concept rather than a critique of a reality"[10] is to recognize that his broadly humanist ideal for the British never had much chance of becoming a reality. Such comments miss an important contribution of the novels—the tying of one historical failure to universal psychological shortcomings and metaphysical problems. Scott's novels transcend their tenor, or immediate historical picture, to say something about the limitations of the human condition. Their view of British failure in India is tied to general human deficiency; they lament in historical terms the failure of an ideal of love that, given the human condition, was never really possible.

This vision is most important, a conception which thematically and symbolically unites political with sociological and psychological components to create a transcendent or mystical vision of love, not as in Dante's *Paradiso*, fulfilled and infinitely fulfilling, but sadly, necessarily, and almost as infinitely thwarted. That the focus of the novels is subtly shifted from external to internal consequences is apparent when we consider that the relation of the rape victim, Daphne Manners, to *The Raj Quartet*'s center of values is more important than that of any political figure, and that even the considerable stature of a character like the Congress Party politician Mohammed Ali Kasim depends in a Dickensian fashion on his proximity to the mystical core of the novels rather than to the center of political and social power.

This mystical vision or core is revealed through telepathic insights which are shared by those characters who embody the values of the novels. The insights are frequently symbolic or analogical and serve structurally to tie together levels of meaning by revealing the history of England in India incarnate in individual lives. Thus the historian Guy Perron, disturbed by a memory of Kumar playing cricket at Chillingborough, sees in Hari's face his own historical awareness "that to misjudge, to mistime," would lead to destruction" (D 107). Barbara Batchelor, the bumbling, retired missionary who is the novels' most explicit, sustained symbol of the British in India, hallucinates what she takes to be the Voice of God saying, "Nothing can bring you peace but yourself. Nothing can bring you peace but the triumph of principles." She cries out in fear, her knees unable to bend, symbolically fixed in this "proud and arrogant position" because "she could not remember what her principles were" (T 202).

Scott employs a circular, partly repetitious writing style in *The Raj Quartet*. His Stranger-Traveller-Writer, returning to India in 1964 after an eighteen-year absence, as Scott himself did, "with lepidopteristic intention to pin down the truth about Miss Crane, Miss

Manners and young Kumar" (J 100), interviews those people still
alive in 1964 who had some acquaintance with the Bibighar case,
the sorry affair stemming from the rape of Daphne Manners in the
Bibighar Gardens during the Quit India riots of August 1942. He is
unable to interview even one of the three characters central to the
affair—Daphne Manners, Hari Kumar, or District Superintendent of
Police Ronald Merrick—but must rely on diaries, letters, journals,
and depositions, which he presents as evidence for us to ponder. In
the succeeding novels, as Scott warms to his technique, the narrator
abandons the use of such devices, and the reader is left to imagine
from his occasional but increasingly infrequent appearances that an
episode told from any character's point of view is the re-creation of
Scott's narrator from his interview material.

Scott uses the narrative method to allow us to compare corresponding or conflicting views of the same character or event, in part
because he is writing about the painful limitations of human perception, the tragic failure of communication between men and nations
(and between parts of ourselves). Besides permitting each novel its
self-containment, the method creates an amazing verisimilitude—
the sense of an entire world with its own dynamic—and allows us to
apprehend the bridges of contact and the unfortunate gaps between
them. The technique is most dramatically successful with strongly
contrasting views of the same event, such as Brigadier-General Reid
vs. District Commissioner White on the Mayapore riots and the
Bibighar disaster, or with the revealing erroneous views of another
character, such as Susan's hero worship of her villain husband,
Merrick.

As early as *The Mark of the Warrior*, Scott had sought to capture
a sense of life's relativity and complexity with the method described in the preface: "Three things are to be considered: a man's
estimate of himself, the face he presents to the world, the estimate
of that man made by other men. Combined they form an aspect of
truth." In *The Raj Quartet* the second-hand conflicting and tangential accounts establish a distance and sense of perspective which
seem to convey an objective truth. Although *The Raj Quartet* is
sometimes compared with Lawrence Durrell's *Alexandria Quartet*
and Japanese filmmaker Akira Kurosawa's *Rashomon*[11] (also about
events concerning a rape), in these works the reader or viewer,
treated to conflicting versions of the same event, despairs of being
able to establish the facts; indeed, that is the point. Scott, however,
is not concerned with the relativity of truth so much as with its
revelation.

Scott's Stranger-Traveller-Writer is a technical device that, like

Melville's use of Ishmael in *Moby Dick*, in no way implies relativity but is merely a device for an omniscient narrator. The narrator, however, does not intrude his point of view, except to point, particularly through the heightened restrained tone, to the tragedy involved. He concentrates on re-creating the affair in its totality and—to all appearances—allows readers to arrive at their own conclusions.

The method is circular, through repetition in varying contexts emphasizing and extracting more meaning from the images presented than is ordinarily possible in a straightforward narrative line. Governor Malcolm of Ranpur in *A Division of the Spoils* provides a clue to Scott's narrative method and the structure of *The Raj Quartet* when he tells his assistant, Nigel Rowan, that "sometimes when faced with [an] apparently insoluble and intricate problem . . . he applied his own theory of relativity, which was that although people seldom argued a point but argued round it, they sometimes found the solution to the problem they were evading by going round in ever increasing circles and disappearing into the centre of those, which, relatively speaking, coincided with the centre of the circle from whose periphery they had evasively spiralled outwards" (318).

The repetitive nature of the narrative, then, grows out of Scott's desire to present a total picture, and his need, in novels published three years apart, to remind the reader of what had gone before.[12] Additionally, the repetition, together with the sheer volume and emphasis on historical facts, contrasting views, and minute realistic details, has another, perhaps more important function in serving to balance the individual mystical insights which direct the reader by making the values of the novels explicit. Our sense of the real must be filled with a solid, comprehensive sense of life before we can accept a guiding mystical dimension, however individually and metaphorically realized.

The circular structural pattern of *The Raj Quartet*, while appropriate for the building of memorable tableaux, is also suitable for the pervasive images of imprisonment. Hari Kumar, Mohammed Ali Kasim, and Colonel Layton are physically imprisoned, but, as we shall see, there are prisons of other kinds. The imprisonment of Daphne and Hari is in the conventions of a society which castigates them and restricts the places where they can safely meet. The promise of Hari to say nothing in regard to where he had been on the night of her Bibighar assault is described as a "promise [that] had betrayed and imprisoned them both" (S 304). Kumar, after his release from the Kandipat jail, is still imprisoned: "You had only to look at Kumar's face to see that Kumar's window onto the world was still closed and darkened" (D 322). When Susan Layton Bingham, in deep postnatal depression after the loss of her husband under fire, declines to madness and tries to kill her newborn son by placing him in a circle of fire, she whispers, "Little prisoner, shall I free you?" (S 494). When she hears of Teddie Bingham's death, retired missionary Barbie Batchelor repeats Susan's thought in her letter to her superior, "Is the Universe an unprincipled design? Does God weep somewhere beyond it crying to its prisoners to free themselves and come to Him?" (T 207). Even the butterflies in a lace christening gown are developed into an appropriate symbol of imprisonment.

The circular pattern and pervasive imprisonment images are appropriate for the strong sense of loss of paradise in *The Raj Quartet*, created by the same conflict of reality with illusion or desire that was played out in the earlier novels. There would appear to be no way out of the sufferings imposed by the human condition, but particularly by those imposed by the turmoil that grew out of the application of the Defense of India laws. This pattern and imagery are keys to the *Quartet*'s central metaphysical ambiguity which, together with the theme of thwarted love or union, is described in the chapters which follow. First, "The Illusion of Principle," mindful of the alienation of England from India, discusses the *Quartet*'s view of the history of India leading up to partition. Although in the main the novels embody a criticism of the Defense of India laws and view the English as having been more concerned with their own moral stance and material gain than with the future of India, structurally the *Quartet* is built around an essential contradiction concerning these laws; much of what the English did during the war, in the view of the *Quartet*, they did because they had no choice.

The next two chapters discuss the thwarted union of individuals: the first identifies a tragic pattern in the life stories of the major protagonists who are diminished or destroyed at the very moment of having their fondest dreams actualized; the second demonstrates the essential barrier to union for Scott and the different forms this barrier takes in the lives of his antagonists.

The following chapter concentrates on British social attitudes toward Indians and the psychological defenses, including racism,[13] which led to British alienation from India. Developed from the imagery of India and England in the four novels, this level of meaning deals psychoanalytically with a thwarted union of body and soul, a condition considered representative of civilized society. The final chapter is a discussion of Scott's unusual narrative technique whereby symbol plays a role in the structure and texture of these novels. The thematic discussion of *The Raj Quartet* has been divided into separate chapters demonstrating historical, social, and psychological levels of meaning to illustrate what is perhaps most extraordinary about the novels—their astonishingly sustained unity of theme and form in conveying a transcendent philosophical and symbolic vision of thwarted union.

7. The Illusion of Principle: British Policy in India

About two hundred years of British ascendancy in India ended on August 15, 1947, in the partition of the country and the communal massacre of perhaps a quarter of a million people. *The Raj Quartet* is concerned with both this political failure and its human consequences. It dramatizes the debacle of division, not only of India and Pakistan, but, more centrally, the divorce of England from the Indian subcontinent in the years leading up to and including partition. Metaphorically, the tales of individual lives caught in the rupture are the vehicle used to illustrate the tenor, the alienation of England from India and the consequent division of the subcontinent.

The Raj Quartet is a melancholy investigation into British failure in India and seeks to understand the complexity of divisive historical and psychological forces that led to partition. For this reason it bombards the reader with such a wealth of historical detail that one critic objected that "we are being fed information about history rather than being told a story."[1] Yet the drama of the narrative is sufficient to hold the weight of its history; in order to place the image of the girl running in its historical context, Scott needed to immerse his reader in accurate detail. He presented a dramatization of what went wrong with British policy in India and also allowed his characters lengthy, often ironic discussions of policy. Just as Melville's *Moby Dick* is enhanced by particulars about whaling, Scott's *Quartet* is textured with the history of England in India, a tragic story which it ties to the shortcomings of human nature. Scott's vision of the inevitable limitations of love in politics must be understood in order to appreciate his admirably sustained three-tiered structure of thwarted union. To demonstrate the *Quartet's* view of how British policy in India was rooted in self-interest, often accompanied by an illusion of sacrifice or principle, I have traced its presentation of history and related its ambiguities to two opposing forces in human nature.

The *Quartet*'s underlying view, shared by a number of historians, is that the political justification for nearly two hundred years of power (first by the East India Company, which in the 1750s began assuming control of Indian states to protect its trading interests, then, two years after the 1857 mutiny, by direct Crown rule) was the evolution of a united and independent India. In 1948, the widow of the former governor of Ranpur, Ethel Manners, a social outcast in British India because she has adopted the illegitimate half-Indian child of her dead niece, Daphne, writes to her Indian friend, Lili Chatterjee, "The creation of Pakistan is our crowning failure. . . . Our only justification for two hundred years of power was unification" (J 473). This opinion echoes that of Hari Kumar, expressed in a letter to his English friend Colin Lindsey—that two hundred years should have been long enough to unify the subcontinent. Scott, who considered himself a liberal humanist,[2] is gravely disappointed by what his narrator reflectively describes as "a cutting off before the prime or in the prime, with all that this suggests in the way of unfinished business" (S 11). A magnificent opportunity had been wasted, and various characters lament being forced to settle for the second-rate. Britain's achievements in India are defined by the narrator as those of a democracy advanced in technical knowledge—the roads, railways and telegraph, the civil service, the legal system and pattern of government, the army, and a social model in the clubs. What Indians wanted, Scott believed,[3] was an English identification with the country they ruled and the eventual embrace of equals. This the British as a whole were unprepared to give. The *Quartet* holds that the ideal to which the best aspired might have set a pattern for the colonial relationship. Instead, with insular and divisive consequences for the modern world, the British "created a precedent for partition just at the moment when the opposite was needed" (J 475).

Scott believed that "some kind of aspiration [was] . . . central . . . to major tragedies and to minor personal ones." There are two aspects to his theory of tragedy: aspiration—to the goal of a united, independent India—and its betrayal by "the insularity, the selfishness, the self-protectiveness, the defensiveness."[4] The link is made clear when Edwina Crane muses:

> For years, since the eighteenth century . . . we have said at home . . .
> that the day would come when our rule in India will end, not bloodily,
> but in peace, in . . . a perfect gesture of equality and friendship and
> love. . . . There has been . . . a seed . . . planted in the Indian imagina-
> tion and in the English imagination. Out of it was to come something
> sane and grave, full of dignity, full of thoughtfulness and kindness and
> peace and wisdom. . . . For years we have been promising and for years

finding means of putting the fulfillment of the promise off until the promise stopped looking like a promise and started looking only like a sinister prevarication, even to me, let alone tó Indians who think and feel and know the same as me. (J 72)

The antagonist credited with the failure to unify India appears in British prevarication, detachment, racism and repression, or less emphatically in Indian childishness, intransigence, and communal violence. This chapter will demonstrate how Scott traces in the past and during the time present of the novels the insular political spirit that revealed itself in the indifference of the British electorate,[5] the delaying and then fatal rushing of independence, the slaughter at Jallianwallah Bagh that turned Gandhi against permanent British rule, the policy of divide and rule, and the lapsing of paramountcy or final abandonment of the princes. So well are the views of the history integrated with the fully believable lives of his characters that the reader has difficulty quarreling with Scott's conclusions.

Although there is always a danger in considering the views of one or more of the characters to be representative, it is fairly safe to assume a philosophy consistent with that of the novels when several sympathetic characters share a view of history and that view is not treated ironically or contradicted by the perspective of other positive figures. Wherever possible, Scott is at pains to show through the views of characters we like and admire that it was not love of India that motivated a nation that prided itself on its principles so much as a concern with retaining its self-image. The saintly Sister Ludmila refers to this concern when she describes the British as "very conscious, as you walk in the sun, of the length or shortness of the shadows that you cast" (J 168), and historian Guy Perron reflects on their empire-building convictions of moral superiority. The impressions of his characters are complemented by Scott's remarks on the Raj in an essay in which he speaks of "an explosion of national pride" in British encompassing expertise and then continues ironically: "Of course no Englishman would say, 'We are great, we know everything, we do everything that much better than anyone else.' Greatness was a mystical inward knowledge and best supported by a deprecating outward modesty, an appearance of ease that amounted to languour, or being awfully ordinary, as greatness was when it was shared by a whole nation."[6]

Indifference of the British Electorate

Scott's opinion is substantiated by a view of British imperialism that points to a disturbing nineteenth-century distinction between principles and practice, or ideals and self-interest. While giving Indians eighteenth-century radical ideals of equality, opportunity, and self-government in their schools, nineteenth-century reactionaries, sustained by ideals of hardship and self-sacrifice popularly reflected in Kipling's poem "The White Man's Burden," held tenaciously to their ideas of racial and moral superiority, and the consequent necessity for staying on indefinitely as a privileged class in an India that would always be incapable of ruling itself. With some notable exceptions, the nineteenth-century Englishman, whatever he thought he was doing, was not interested in helping Indians to attain self-government except in theory, in some distant time, beyond his own lifetime certainly. Perhaps the central paradox is contained in the fact that while the British were on the one hand exploiting India for their own material and psychological purposes, they believed, in the nineteenth century, that they held the country by virtue of moral force.[7] True principle, which would have entailed economic sacrifice, was not as important as its more comfortable illusion, which could allow pragmatic advantage while permitting the retention of a superior racial and national self-image.

Reflecting the fact that, as District Commissioner White realizes, most of the British were in India for what they could get out of it, or that all too often the attitude toward India was what Governor Malcolm's assistant Guy Rowan describes as "a bit of window dressing in Westminster and damn the consequences in Delhi" (D 269), the *Quartet* records British self-serving behavior on the subcontinent. Policy was controlled not by the government of India but by the government at home. Though generally well intentioned, indeed, most often more liberal than the hard-core reactionaries who formed the base of the community in India, the British government as well as the average Englishman was appallingly ignorant about India. Perhaps "well intentioned" or "benevolently indifferent" would be the best way of describing Whitehall's attitude. The three senior ministers of the 1946 Cabinet, sent to heal the wounds of British policy of divide and rule and to bring about a united, independent India, show an astonishing ignorance of the map of the subcontinent in *A Division of the Spoils*. And Perron writes that "for the majority who voted [to bring in the Labour Party, which would dismantle the empire] India does not even begin to exist" (D 106). The attitude of the British electorate is satirized in his view of his pragmatic Aunt Charlotte. Though she is profoundly aware of the self-interest underlying policy in India and though she had voted for the Labour Party, Aunt Charlotte does not consider herself in the least responsible for the hundreds of thousands of deaths that ensued. Her quick and unqualified repudiation of British responsibility is a strangely blind denial, for one so perceptive, of the imperial role and confirms her nephew's impression of the enormous importance in the failure of the British-Indian relationship of the role played by "the indifference and ignorance of the English at home" (D 222).

The Rushing of Independence

The demission of power occurred in August 1947, almost a full year before the first-announced target date. In February 1947, Lord Wavell, the viceroy strongly opposed to partition because he believed (prophetically) that the artificial division of the subcontinent by religion would cause further division, was sacked. His replacement was the uncle of the duke of Edinburgh, Lord Louis Mountbatten, a man remarkable for his energetic determination to get the job done, and as quickly as possible. When Mountbatten announced publicly early in June of 1947 that India would be granted independence on August 15, 1947, a date only ten weeks away, it is suggested in *A Division of the Spoils* that members of the Bengal Club, on hearing this announcement, must have looked as if stricken by apoplexy. In England, however, there would be few pangs of conscience, as Perron notes, India being no longer a part of the British self-image.

Repeatedly, the ideals of dedication, service, and eventual self-government for India played a subordinate role to British interests when the two conflicted. Politically astute Aunt Charlotte sees through the politicians' benevolent sham to posit what she called "Bunburyism"—"clear evidence of pre-arrangements between . . . [the] viceroys and . . . [the] Secretary of State for India in Whitehall to ensure the continuation of whatever policy the British government was currently pursuing in regard to the sub-continent" (D 217). Elsewhere we learn that when the British wanted to hold on to the country, Indians were considered too immature to govern themselves; but, after World War II, when people at home wanted to get out of a country that was increasingly an administrative burden and economic drain, many had a sudden perception of the immorality of colonialism.

Though official government policy would call attention to the fulfillment of a promise, a number of historians agree that the rushing of independence was a major cause of the bloodshed and the division of the country. Scott's perceptive Major Clark, who sardonically compares the government's relinquishing of India to the amputation of a gangrenous leg, asserts that though the British at home would pretend to have fulfilled a moral obligation, in fact India was to be disposed of for economic reasons. As Lady Manners comments, "The slogan is still insular. India's independence at any cost, not for India's sake, but for our own" (J 473).

Slaughter in Jallianwallah Bagh

The focus of opinion in the novels is especially on the critical period after World War I when the Rowlatt Acts bred fear and suspicion and led to the massacre at Amritsar. The *Quartet* corroborates the view of many historians that the Jallianwallah Bagh slaughter proved the turning point in British-Indian relations. As Sir Ahmed Akbar Kasim had told his son Mohammed Ali, though Indians were killed at Jallianwallah Bagh, the massacre was also the scene of British India's suicide. Although there had been nationalist agitation before the war, British rule had never seriously been called into question. When many Indian nationalists hastened to join the war effort, thinking they would be rewarded by some kind of progress toward independence, the British government, feeling the need for Indian enthusiasm, issued for the first time a statement of belief in the peoples' ability to govern themselves responsibly. But Indians soon discovered that Allied insistence that the war was being fought to ensure self-determination of all peoples did not apply to India, and the reward for military service turned out to be political and administrative repression. The end of the war brought back arrogant British administrators and returned Indians to their subordinate positions in the administration. Far worse, the government of India imposed the repressive Rowlatt Acts, which tried political cases without jury and could imprison arbitrarily under the Defence of India rules. District Commissioner White points out the contradiction in policy when he asks, "What in hell was the good of declaring Dominion status as our aim for India in 1917 and not much more than a year later instituting trial without jury for political crimes and powers of detention at the provincial level under the Defense of India rules, ostensibly to deal with so-called anarchists but in practice to make any expression of free-will and free-opinion technically punishable" (J 346). Added to problems of high prices and unemployment for many returning soldiers, these acts caused a loud public outcry, and the resulting riots, as White explains, led to the massacre at Amritsar.

On April 10, 1919, a mob protesting the deportation of two nationalist leaders murdered four Europeans and attacked others, one of whom, the English missionary Marcella Sherwood, was left for dead.

Mass meetings were forbidden, and when a large crowd assembled in Jallianwallah Bagh on April 13, Brigadier-General Dyer arrived with his troops, blocked the exits, and ordered his men to fire repeatedly at the crowd. ("It was no longer a question," he said, "of merely dispersing the crowd, but one of producing a sufficient moral effect from a military point of view not only on those who were present but more especially throughout the Punjab."[8] According to official figures, 379 were killed and 1,200 were wounded, including men, women, and children. Martial law was then declared, and for a period of eight weeks Indians were forced, among other humiliations, to walk on all fours past the spot where Sherwood had been attacked. Indian reaction must have been all the more bitter because Dyer's actions were approved by the provincial government, and official reproofs by a commission of inquiry set up by the London government were mild: General Dyer's actions were "unfortunate" or "injudicious." Most of the British, including members of Parliament and the press, were vindictively proud of his behavior and collected twenty-six thousand pounds when it was deemed judicious to retire him.

The slaughter destroyed the trust between rulers and ruled; Indians increasingly determined to rid themselves of a community in which men like Robin White and women like Sarah Layton were distinctly in the minority. The special significance of these events on Scott's imagination is evident from innumerable references to them. Aside from Mabel Layton's recurrent nightmares, these include a suggestion in *A Division of the Spoils* that the root cause of the massacre was Dyer's amoebiasis and the reminder that Brigadier-General Reid's name in the *Quartet* is Dyer spelled backwards.

Hari Kumar also blames Amritsar and the two-handed practice of promising independence while imposing repression for the failure of the British-Indian relationship. He traces Indian skepticism about vague World War II promises to the World War I promises which ended in the massacre. Congress's fears were not unfounded. In a startling parallel to World War I policies, Congress learned during the summer of 1941 that the Atlantic Charter's claim that the British and American governments respected the right of all peoples to choose their own government did not apply to Indians; Mohammed Ali Kasim reflects bitterly on this injustice from the fort at Premanagar where he is imprisoned. When the secretary of state repeated his promise that India would be free to choose its own government after the war, there were, not surprisingly, few Indians who believed him. And the Cripps mission of 1942, which conceded India's right to draft a new constitution with reduced British obligations and the right to leave the Commonwealth if it wished, was popularly interpreted as "a typical Churchillian move, made to dress the window and make friends and influence people abroad after the defeat in Asia but which amounted in itself to no more than a grudging repetition of old promises and even older reservations" (J 356). As far as Indians were concerned, Hari Kumar says, the British showed their real feelings about self-government when, for all their promises of dominion status for India, they failed to give it the dignity of consulting with Indian leaders before declaring war on Germany on its behalf.

Indian Responsibility

The historical view which the *Quartet* corroborates is that Indians were not without their share of responsibility for the division of the country and the bloodshed. If the British provoked the Congress Party by failing even to go through the motions of consulting it about the declaration of war, a major step leading to the creation of Pakistan turned out to be the Congress resignation of its provincial ministries in 1939, a resignation, as Edwina Crane sees it, "in a fit of pique" (J 45) over what Srinivasan calls "the ridiculous point of order raised on the Viceroy's declaration of war on Germany" (J 201). The view of the *Quartet* is that the resignation, though provoked, was a childish intransigence which made nonsense of the Congress Party's claims to represent all India and enabled the Muslim League to extend considerably its political influence in the years immediately before partition. Hari Kumar feels that by allowing the provinces to revert to the old-style rule of an autocratic British governor and nominated council, Indians must share the blame for delay in independence (J 270). The aim of the Congress Party should have been focused not on getting rid of the British, in Governor Malcolm's opinion a foregone conclusion since the creation of Indian provincial ministries in 1937, but on extending its own political base. "When you all resigned the power you'd got," Malcolm tells Kasim, "in the belief that you weren't striking another blow for India's independence, you weren't striking a blow for that at all. You were striking a blow at your own existing and potential political power" (S 23). Not only did Congress deprive itself of influence in the resignation of the provincial ministries, but by advising the British to quit India and threatening civil insurrection with the Japanese pounding on the back door, Congress invited, whether consciously or not, the arrest and incarceration of its leaders and a further extension of Jinnah's powers.

Though the *Quartet* is anti–Muslim League, as it is against any divisive political force, Scott's main concern is with British un- fulfilled responsibility. In the words of Robin White and in Scott's best imperialistic tradition, "The onus of moral leadership falls naturally on the people who rank as superior" (J 340). Ethel Manners writes of the inability of India to "withstand the pressure of the leg- acy of the division we English have allowed her to impose on herself and are morally responsible for" (J 475). British prevarication over independence, according to Hari Kumar, led Muslims to seize the political opportunity that would result in the creation of Pakistan. If Indians doubted British sincerity even when Britain was sincere, the *Quartet* implies that their doubts were due largely to their experi- ence of British equivocation. Though the novels portray Indians, Hindus, and Muslims alike as having played their part in fanning sectarian differences, the emphasis is on the British advisory role.

Divide and Rule

Historically, it was in Britain's interest to follow a policy of divide and rule. Particularly after the Sepoy Mutiny of 1857, the British felt a need for security in a foreign country in which they were greatly outnumbered. When Muslims demanded separate electorates in the early part of the century, Lord Minto believed, perhaps sincerely, that he was acting to protect the interests of a minority. But, though the British never intended bloody warfare to break out between pro- ponents of the two religions, by yielding to Muslim pressure for sep- arate electorates, Lord Minto succeeded in institutionalizing the communal differences that would play a part in the eventual parti- tion of India. The historical relevance for 1945 affairs is dramatized in the *Quartet* by the story of Fazal Haq Rahman, a Congress Mus- lim taking Kasim's place, who will lose the cold-weather elections, in Kasim's opinion, because "communalism [having] been written into our political structure by the *raj*, . . . the . . . elections will be fought on a religious not a political issue" (D 444). British preference of Muslims (because they were perceived as manlier than Hindus and worshipped a deity closer to the Western god) exacerbated com- munal differences. Too often district commissioners provided an in- sular example like Stead, White's predecessor in Mayapore, who (though contemptuous of all Indians) made no secret of his prefer- ence for Muslims and appointed a militant Muslim as assistant commissioner and joint magistrate in Congress-run Mayapore. By Srinivasan's account, this action aggravated sectarian feelings be- cause Hindu offenders were treated harshly and Muslims leniently.

Hindu retaliation requiring all Muslim children in the village schools to sing Congress songs and salute the Congress flag led to rioting in Tanpur. This kind of model made it easier for Congress to become increasingly Hindu-dominated and exclusive.

"Whether intentionally or not," Hari Kumar writes in 1942, "in the last twenty years . . . the English have succeeded in dividing and ruling" (J 275). In his capacity as *Mayapore Gazette* reporter, Kumar overhears conversations which lead him to believe that the English openly depend on Indian political division to extend their own rule. His notion of British interest in perpetuating communal differences is echoed a few years later in *A Division of the Spoils.* The cartoonist Halki draws an illustration of Winston Churchill looking approvingly at Kasim, the nawab of Mirat and Jinnah, in which Churchill's face is smugly satisfied at the thought that the Muslim League and the princes, who know independence to be in-imical to their interests, would together so hinder every move the Congress made toward a Hindu-dominated independence that Brit-ish rule "could comfortably be extended far enough into the future for the phrase 'indefinitely if not in perpetuity' not to seem inap-propriate" (D 6).

In the final analysis, the British lost control of the policy of divide and rule. As Srinivasan says, "Communal differences have always tended to snowball" (J 198). The insular British had divided only too well, played upon the ancient antipathy of the Hindus and the people who had once ruled them, and could not overcome commu-nal feelings when they wanted to. The result was the tragic division of the country and the "damned bloody senseless mess" (D 592) most poignantly dramatized in the train-compartment murder of Ahmed Kasim.

The Princely States and Paramountcy

The country was divided not only into Hindu and Muslim commu-nities but also into an India that modeled itself along democratic lines and an India that consisted of hundreds of Princely States. Be-fore quitting India "honorably," Britain had to settle the problem the departure would cause these autocracies. While Britain had prom-ised self-government to Congress India, it was also committed under the terms of the agreement with each government to protect the rights of the princes. The essential contradiction of the two policies, presented in the *Quartet* in an editorial from the *Ranpur Gazette* entitled "Pandora's Box," is reminiscent of the game of chess be-tween William Conway and his father in *The Birds of Paradise:*

Unfortunately, the doctrine of paramountcy has run counter to the doctrine of eventual self-government for those provinces ruled directly by the British parliament, through the Government of India. Paramountcy has always been illogical in the long run, and this illogicality is best exemplified by the dual role assigned to the Viceroy. In his role as Governor-General, it has been his duty to govern and guide and encourage the British-Indian provinces towards democratic parliamentary self-rule. As Crown Representative, it has been his duty to uphold, secure, oversee and defend the autocratic rule of several hundred princes.

[This rule is] alien in nature to the form of government [Britain] advocates and which the British people themselves enjoy at home and seem convinced is everyone's birthright. You can hardly wonder that this left-hand/right-hand policy was entrusted to one man, the Viceroy, in order to create the illusion that there was a unity of purpose. (D 523–524)

The two principles, antithetical in nature, were certain to clash during the transfer of power. The difficulty had its beginnings immediately following the mutiny, when Britain decided it might provoke the people less by ceasing to annex new territory and declaring "no further territorial ambitions" (D 522). Additionally, most of the princes had remained loyal during the mutiny, and by keeping princely India divided from British India, England undoubtedly saw itself as gaining in security what it lost in territory from a policy of divide and rule. The territory was not truly lost either, since under the conditions of paramountcy, the ruler, though free to exercise autocratic rule over his subjects, owed primary allegiance to the Crown. But when partition was decided upon, Britain was faced with the added problem of what to do with 562 Princely States scattered throughout the Indian subcontinent, many of which were anachronistic and corrupt.

Separate Princely States made no sense. In terms of economics and administration, the states had always been linked with British India. If the princes were left in power, the India-Pakistan partition would be greatly aggravated. And if they were left in power without an agreement of paramountcy with the British, effectively a guarantee of sovereignty, the Congress-run Indian government could take them over immediately after independence. Mountbatten, fearing that the question of the princes might destroy the delicate balance achieved between Congress and the Muslim League, tried unsuccessfully to have inserted into the Indian independence bill a clause limiting the powers of the Princely States and automatically transferring paramountcy over the smaller ones to India or Pakistan. But the request was refused because, the secretary of state declared, the clause could not be added without changing the government's "publicly declared policy towards the princes."⁹ Indeed, the government preferred to observe its treaties to the letter of the law and let paramountcy lapse. Numbed, the princes had little choice but to sign their individual Instruments of Accession, which meant incorporation into either India or Pakistan. A few, however, refused to comply.

The situation was especially complicated when there was, as in the case of Junagadh and Hyderabad and Scott's Mirat, a Muslim ruling a Hindu state, or in the case of Kashmir, a Hindu ruling a Muslim state. Since at the time of partition Kashmir had not acceded to either India or Pakistan (if the ruler chose Pakistan he would himself have had to abdicate; if India, he would be acting contrary to Kashmir's geographic, religious, and economic interests), communal tensions were intensified. In Scott's Mirat, the understandable hesitation of the Muslim nawab in signing an affiliation with India and the possibility of his signing with Pakistan led to violence by Hindu extremists against Muslims and Muslim retaliation.

Though the accounts of historians suggest that India was well rid of the princes and their extravagant abuses, Scott makes his Mirat a virtuous state. He claimed that "quite a number [of the states] were as virtuous as Mirat, if they were well advised and had progressively minded rulers. . . . you seldom *heard* about them, because scandal and bad news are always more memorable than virtue and good news. If I had made Mirat a hotbed of autocratic corruption I would have thought myself guilty of following an easy, a popular line."¹⁰ It is clear too that Mirat as a progressive state better dramatizes both the impossibility of reconciling opposing rights and the sufferings inflicted on the princes by the implicit contradictions in British policy. The two strongest political unifying figures in the novels, Mirat's Russian émigré wazir, Count Bronowsky, and Congress's former chief minister of Ranpur, Mohammed Ali Kasim, are politically opposed to a decree that precludes personal intimacy. Mohammed Ali Kasim mentions that Bronowsky is "dedicated to the continuing autocratic authority of the Nawab," while he himself is "dedicated to the diminution and final extinction of the autocratic authority of *all* the Indian princes" (D 407). On Bronowsky's sound advice, Mirat had been transformed from a feudal autocracy into a semidemocratic state with a judiciary separate from the executive, which had largely taken care of its communal problems by providing equal opportunities. Although the state is a model from the British point of view, it does not have a Resident of its own but must borrow that of a larger neighbor. British economy cost Mirat dearly during partition, when communal riots resulted from the delay in accession to either India or Pakistan (the nawab followed the advice of Sir Robert Conway, who is indifferent to Mirat's fate, to do nothing until the lapse of paramountcy on August 15).

To protect their image, the British government was true to what the *Ranpur Gazette* editorial names "a farce"—the letter of their agreement with the princes; they did not turn paramountcy over to their successors but instead assured the princes that paramountcy would be allowed to lapse. But, as Congress leader Sardar Patel realized, the lapse would only enable Congress more freely to impose its own rule. When the British leave, paramountcy would be without meaning, and the princes would be abandoned to their fate. The perceptive wazir, Dmitri Bronowski, sums it all up when he tells Governor Malcolm's assistant, Nigel Rowan, why he hopes he does not live to see the British leave:

> when you go the princes will be abandoned. In spite of all your protesta-
> tions to the contrary. . . . Nawab Sahib . . . pretends not to believe it. I
> show him the map. I point to the tiny isolated yellow speck that is
> Mirat and to the pink areas that surround it which are the provinces
> directly ruled by the British. Since India passed under the Crown, I say
> to him, you have relied on the pink bits to honour the treaty that allows
> the yellow speck to exist. But you cannot have a treaty with people who
> have disappeared and taken the crown with them. The treaty will not be
> torn up but it will have no validity. It will be a piece of paper. (D 166)

Under the circumstances, Dmitri would settle for "honourable integration" (D 497), which must be immediate if integration is to be attained by agreement rather than by physical coercion, and if something of fortune and privilege is to be preserved for the nawab. He is, however, for the first time unable to persuade his prince to act. The nawab, with one son an officer in the Indian air force and his private army handed over to the British and captured by the Japanese, cannot relinquish his sense of trust. Against all logic, he prefers to keep his illusions and considers his wazir's arguments simplistic. When he is told that the British are pledged in two directions at once and can only go in one, he replies, "That, Dmitri, is where they are so cunning" (D 166), and does not allow himself to think further. The pathos of the situation is again pointed to by Bronowsky when he remembers the bewildered nawab watching Mirat's communal fires burn and sadly wondering "what he has done wrong, or what I have ever done right" (D 551).

The British arrangement, then, threw the princes into an extraordinary predicament as they reluctantly came to realize that nontransference of paramountcy was tantamount to ensuring that they would lose their power to the new India or Pakistan, and that British assurances that paramountcy would not be transferred were meaningless promises. In view of the fostering of differences between the Princely States and Congress India as well as the abandonment of the princes, Scott treats with irony British adherence to the illusion of principle. In a conversation between Nigel Rowan and Guy Perron, Nigel begins:

> "From what I've seen going on in the past few weeks I sometimes wonder whether the Political Department cares [what happens to the Princely States], so long as it can close itself down convinced that it's upheld the principles of the whole past relationship between the States and the Crown."
> "Nothing can bring you peace but yourself," Perron quoted. "Nothing can bring you peace but the triumph of principles."
> "What?"
> "Emerson."
> "Oh," Nigel smiled. "Did he say that? How apt. That sums up my department's attitude admirably."
> "Not just your department's. I think it sums up the attitude of everybody who's concerned in what happens on August fifteen." (D 497–498)

The Well-Intentioned Raj

Despite the recording of actions based on self-interest and justified by the illusion of principle, the *Quartet* is at pains to show "as inaccurate, [the] picture of a tyrannical and imperialistic power grinding the faces of its coloured subjects in the dust" (J 356). The Raj had meant well, and the *Quartet* records its good intentions. Policy from Whitehall sought to be impartial when British interests were not directly at stake, and, like Robin White, many dedicated civil servants worked diligently to heal communal differences and overcome racial prejudice. But British policy in India was complex and by no means consistent, and individual efforts tended to be overshadowed.

The parliamentary form of government assured that, periodically, different approaches would be implemented; in the ongoing dialogue over the governing of India, policy was the product of opposing factions. Churchill wanted to keep India; Atlee did not. In the *Quartet*, Mohammed Ali Kasim has been told by his father that the English can never be charged with hypocrisy, "only . . . with sincerity and [with] being divided among themselves about what it is right to be sincere about" (S 70). Not just the ruling elites were divided; relatively liberal policy makers in Whitehall were just as often divided from reactionary policy enforcers, like Mr. Stead. Conversely, rather than risk chaos, well-meaning administrators in India sometimes had to implement policies they knew to be mistaken. White unhappily muses over his arrest of Congress leaders in 1942, a policy he carried out against his better judgment: "Doubts and all I locked up X, Y and Z. And I think it was wrong. The men who ordered me to lock them up had probably had similar doubts before initiating the policy, but once it was laid on none of us was left with any official alternative but to carry it out" (J 345). The influence of benevolent officials like White, who braved social humiliation by taking three Indian associates to the club with him, is limited on the one hand by their having to carry out policies of the government of India they feel to be mistaken, and on the other by vindictive officials like Ronald Merrick, who punishes an innocent man because he confuses his own depraved response to him with justice.

If the *Quartet* posits English responsibility for the suffering of India, it also seeks to recapture, in evoking the total experience of living in British India in the convulsive 1940s, a sense of the overwhelming complexity of political, social, and psychological causes of disaster. Like all art, it eludes complete analysis.[11] Insofar as Scott's work is a rendering of life, it shares life's ambiguities and apparent random patterning. For any one event which led to the misformed fruit of the labor, we could say with White, "When I attempt to relate the theory to all the events in the lives of all the people who were connected with the action—however directly or remotely— my mind simply won't take in the complex of emotions and ambitions and reactions that led, say, to any one of the single actions that was part of the general describable pattern." No attitude toward the actions can be considered truth, he says, for "The action of such an attitude is rather like that of a sieve. Only what is relevant to the attitude gets through" (J 357–358). For any event, we can provide or infer views from the *Quartet* favorable to both sides. White, a man who looks for complexity, describes such dual interpretations for the Indian rejections of the 1935 scheme for federation and the failure of the Cripps mission (J 356), while Mohammed Ali Kasim points out to Governor Malcolm the simplistic argument on both sides which somehow eludes the truth:

> We could accuse the British of trying to blackmail us into putting everything into the war effort with false promises of independence when the war is won. You would answer that by saying they are not false, although you cannot prove that to us, and Churchill has made it clear that the rights and freedoms embodied in the Atlantic Charter do not apply to India so far as he is concerned. We, for our part, would answer your

charge of blackmail by pointing out that the war is irrelevant to the situation because we are demanding nothing that we have not been demanding for years. (S 42)

Scott's extraordinary talents in developing opposing and tangential points of view and the characters who hold them can lead some critics to criticize the *Quartet* for having on some issues no views of its own. Benita Parry, referring to what she aptly calls the "contention between two conflicting conceptions of right" (as represented by Mohammed Ali Kasim and his son Sayed, who perceive the Indian National Army as treasonous and patriotic respectively), claims that "there are areas where such apparent disengagement can be unsatisfactory and disturbing, for when political conflict and moral choices are opened to too many possible constructions, the definition of an author's own controlling intelligence is obscured."[12]

My own view is that our sense of the tragic is increased by the balanced view presented, and I am reminded that Hegel defined tragedy as the conflict of two opposing rights. Yet, while ambiguity is widely accepted as a component of great fiction, the larger artistic question is whether such a balance of opposing forces is acceptable within the larger context of a series of novels which appear to have a definite point of view. In this larger context the position of the novels is clear. However Scott may have sympathized with men like Sayed, his own anti–Indian National Army view[13] remains implicit in the emphasis of the novels on union and their use of union-seeking characters like Mohammed Ali Kasim as protagonists. Scott himself had an enormous admiration for intensity of effect, which he relates, in a review of a James Hanley novel, to the absence of any guiding hand of the writer, whose purpose is by definition moral, rooted in "human compassion and social inspiration."[14]

District Commissioner White suggests that perhaps "the mind can respond to a sense of a cumulative, impersonal justice" (J 358), and what he and Scott refuse to do in the *Quartet* is to accept any of the simplistic points of view favoring one side or the other, about an area of history whose interpretation is, and probably will always be, the source of controversy among historians. What Scott has recaptured, in the presentation of contrasting views, is a sense of the complex interlace of cause and effect, hopeless of disentanglement, and of the people helplessly caught in the net. This is not to say that the combined weight of conflicting perceptions of protagonists and antagonists, both British and Indian, does not provide a view, but the view is, at least in part, that the historical interpretation cannot be completely understood. To pretend otherwise would be an over-simplification and less of a re-creation. Scott's control of distance is such that he is able to give the appearance of complete objectivity, seemingly without intruding his own point of view. In fact, his vision, though complex and even at times contradictory, is not obscured. If we are unable to say, for example, just where Scott stands on who is to blame for the failure of the Cripps mission, it is because we sense, from the wealth of detail and multiplicity of viewpoints, the interrelating causes.

In this regard, neither English insularity nor narrow Indian response, nor both together by themselves led to the tragic outcome of the British-Indian encounter. One feels that there is something more, something cumulative, some kind of "malign spirit" at work to destroy the characters and prevent the unification of the country. The *Quartet* gives a sense of the time being out of joint, of opposing forces gaining momentum and clashing together, crushing people caught between them at a time of increased stress.[15] The British often appear as bewildered at the fate that is overtaking them as their Indian victims. The ordinary soldier is hard put to understand civil unrest when Britain is at war fighting for India; Brigadier-General Reid, perceiving the strength of the forces that seem to be lined up against them, asks his journal plaintively, "In what way are we at fault? In what way have I personally failed" (J 322), and the narrator feels "caught up by his own people's history and the thrust of a current that simply would not wait for them . . . to comprehend its force" (J 171).

We have seen that if the British are confounded, the political cause of the failure cannot be neatly pinpointed. Just as communal differences increased rapidly, short-sighted policy moves on both sides multiplied until people were caught up in an ethical net from which they could break free only by destroying the imprisoning ties of love and moral obligation. Much of what Britain did in the final years leading to partition it did because, in pragmatic terms, there was little choice. In all fairness the pursuit by the British of a deliberate policy of divide and rule to keep the Princely States separate from democratic India is understandable in view of the mutiny and their own small numbers. Additionally, the *Quartet* notes that, if the princes were in 1947 placed in an untenable position, they had refused the 1935 scheme for federation, which would have brought them loosely into the central government. And the British could not practically have defended hundreds of small states within the boundaries of the country they were leaving. In the problems of paramountcy as well as those of the Quit India and Indian National Army movements, the *Quartet* records a Britain caught up in a vortex not entirely of its own making.

When, with the Japanese "practically hammering at the door" (J 339), Gandhi and the Congress Party threatened civil disobedience, the British were forced to use the repressive measures detailed in *The Jewel in the Crown* that led men like Sayed Kasim to join the Indian National Army. For it was "a resolution under which the British would be called upon to leave India on pain of finding the realm impossible to defend, their armies of the Assam-Burma frontier impossible to feed, clothe, arm or support; impossible, for the simple reason that there would be no one who was willing to operate the railways, . . . the banks, the offices, or any of the administrative and productive services" (J 45). The society, in the midst of a war, would have ground to a halt. Perron and Malcolm both share Rowan's view of the necessity of repressive measures in context:

> If there were cases of unduly repressive measures there were an infinitely greater number of cases of intense and by no means invariably non-violent provocation. You have to put both the provocation and the methods used to meet it in the context of the atmosphere prevailing at the time, and that was a pretty tricky one. The Japanese were on the Chindwin, Singapore had gone and Burma had gone. Most of Europe had gone and North Africa was a mess. The plain fact is that strategically and . . . morally, India had to be held on to. And I honestly don't see that any Indian leader who incited people to rebel against the *raj* and obstruct or sabotage its war effort has any right whatsoever to complain if quite a few of them got harshly treated. (D 269)

And District Commissioner White, while sympathetic to the Indian side, yet compares the situation to "the one a quarrelsome household would face if they looked out of the window and saw burglars trying to get in, or a gang of hooligans preparing to burn the house down. The head of the house would immediately feel obliged to take a lead and stand no nonsense from inside" (J 339). Reflecting the novels' recapturing of causative complexity, White then uses the voluminous balance of the house analogy to show how Britain is indeed to blame.

The force of the apparent contradiction in the *Quartet* is further evident when we recall that the novels are a dramatization of the injustice of the Defense of India rules, portraying with a controlled emotion no argument could capture the violations of civil liberties, the hardships of people arrested on suspicion of being political activists or members of an outlawed party. It will be remembered that it was the incarceration of Congress leaders that led to the suffering of Mohammed Ali Kasim and the consequent desertion of his son to the Japanese-led Indian National Army and to the riots responsible for the slaying of Edwina Crane's Indian colleague, Chaudhuri, the rape of Daphne Manners, and the imprisonment of Hari Kumar. Clearly, the text is conflicted. Scott is acknowledging the inevitability, given the war, of certain repressive measures while deploring the suffering caused by them.

In *The Scarlet Letter* the central ambiguity is between Hawthorne's feelings toward illegitimate passion, which he admires but finds sinful, and his feelings toward puritanism, which he dislikes but must respect.[16] There is a certain ambivalence in *The Raj Quartet* between self-sacrifice on the grounds of principle, such as a character like Mohammed Ali Kasim embodies, and the need for a certain amount of healthy self-interest. It can be said, perhaps, that in the *Quartet* there is too much of the one at the expense of the other, too much lamenting over what the British could have done in India and not enough emphasis on what they actually did accomplish. To say this is to quarrel with Scott's focus and his subject. It will be remembered that he saw the novel as a metaphor for a view of life, that in the *Quartet* one historical failure is tied to universal psychological shortcomings and metaphysical problems. The implicit conclusion with which Scott leaves his readers is that the British presence in India at its best embodied an ideal of love that could never be implemented consistently.

We have seen that Scott's theory of tragedy, whether national or personal, posits insular forces as largely responsible for frustrating the fulfilment of human aspirations. Yet the *Quartet* does not seek to blame the British for the suffering of India so much as it grieves for their lost aspirations, their *"love never made manifest"* (J 147). To have helped India gain independence and peaceful, prosperous, enlightened self-government, without the violence and human loss generated with tragic implications for our own times, England would have had to have been heroic, not simply "great" in demeanor; for India's sake, England would have had to take some voluntary economic and perhaps military losses as well. After the devastation of World War II, England was unprepared to do this. In addition to Indian pressures, the United States was pushing toward independence for India, as was the ascendant Labour Party, which saw India as an economic drain and chose rather to abandon the country rather than pay the heavy cost of bringing it gradually into the twentieth century and remaining until the unification of the country was completed. In one way, England had always and would always be unprepared because, with notable exceptions, its interest lay not with helping India so much as with the image of itself doing so. In the view of *The Raj Quartet,* British aspirations for India prove to have been the stuff of dreams.

8. The Tragic Pattern

Paul Scott once said that he envisioned every page of a novel in a proscenium arch.[1] He longed to see his work on stage, and the enormous success of Granada Television's Masterpiece Theatre production of *The Raj Quartet* attests to his skills as a dramatist. The narrative complexities of his masterpiece, the differing views of historical events, the way the events of the story are pieced together by a narrator from diaries, letters, depositions, and memories of peripheral characters, may hide from the uninitiated reader the fact that the stories are intensely dramatic. Like Ibsen, Scott portrays primarily middle-class people of supposedly free will caught inextricably in a web of fate growing out of political and social problems and issues. He goes further in portraying antagonists as well as protagonists, minor characters and major, all as "the chance victims of the hazards of a colonial ambition" (J 82).

When he died at fifty-seven, just at the start of his recognition as a major twentieth-century writer, Scott was, however reluctantly, true to the tragic pattern of his fiction. We have seen in the preceding chapter that Scott posited "some kind of aspiration . . . as central to major tragedies and to minor personal ones."[2] That chapter demonstrated the aspiration to a free, unified subcontinent thwarted at the last moment by an insular spirit. In the *Quartet*'s view policy was based on a convenient illusion of principle which allowed England to keep its convictions of moral superiority without the political, economic, and military sacrifice that true principle would have required. England abandoned India when keeping the country was no longer in its interest. For Scott, England's tragedy is its unrealized potential, what it could have been, and what a difference it might have made for India and the civilized world.

There is a change of emphasis on the personal level; the protagonists have the courage of their convictions and do not hide behind an illusion of principle. Their lives dramatize a thwarted or aborted attempt to actualize an aspiration toward union through love or work, and the price exacted for the attempt. "Death is the price the world demands for love" (217), Thelma Craddock concludes in *The Corrida at San Feliu*. In *The Raj Quartet* the particular behavioral pattern which leaves the narrator and his reader with a heightened sense of life's tragedy is identified by an attempt at union which is disastrously, even fatally, thwarted at the moment of actualization. This is the heart of Scott's sense of the tragic in *The Raj Quartet*. His protagonists sacrifice themselves because of a "thrust for freedom"[3] from the confines of their social or political mores, or of the physical laws which rule the universe. Despite their initial ordinariness, they are transformed into heroic figures by the intensity of their commitments. Their actions are given magnitude not by their social status but by their philosophical nearness to the mystical and moral core of the novels. As a character draws closer to this center, his or her life becomes more psychologically meaningful and more besieged by hostile forces. Consistent with the idea of tragedy since Nietzsche, the significance of the fatal choice or way of life is not dictated by the character's flaw, as in classical and romantic tragedy, so much as by his or her virtue.

For Scott the exalting struggle to achieve communion with other human beings, particularly those of races, religions, or social classes considered by some to be inferior, is synonymous with worthy principle or love, the novels' major positive value or true protagonist. (The peculiar structure of Scott's novels, with their shifting central focus, leads us to conclude that the *Quartet* has no one human protagonist and obliges us to take as major protagonist the structurally unifying idea of love or union and to consider as human protagonists each of the major figures who embody this love.) Each of his human protagonists aspires to cut across communal, racial, political, or psychological barriers to some form of union, usually with or for India or Indians. Missionary Edwina Crane has a mystical love for the country and yearns for spiritual union with an abstract Indian; Daphne Manners falls in love with the anglicized Indian Hari Kumar, who provides a mirror image of the English protagonists by cutting across race barriers to return her love; Count Bronowsky's and former Congress minister Kasim's union-seeking aspirations are defined in terms of their work. Bronowsky wants equal privileges for Mirat's Hindus and Muslims, joined harmoniously under his prince; Mohammed Ali Kasim works toward a united, independent India. These are the ideals. But their achievement is too often possible only in dreams. Almost all of the people who embody the *Quartet*'s values are betrayed by a combination of political, social, and psychological forces.

Characters who aspire to union, whether through love or work, leave the dull but protective safety of the community to plunge into "the destructive element," which for Scott in the *Quartet* is not the dream—which, actualized, would be better identified with paradise—so much as "the destructive counter-element of reality that entered any state of intended happiness" (S 183). For Scott, dreams without the ballast of reality are deadening, as they are for the English memsahibs who live in the unreal world of the club, but dreams at the point of actualization are most dangerous. This pattern was apparent in Tom Brent's loss of the elusive prostitute Teena Chang at the very moment he was going to ask her to go away with him, out of the Chinese love pavilion and its world of illusion into the real world. Scott's "destructive element" in the *Quartet* is not quite the same as Stein's view of the dream in Conrad's *Lord Jim*, where Stein admires Jim for immersing himself in "the destructive element." Although the pattern may be similar (the pursuit of an ideal which then leads to disaster), Scott is not even ambivalently critical of Daphne's dream, as Conrad is of Jim's when Marlowe marvels at "the exalted egoism of a man who goes away from a living woman to celebrate his pitiless wedding with a shadowy ideal of conduct" (307). In the passage closest to the mystical and moral core of the novels, Sister Ludmila admires Daphne's courage to leap metaphorically from the MacGregor House, the place of the white, to the Bibighar, the place of the black, a courage involving a plunge into the very heart of life:

> To get from one to the other you could not cross by a bridge but had
> to take your courage in your hands and enter the flood and let yourself
> be taken with it, lead where it may. This is a courage Miss Manners
> had. . . .
>   It is as if she said to herself: Well, life is not just a business of standing
> on dry land and occasionally getting your feet wet. It is merely an illu-
> sion that some of us stand on one bank and some on the opposite. So
> long as we stand like that we are not living at all but dreaming. So jump,
> jump in, and let the shock wake us up. Even if we drown, at least for a
> moment or two before we die we shall be awake and alive. (J 151)

Daphne's desire to cross to the Indian side of the river is representative of her wish to actualize a dream of love and union. Her tragedy is that she does indeed "drown," having had only "a moment or two" of exhilarating joy in the Bibighar Gardens when she and Hari Kumar consummate their relationship.

The theme of the crucifixion of love in its encounter with destructive forces achieves a cosmic magnitude as the echo of Daphne and Hari's aborted love reverberates through Scott's Raj. The theme is even present in the cartoons of the *Ranpur Gazette*'s Halki and in such imagery as that of "one naked electric bulb around which moths and insects danced their nightly ritual of primitive desire for what might burn their wings" (J 54). The historian Guy Perron relates that his Uncle George once said that "the only reward in life for being fair is an obscure death" (D 267). Immediately after the Bibighar and Dibrapur disasters, the English community is aware that "the victims must have been people in whom the impulse to show as well as feel affection in the performance of their duty had been stronger than was usual, even than was wise" (T 82). Ahmed Kasim, at the point of finally getting to know his father, sacrifices himself because he cannot risk endangering his friends during the communal riots on Independence Day. Scott's restrained eloquence reflects his admiration for the heroism of Ahmed's act: "He is said to have gestured at the shuttered window of the compartment door on which strangers outside were banging [while calling out his name], and said 'It seems to be me they want,' and then smiled at his shocked fellow-passengers, as if he had recognized a brilliant and totally unexpected opportunity" (D 112). And Edwina Crane's last statement, expressed posthumously to Barbara Batchelor by Captain Merrick, who had gone through her things, and Merrick's reaction to it express Scott's grief that the price of love is often death, whether in the literal sense or the symbolic sense of diminution. Merrick says she wrote, "There is no God. Not even on the road from Dibrapur."[4] The passage continues:

> An invisible lightning struck the verandah. The purity of its colourless fire etched shadows on his face. The cross glowed on her breast and then seemed to burn out.
> "Not even on the road from Dibrapur?"
> He nodded.
> For a moment she felt herself drawn to him. He offered recompense. He looked desolated as if Edwina's discovery were a knowledge he had been born with and could not bear because he had been born as well with a tribal memory of a time when God leaned His weight upon the world. He needed consolation. (T 386)

The "thrust for freedom" that costs Daphne her life leads to a feeling of moral incongruity between what is and what should be.[5]

Thus, tragic figures are often brought face to face with the lack of correspondence between their inner and the outer world, and the reader as well is made to see the indifference of the world to human desires and noble ideals. As the narrator notes the "grand irrelevance of history to the things that people wanted for themselves" (D 84), the unrealized aspirations of the protagonists are considered idealistic illusions. Tragically, the price of attempted freedom from the confining mores of the society is often some form of diminution. When disaster strikes, those who are not left ravaged, despairing, mad, or dead are, like Hari Kumar, poignantly saddened. Through their heroic acceptance of their undeserved fates, Scott evokes in the reader a sense of pity or compassion and muted fear paralleling the feelings of the narrator and leading to a cathartic, majestic sadness.

We shall see in the individual stories that follow people whose dreams of love and union lead them to an attempt to cross the confining social and political mores of their society. These characters see their fondest hopes destroyed just at the point of fulfillment, leading to an identity crisis and death or a diminution of the circumstances of their lives. Edwina Crane's is the first disaster, and she is a prototype of the more cognizant heroine, Daphne Manners.

Miss Crane is an intelligent but unsophisticated spinster, a mission administrator who is laughed at for her idiosyncrasies at the same time that she is grudgingly admired for her courage in once refusing a band of Indian rioters entry into her schoolhouse. She is an independent woman whose problems stem from plain looks, poverty, a lack of education, her own unrealistic taste in men, and no family other than a burdensome, drunken father. Without friends, she translates her erotic impulse into a selfless though abstract love for India. She aspires to the imperial ideal, believes in "the importance of courageously accepting duties and obligations, not for self-aggrandizement, but in self-denial, in order to promote a wider happiness and well-being, in order to rid the world of . . . poverty, disease, misery, ignorance and injustice" (J 30). She believes too that the British promise of independence will be fulfilled.

In an idealistic fashion Edwina longs to break through the racial barrier imposed by the society to experience a genuine relationship with an Indian; she attempts a friendship with Mr. Chaudhuri, the dedicated mission teacher, but is unable to get past his reserve. Not until she and Chaudhuri are braving the road from Dibrapur back to Mayapore during the riots of August 9, 1942, does she lose her inhibitions and feel herself on the verge of true contact. She senses between them "an unexpected mutual confidence . . . [and has] a feeling in the bones of her shoulders and in the base of her skull that she was about to go over the hump [of racial difference] thirty-five years of effort and willingness had never really got her over" (J 64). Exhilarated, she sings the mission song, not timidly or piously, but strongly and joyously, so that Chaudhuri catches her enthusiasm and joins in, only to find the rioters immediately ahead, blocking their way.

In Miss Crane's case, aspiration to selflessness and union with India is abstract and, in a sense, illusory. Worldly Lili Chatterjee offers a shrewd analysis when she muses that Edwina was living her life in an idealistic vacuum, that she made friendships in her head rather than her heart, and that "She loved India and all Indians but no particular Indian" (J 117). Miss Crane also believes naively in the power of right behavior. In her desire to courageously fulfill her responsibilities at the mission school, she never considered that she might be endangering Chaudhuri's life. Her illusions are shattered when Chaudhuri is killed coming to her defense and, symbolizing Scott's feelings about the British in India, Edwina sits in the roadside holding the dead Indian's hand and muttering, "It's taken a long time. . . . I'm sorry it was too late" (J 69). Holding his hand is an act of love and desire for atonement, just as her suttee for her dead mate, India, is really an act of atonement for being out of touch with the world around her. Edwina despairs because her belief in the power of selfless love and courage is destroyed; she has physical courage and immolates herself because she can in no way face her unwilling role in Chaudhuri's death. Her posthumous revelation that there is no God expresses the lack of correspondence between her inner world and the outer world and conveys also her emotional realization of the tragic flaw in the universe.

There are important similarities between the fate of Edwina Crane and that of Daphne Manners. Like Edwina, Daphne has lost her family, makes a point of working for charitable organizations, and genuinely likes India. But she is a much less limited and more realistically committed person. She has a love of the universal in human beings and a corresponding disdain for insular divisiveness. Where Edwina (in Lili Chatterjee's words) does "all her good works . . . in a vacuum" and "never dirtie[s] her hands" (J 117), Daphne, though shy, makes a point of extending herself and of getting her hands grubby, for she believes philosophically in challenging the confining mores of her society—in "put[ting] ourselves out on a limb, dar[ing] other people to saw the limb off, whoever they are, black or white" (J 116).

There were difficulties with Daphne and Hari's relationship from the beginning. They had to combat not only social pressure and prejudice but their own internal fears and defenses. If Daphne fears that she is merely appealing to his vanity, Hari, educated in England since the age of two, is ashamed of his poverty, bitter at his exclusion from English society in India, and too proud to accept what he must consider Daphne's liberal condescension. After he stops contacting Daphne and fails to keep an appointment at Sister Ludmila's Sanctuary, she finds him alone in the Bibighar Gardens and wills him to love her. He takes her roughly at first, an indication of the strength of the barriers that must be overcome before they can experience the joy of union: "There was nothing gentle in the way he took me. . . . He tore at my underclothes and pressed down on me with all his strength. But this was not me and Hari. Entering me he made me cry out. And then it was us" (J 433). As in the Crane-Chaudhuri relationship, overwhelming, hostile forces intervene at the critical moment. Racial taboos having been broken, Daphne is raped by rampaging lower-class Indian hooligans immediately after the consummation of her love with Hari. But the British Raj visits upon her a worse indignity. By indefinitely incarcerating Hari under the convenient Defense of India laws, they prevent her from seeing again the only man she has loved.

Daphne Manners could fall in love with Hari Kumar because she refused to don the armor of contempt the other English women wore for their Indian encounters. When Daphne makes prosecution of the men arrested for the rape impossible by refusing to testify at the trial, and later, when she decides to have the baby she believes is Hari's, she is insisting on implementing the values of love, whatever the consequences. And the same insistence on living her life the way she believes it should be lived leads her to have her child naturally at home after her doctor advises a Caesarian. If there is any negative aspect to the risk she takes, any death wish or attraction to the forbidden and the dangerous, Scott shows little if any awareness of it but clearly admires her single-minded pursuit of the natural. She wants "to do this thing properly. I don't want to be cut open, to have the child torn out like that. I want to bear it. I want to give it life . . . [and] to try my best to end with a good conscience what I began with one" (J 374). The Caesarian has to be performed anyway, and Daphne, at home rather than in hospital, weakened from a forty-eight hour labor, together with the slight additional "debit" of her heart problem, dies from peritonitis. Sister Ludmila thinks that without possessing striking features, she was a beautiful woman. For Scott it is ironically and tragically Daphne's remarkable stature, her closeness to the mystical and moral core of the novels implicit in her refusal to compromise with the desire to live fully, that leads to the Bibighar disaster and her death. Symbolically and despite her wholeness, she can be seen as one of his birds of paradise living on the "celestial dew" of love, dead from contamination by the real world.

In her values and her courage, Daphne is replaced in *The Day of the Scorpion* by Sarah Layton, the only English person to visit Lady Manners, who has been shunned after adopting Daphne's daughter Parvati. Like historian Guy Perron, however, her role as a participant in the drama is not as important as her role as a stoic observer of the dying Anglo-Indian scene, an "ideal daughter" reflecting Scott's views.[6] Sarah serves as a foil for her spoiled sister, Susan. She exemplifies selfless love and responsibility but is merely a muted example of the tragic pattern, for she has no endangering aspiration. Although she is close to Ahmed Kasim, she has no desire to become his lover. Her imprisonment is not by tightly structured Anglo-Indian society so much as by "the net" (D 372) of her own family responsibilities. Unstable Susan is in constant need of attention, and Mabel Layton's companion, Barbie Batchelor, warns Sarah that Susan's needs may prevent her own marriage: "Some people are made to live and others are made to help them. If you stay [with the family] you'll end up like that, like me" (D 386–387). Barbie's prophecy is fulfilled for the remainder of the *Quartet* when Susan's marriage to Ronald Merrick prevents Sarah's desired union with Nigel Rowan, the governor's assistant. Weeping privately, she senses that Rowan, a man with a strong, even squeamish sense of what is proper, cannot ask her to marry him once it is clear that Merrick is to be her brother-in-law. The *Quartet* ends on a hopeful note for Sarah, however, as she continues to play an important part in the thoughts of Guy Perron.

In Hari Kumar's case, the contributing aspiration was his father's. Duleep Kumar's dream of egalitarian dignity was no match for the real world in his own life. Duleep[7] was a man of strong ambitions and limited abilities who rebelled against the narrowness of orthodox Hindu tradition and aspired to British education and responsibility. Continually caught between his English goals and his Indian traditions, Duleep, who has wanted to go to England to study for the civil service, obeyed his father, married at an inauspicious moment, left his new wife in India, and went to England to study law. Probably less suited for law than for civil service, he failed his bar exam and returned after several years to India. Duleep concludes that "if you looked at the situation squarely he had managed to get for himself the worst of both worlds" (J 227).

After his wife died in giving him the son they wanted, Duleep de-

termined that Hari should fulfill his English ambitions. He took him
to Britain at the age of two because he believed that bringing up Hari
as an Englishman would bring him English privileges: "It is not only
that if *you* answer the phone a stranger on the other end would
think he was speaking to an English boy of the upper classes," he
told his son. "It is that you *are* that boy in your mind and behaviour"
(J 215). Again, the pattern of disaster that intrudes on the verge of
fulfillment repeats itself. Hari had been educated at England's elite
public school, Chillingborough, and had hoped to enter the Indian
Civil Service, the only conceivable way of bridging the gulf between
the English and educated Indians. But after his father loses his financial empire and commits suicide, Hari finds himself back in India in
a most unenviable position. Living with his Aunt Shalini under conditions that appall his civilized sense, he is dependent financially
on his miserly *bania* uncle and shunned by English and Indian alike
for his British upper-class manner. Slowly and painfully he realizes
that his situation is impossible and that "his father's plans for him
had been based upon an illusion. In India an Indian and an Englishman could never meet on equal terms" (J 260).

His wealth and schooling gave Hari qualities that could only hurt
an impoverished Indian back in India: a British sense of alienation
from the country, an upper-class British accent, and a public-school
air of superiority which will not permit him to humble himself.
When Hari applies for a position at British Electrical, he is turned
down; his manner and "sharp clipped-spoken accents of privilege
and power" (J 145) are intimidating to a less well educated Englishman. The same need to retain his personal dignity[8] is what brings
him to the fatal attention of the district superintendent of police in
Sister Ludmila's Sanctuary, where he is brought drunk and unconscious. Hari treats Merrick as he would any man who has just in-
sulted him. Because he does not answer in a properly submissive
fashion, he is punched and shoved by Merrick's Indian subordinate
into the police van for further questioning and marked out by Merrick as a future victim.

What finally destroys his life's hope is falling in love with an English girl. Arrested for her rape and tortured by Merrick, he says
nothing in his own defense and makes no complaint to outside authorities when given the opportunity. When Kumar is released several years later, a shadow of himself, it is to find Daphne dead and to
be forever barred from the administrative post for which he was educated and from the life he had once loved. Living in a miserable
hovel and trying to make the best of his situation, Kumar is "a man
who [feels] in the end that he [has] lost everything" (J 355). He has

neither India nor England; not his English friend Colin, whose lack of recognition is a betrayal, not Daphne, not his daughter, Parvati, whom he has never met. He has only his memories, his dreams of the splendid opportunities life had once seemed to offer.

Personal aspirations are betrayed, then, in the lives of Edwina Crane, Daphne Manners, Sarah Layton, and Duleep and Hari Kumar. The leading political figures show political aspirations betrayed as well. Although the wazir of Mirat, Count Dmitri Bronowski, plays a smaller role in the *Quartet* than some of the major figures, his union-seeking values suggest that his story should be told as an illustration of Scott's tragic pattern. Count Bronowsky, a Russian émigré whose life has been devoted to preserving peace, communal unity, and power for his prince, lives to see his dreams destroyed. Placing loyalty to his prince even above his secret love for Ahmed Kasim, Bronowsky has transformed Nawab Sahib from an extravagant libertine to a ruler-statesman, brought Hindu-dominated Mirat into the twentieth century by modernizing the machinery of government, and, most important, lessened communal differences for his Muslim prince. "My life in Mirat," he tells Rowan, "has been spent trying to ensure that the two communities have equal opportunities . . . that they live in amity and have reason to be perfectly content to live as subjects of the Nawab, and do not hanker after the democratic millennium promised by Gandhiji on the one hand or the theistic state on earth envisaged by Mr Jinnah on the other" (D 165). As astute observer who enjoys intrigue, Bronowsky is well aware of any threat to the welfare of Mirat and his prince, and has an eye out for subversives from Congress-run India. In the end, though, even he cannot stop the communal violence that breaks out in Mirat when the British make known their policies concerning the Princely States. When Ahmed, whom he hoped would marry the nawab's daughter and ensure Mirat's succession for his prince, is brutally murdered, Bronowsky blames himself for not anticipating the train massacre. "My life has been wasted" (D 560), he says, approaching tragic stature as he and the bewildered and despairing nawab watch with a sense of unreality as Mirat is abandoned and destroyed in flames. Bronowsky is not fully a tragic figure; unlike the case of his kinsman Kasim, the destruction of his life's work represents more a political defeat than a personal crucifixion.

Like Bronowsky, Mohammed Ali Kasim is a man of strong principles. His dream is Akbar's, of a united India, which he believes can only be achieved through the Congress Party, however foolish its dictates sometimes appear to him. Because Kasim is a man consistently true to his principles, he is caught between British Raj and

Congress Party manipulations. In 1937, Kasim, unwilling to split the party, was forced by Congress to resign his provincial ministry, a move which left the way open for Jinnah's divisive Muslim League to strengthen its position. Later, he will not let either the threat of prison or the lure of a seat on the governor's Executive Council tempt him to resign from the party and appear a lackey of the British. Nothing can sway him from his purpose, not even Governor Malcolm's suggestion that news of his father's imprisonment by the British might well turn Kasim's prisoner-of-war son Sayed into an Indian National Army man fighting side by side with the Japanese.

Physically wasted by the prison experience and suffering from a sense of loneliness and helplessness, he pays dearly for his choice. But the hardest blow is the shock of learning that Sayed has in fact betrayed his commission and joined the Indian National Army. His anguish is terrible. What kind of independence will it be, he says, without people faithful to their national responsibility? He continues:

> When the British invited Indians to take the King's commission, they were proving what my father called their sincerity. You do not hand your armed forces over to the command of men who will turn it against you. What kind of an army will it be [when the British leave] if its officers think of their commissions as meaningless bits of paper. It is a contract, a contract. All of Muslim law is based on the sanctity of contract, of one man's word to another. You must be prepared to suffer and die for it. It is written. It is revealed. It is in our hearts. What are you telling me? That it is not in Sayed's? That he is not a man to keep his contract? That he is an opportunist? A cowardly scoundrel? Without a thought for his own honour or for mine, or his mother's or for yours? Are you telling me this is the kind of India I have gone to prison for? If you are, you had better leave me here. I do not know that kind of India. I do not know that kind of man. He is not Sayed. He is not my son. (S 480)

Not only is Kasim's favorite son lost to him, but Sayed's desertion and Kasim's own refusal to defend his son and the Indian National Army cost him his political office. Kasim is a man caught between systems and a web of his own principles, which necessarily limits his options. Though staggered by Sayed's desertion, Kasim refuses to become an instrument of the British by publicly criticizing his son and the INA. At the same time he will not defend Sayed and encourage the idea that the officers of the INA are heroes. He believes that a man who would throw away his commission is one who might be tempted to overthrow a properly constituted civil authority and pave the way for military dictatorship in India. The political cost is his Congress seat. He resigns from the public life he holds dear, knowing that with the institutionalization of religious differences into India's political system, his replacement will almost certainly lose the seat to the divisive Muslim League.

Kasim cannot betray his principles to join Jinnah, who would probably give him a ministership in Pakistan's central government. He also cannot bring himself to accept the governorship that Malcolm offers him because he is unwilling to appear a British lackey, but the difference between what he wants and what he must do is apparent in the sense of unreality that accompanies his refusal as he hears himself telling the governor why he cannot take the position. The price of principle for Kasim is loneliness in his mature years. If there is anything unnecessarily self-destructive in his total refusal to compromise, Scott's narrative shows only admiration for his courage. Kasim is left with nothing: his wife dead; his favorite son a detested INA hero; his son Ahmed, whom he was just getting to know and respect, killed in the communal riots; his own position lost; India divided; "his youthful longing and commitment . . . [un]fulfilled." Everything he had loved and worked for is destroyed. Indicative of his crucifixion, Kasim bids Ahmed place his Congress cap on his head "straight and firm . . . like a crown of thorns" (S 486).

Characters like Kasim, Sarah, and Daphne, whose union-seeking values reflect the dominant norm of the *Quartet*, are not the only people whose courage Scott admires, even though some of the others do not share his values. What they do share is an aspiration, or love principle, which is in some way defeated. But many of the aspirations of these characters, particularly of the antagonists, appear misguided. Mildred Layton wants the privileges her father enjoyed and is bitter at losing them; in her Scott demonstrates the resentment of people who feel they have been deprived of an inheritance—India (D 271). Ronald Merrick, whose would-be paradise is also one of power and mastery, wants to belong to the upper classes in India; Susan struggles to feel herself a member of the group just as much as Sarah fights to retain her individuality; Teddie insists on believing in the reality of the glorious British Empire of legend—duty on one side and loyalty on the other.

Sometimes, as in the sacrifices of Officer Teddie Bingham for the regiment's turncoat INA men,[9] and Officer Ronald Merrick for Teddie (despite what Merrick says to the contrary), the antagonists loom larger than life, into an heroic grandeur undiminished for the moment either by the foolish illusion for which Teddie sacrifices himself or by the cruelty of Ronald Merrick. In the price they pay for their courage and intensity of commitment, they transcend the ordinary limitations of their characters to achieve an instant proximity to the mystical and moral core of the novels, a proximity which confers heroic stature upon them. In a moment of insight Sarah muses:

> I don't know, I don't know, where that kind of courage comes from or why or what its purpose is, but I know it has a purpose. It's a kind of madness, a sublime insanity which even Ronald who's experienced it can't explain. He wanted to diminish Teddie for me but Teddie isn't diminished. He began to diminish himself, but now he isn't diminished either. For a moment they are both larger than life. Teddie calling stupidly for those men, and Ronald stupidly risking death to try and save him. And that's how I shall remember them. Without understanding why it makes them larger. (S 402)

And even while intuiting him as the devil, Barbara Batchelor is "hit by the terrible consequences for Captain Merrick of his heroic act, hit as never before because she hadn't known the man or been able to imagine in detail the ruined face and the awful artificial arm" (T 377). What makes the characters larger than life is their willingness, at a critical time, to forget their human limitations, to "risk all"[10] in the service of the unifying instinct. The price they pay for their courage is what gives these far from admirable characters a tragic dimension.

Scott has an uncanny gift for transforming his antagonists—either unsympathetic people like Mildred or Merrick, or relatively likeable but misguided people like Teddie and Susan—by some heroism or overwhelming loss. He transforms them for the moment not just into victims but into tragic figures, a stature usually reserved for the protagonists. All of his characters are imprisoned, like the blind lace-maker Claudine's exquisite butterflies, unable to "fly out of the prison of the lace and make love in the sunshine" (S 367), or caught, like the symbolic scorpion, in a circle of fire, unable to protect themselves because of the tenderness of their skins. The characters, protagonists and antagonists alike, share, in Kasim's words, "a special sense of impotence, of powerlessness to do anything that will help to alter things in any way" (S 43). Bronowsky feels the same when he looks at Mirat in flames and thinks that his life has been wasted. Hari Kumar sees his father's financial disaster and suicide, his own alienation from Colin Lindsey, and his miserable position as the work of a "malign spirit." Sister Ludmila, impotently sensing character as fate, tells the narrator that the Bibighar disaster had begun in the very first seconds of the initial meeting of Merrick and Kumar. And she relates how helpless she felt when, in her anxiety over Daphne's disappearance, she mentioned that Daphne might have gone to Mrs. Gupta Sen's and triggered in Merrick's mind the thought "Hari

Kumar": "I had that sensation which sometimes comes to us all of returning to a situation that had already been resolved on some previous occasion, of being again committed to a tragic course of action" (J 158).

Miss Crane feels that special sense of helplessness immediately after Mr. Chaudhuri is killed when, distracted, she walks unsteadily in the rain muttering, "Nothing I can do. Nothing. Nothing" (J 69); and later when, unable to alter the tragic events, she declines into insanity and takes her own life. Sarah is helpless immediately after Ahmed's murder when she speaks painfully of just sitting there and letting him go. And her feelings are the same later when, amidst the frightful slaughter, she kneels at the tap, trying to fill cups of water for the dying, thinking that what she is doing was "just as useless as what he'd just done" (D 592). Daphne has intimations of disaster when she compares the club to a Titaniclike vessel "with all the lights blazing and the bands playing, heading into the dark, with no one at the bridge" (J 389). And she experiences a sense of impotence when she says that somehow her relationship with Hari never had a chance and that she had given up hope of ever seeing him again. Her frustration is also apparent when, convinced that she must keep silent for Hari's good once he is imprisoned, she is led to echo the words of Edwina Crane and wonder where she has heard them before.

The helplessness of the characters to combat destructive forces creates pity and fear, particularly when the narrator describes people as toys in the hands of alien forces. Reflecting on the tragedies of Daphne and Edwina, he shows them helpless in the grip of the gods:

> The story goes that for this act of becoming suttee . . . she dressed for the first time in her life in a white saree, the saree for her adopted country, the whiteness for widowhood and mourning. And there is a tale that Joseph, returning empty-handed from some wild-goose errand she had sent him on, fell on his knees in the compound and cried to the smouldering pyre, 'Oh, Madam, Madam' just as, several weeks before, Miss Manners, falling on her knees, had looked up and said, 'Oh, Auntie.'
>
> In such a fashion human beings call for explanations of the things that happen to them and in such a way scenes and characters are set for exploration, like toys set out by kneeling children intent on pursuing their grim but necessary games. (J 123)

Scott's novels leave us with a sense of majestic sadness that can only be called cathartic. As the characters are overwhelmed and in some sense destroyed by the array of destructive forces that con-

fronts them, as they see their fondest hopes die, there is a realization and cumulative effect of profound melancholy about shattered
ideals. Edwina Crane kills herself; Daphne dies in childbirth; blinded
by age, Sister Ludmila remembers again and again how her charity
and chance remark to Ronald Merrick brought on the Bibighar affair;
Teddie is killed; Susan goes mad and only partially recovers; Merrick and Ahmed are murdered; and Hari Kumar is left alone in his
ingrown little hovel, so depressing that it frightens historian Guy
Perron in the concluding novel.

Years before, Miss Crane had entered a church in the Punjab "looking for an image of herself that would not diminish her" (J 193).
Though it is too late for her, she finds what the other protagonists
possess throughout the novels—an image of herself capable of leading to "a further union, a deeper communion." Though the characters are at the end diminished by circumstances, the protagonists at
least remain "imprisoned but free, diminished by everything that
loomed from outside, *but not diminished from the inside*" (J 405).
Daphne's words are intended to describe her own restricted social
situation; it is fair to say that they describe as well the situation of
the other protagonists and demonstrate the lack of correspondence
between their inner and outer worlds.

It has been said that a play cannot be tragic if right is victorious at
the end, if the writer is emotionally satisfied with its answers, as
were writers of the miracle and morality plays of the Middle Ages.
Scott, who felt that the job of the novelist was not to solve problems
but to ask questions, is clearly troubled by the fate of love in its confrontation with destructive forces. His tragic realization is that even
when illusion does not, as it so often does, blind people to the life
of love, *Amor omnia vincit* is not true in public or private affairs.
His novels achieve a larger part of their emotional power from the
strength of this metaphysical conflict.

If Scott moves us by his portrayal of love, of its strength, self-
lessness, creativity, and joy, it is from the perspective of one who has
recognized and accepted the limitations of such love in the real
world. The function of the tragic writer is not to blame but to
mourn, and Scott once identified the subject of the *Quartet* as,
among other things, his "sadness that things had to work that way
and probably will always have to work that way."[11] In one existentialist definition of tragic possibility, the protagonist seeks to retain
control over his or her own destiny, knowing the possible consequences of not bowing to hostile forces in the real world. In *The Raj
Quartet* there is a sense of free moral choice in the face of overwhelming odds, and the determination to abide by the consequences

of one's own decisions however absurd they may turn out to be. The ultimate human dignity for Scott lies in a courageous, existentialist acceptance of one's tragic fate.

Unlike the works of contemporary literature that portray the relations of a few people in an empty universe, Scott's work has a nineteenth-century broadness of scope and solidity of value. Where much of contemporary literature emphasizes the alienation of individuals from their universe, viewing life as either comic or absurd and meaningless, Scott's protagonists, though living in a dying world, possess a moral certainty and, despite their ordinariness, a heroic stature. From Ibsen Scott takes his sense of the tragic—of men like Dr. Stockman in *An Enemy of the People,* caught in the grip of a fate that does not deny free will, and of the sacrifice of people for their ideals.

Such is the power of Scott's artistry that only on reflection do we admit that his major protagonists will occasionally behave in a way that seems unnecessarily foolish to us but not to his narrative voice. (The most obvious example is Daphne's disregard of her doctor's advice.) This quality suggests in their author a "ramrod core" (CSF 166) and a touch of the moral absolutism that plagued Melville. We must remember, however, that the protagonists' uncompromising sense of living their lives the way they believe their lives should be lived serves a dramatic purpose. In tragedy, catharsis is achieved by a resolution through the sacrifice of the protagonist of universal conflicting principles in public and private affairs and in the mind, leaving in us a serenity that is a vicarious acceptance of conditions that would destroy us if we encountered them in life. Thus, it enables us to peacefully accept and even applaud the limitation that, for survival, we have imposed on our own freedom of action.

9. Antagonists and Protagonists: Insular Form against Union

In one of Barbara Batchelor's mad fantasies of symbolic truth in *The Towers of Silence,* Ronald Merrick's face fades into Mildred Layton's (391). For Scott, the heart of British insularity in its worst aspects is the will to power and mastery these characters embody. Most people had better intentions but shared some responsibility for the failure to unify India and the human tragedy that ensued. Scott believed that it was the English sense of alienation from India that caused the tragedy. Yet the conflict presented in *The Raj Quartet* is not simply between "a sense of duty and alienation from the people to whom that duty is owed."[1] With a novelist's prerogative, he has imposed his own values on the conflict; despite his profound sympathy for all of his characters, he finds English alienation from the Indians they were supposed to serve morally and psychologically reprehensible. In the *Quartet's* view, the insular spirit was not only responsible for British failure in India; by its nature it affected the ability of the antagonists to enjoy their lives.

In Scott's Raj, both politically and personally, adherence to "form," meaning the shape or structure of something as opposed to the meaning or material of which it is composed, stands in the way of the implementation of love. Scott is a subtle as well as a difficult writer; in *The Death of Ivan Ilyitch,* Tolstoy portrays as barriers to human feeling conventions or established modes of behavior. But the subject is rarely dramatized in fiction. Chapter 7 demonstrated how British policy in India sought to retain the appearance (the form) of principle when British insular interest demanded a policy not beneficial to India. Additionally, in the view of the *Quartet,* in class and race distinctions and the paternalistic philosophy of *man-bap,*[2] the British substituted adherence to form for concern about people. And by nostalgically clinging to the dead forms of past privilege and refusing to accept the reality of their inevitable departure, they became bitter, hollow men and women living in a charade that was increasingly and dangerously unreal.

The origin of these themes is suggested in a passage from T. S. Eliot's "East Coker," which Scott loved so well:

> Had they deceived us
> Or deceived themselves, the quiet-voiced elders,
> Bequeathing us merely a receipt for deceit?
> The serenity only a deliberate hebetude
> The wisdom only the knowledge of dead secrets
> Useless in the darkness into which they peered
> Or from which they turned their eyes. There is, it seems to us
> At best, only a limited value
> In the knowledge derived from experience.
> For knowledge imposes a pattern and falsifies,
> For the pattern is new in every moment
> And every moment is a new and shocking
> Valuation of all we have been.

The *Quartet*'s development of this philosophy suggests that forms are an escapable part of the human condition. Nonetheless, the novels demonstrate that form is best used not as a barrier and a substitute for feeling but as a way of implementing the values of creative egalitarian love. Sister Ludmila uses a form of love, for example, when she dresses in the habit of a nun to care for the destitute dying. Sarah Layton laments that Ahmed Kasim was killed because he was "following the bloody code" when he knowingly stepped off the train to be hacked to death by the mob. She speaks angrily but with admiration because his action was dictated by his desire not to sacrifice his fellow passengers. The books are textured with the lives of two kinds of people: conformists, whose behavior and rational thought is limited by certain defenses, and individualists willing to sacrifice themselves for a higher purpose. Scott's protagonists tend to be people who attempt to erase the barriers imposed by form, while his antagonists seek to erect or sustain them. Sometimes, however, the conformists are people with whom we are largely sympathetic, or who show a willingness to sacrifice themselves, and then it appears that not they but the molds or defenses that imprison them are the true antagonists of *The Raj Quartet*.

Perhaps the most evident use of form in the *Quartet* is the artificial separation imposed by class and race distinctions. Paul Scott once remarked that he considered the class structure to be at the heart of English insularity and that its nuances became stronger when transferred to India.[3] It seems obvious to say that class and race distinctions are the most evident barriers between people in Scott's fiction. If racial prejudice in India was largely responsible for the tragedy of thwarted lovers Hari Kumar and Daphne Manners, class privilege in England sometimes sent lower-middle-class reactionaries like Ronald Merrick across the seas to India where they could lord it over the natives. Instances abound in the *Quartet* of lower-class Englishmen insulting Indians and even occasionally of Indian arrogance toward those with no power (D 392). As we have seen, the essential source of conflict is, ironically, between two who were most abused by the system: Merrick for his class in England and Kumar for his race in India. Kumar is the obvious one, but Scott regards them both as victims. Specific references to Merrick as psychologically wounded appear at least twice in the *Quartet*, in Sarah Layton's reference to his need "to heal a wound" (S 406), and in an identification, with Kumar, as Philoctetes, the great archer and friend of Hercules who was abandoned by his comrades on the voyage home from the Trojan War because they could not stand the smell of his wound (D 550–551).

Not only does Scott dramatize in the tragic encounter of Merrick and Kumar the victimization that class and race distinctions impose, he insists that we get the point by having some of his most sympathetic characters ponder it. Sarah Layton speaks of her ability to get an abortion that a lower-class girl could not obtain. Historian Guy Perron, born to privilege yet an army sergeant by choice, shares the same perception of society's double-handedness when he tells Rowan—to the perplexity of the reader—that he has been driven to a refutation of the Emersonian philosophy: "Society is a wave. The wave moves onward, but the water of which it is composed does not. The same particle does not rise from the valley to the ridge. Its unity is only phenomenal. The persons who make up a nation today, next year die, and their experience with them" (D 207). The reader is enlightened when Perron tells Rowan that Emerson did not understand that the upper classes avoid drowning by moving along with the wave. Unlike Hari Kumar or Muzzafir Khan, a havildar who is driven to suicide, Sergeant Perron can use his family's influence to get himself transferred back home, out of Merrick's reach.

Class and race distinctions are not the only forms of power and privilege. Other beliefs, codified and calcified, are outdated and unreal, yet the community tries stubbornly to retain them and with them its grip on moral certainty. Longing for the nineteenth century, the soldier Clancey tells Edwina Crane nostalgically, "Things were different those days, sort of simpler, sort of cut and dried" (J 33).

Then, he believes, a man saw his duty—help the Indians and save the Empire—and did it. Now all beliefs are called into question, and doing one's duty, as Teddie Bingham or Mildred Layton or Nicky Paynton discover, seems almost an exercise in futility. For so many of the characters there is, as for Bronowsky when Mirat is in flames, "a strange feeling of being suspended between . . . two worlds" (D 551). Matthew Arnold in "Stanzas from the Grande Chartreuse" writes of "Wandering between two worlds, one dead, / The other powerless to be born." These lines must have influenced Scott when he wrote that Sarah had "no clearly defined world to inhabit, but one poised between the old for which she had been prepared, but which seemed to be dying, and the new for which she had not been prepared at all" (T 278–279). The characters share a sense of flux and of loss; Sarah Layton in a revealing moment feels herself a shell until she can replace the values and expectations of her childhood, but she does not make the mistake of the community at large, of clinging to past rituals in a transitional era. To some extent, she finds her identity in her awakening awareness of their false position. She thinks of the social situation in which she finds herself as playacting, a game in which one is supposed to know the rules before being allowed to play, because "without them the game can be seen to be a game, and . . . [then] all the magic of the game will evaporate, the Fort will be seen to have been made of paper, the soldiers of lead and tin, and I of wax or china or pot" (S 76).

Explicitly and symbolically, the reader is told that antiquated practices must be discarded. Retired missionary Barbara Batchelor, the instrument of Scott's truth in *The Towers of Silence*, realizes that power and privilege must be relinquished when she thinks, in words similar to MacKendrick's (AS 75), "The word was 'dead.' Dead. Dead . . . the edifice had crumbled and the façade fooled nobody. One could only pray for a wind to blow it all away" (T 229). Scott's message is also contained in his title. Mad and speechless at the end of the novel, Barbie retains her visionary characteristic, writing "Birds" on her pad before going with Sarah to the barred windows to watch the vultures. This symbolism is established in *The Day of the Scorpion* when Major Clark tells Sarah that the body of the Raj, dead since the Great War and stinking, needs to be exposed, in Parsee-burial fashion, to the vultures on the towers of silence. Ideals not actualized—the form without the substance—must be abandoned.

In the *Quartet* the development of the ideal, the creative, union-speaking spirit, is hampered politically not just by feelings of class and race superiority and adherence to past mores, but by the nature of political administrations. Systems are intrinsically reactionary and artificial; they are based on generalizations (which, even when accurate, must include a wide margin of error when applied to specific cases) and past experience, which "imposes a pattern and falsifies" (or may not be suitable to present needs). Additionally, the man at the head of the chain of command, although often far from the scene, makes decisions which his subordinates must carry out mechanically, while the man at the bottom can make an error which his superiors feel obliged to perpetuate. Thus District Commissioner White arrests Congress members against his better judgment, and Governor Malcolm cannot for years find the means of releasing an Indian wrongly imprisoned. The English, Daphne writes, despite their good intentions, have "created a blundering, judicial [white] robot [which] works . . . even when . . . [they] least want it to . . . and . . . can't distinguish between love and rape" (J 452–453). Even Ronald Merrick complains about the "rubber-stamp" character of the administration and adds, with devastating irony, that even if he had done something dreadfully wrong, the system would have perpetuated his error.

The system requires the manipulation of men and women, even by those with good intentions; administrators must deal in generalities, their role obligations taking precedence over their feelings for individuals. The correctness of the form must be upheld over the value of its substance. That is why Governor Malcolm arrests, along with the other Indians loyal to the Congress Party, the former chief minister of Ranpur, even though Kasim privately disagrees with Congress's provoking Quit India message to the British and Malcolm would prefer to have Kasim on his Executive Council. Some of Scott's regrets at administrative barriers are apparent in White's wistful musing about what would have happened if he had had the courage to step out of his role and, Gandhilike, address the crowd on the pros and cons of what he had been ordered to do (J 345). The prevailing sadness can be heard too in Kasim's assessment that it has not been politically expedient for the governor to write to him in prison: "I understand . . . why this should be. But to understand does not warm the heart" (S 47).

If forms, systems, and defenses prevent communion between people and nations, those characters who embody the novels' values and see through the falsehood of race and class distinctions are anxious to bury the dead Raj and are impatient with the artificial, robotlike quality of systems (even when they find themselves playing their prescribed roles). Those opposed, on the other hand, tend to be defensive people who find their security in adhering to traditions which proclaim their racial, moral, or psychological superiority.

Marked by conformity, the antagonists do not outwardly diverge from socially acceptable behavior (though Mildred's elegantly disguised alcoholism and Merrick's private mistreatment of prisoners and sexual sadism evidence hidden deviation). They hold themselves aloof; they do not become involved with India or Indians, who—being brown—are "invisible" to them. Merrick is a man who had "perhaps never leapt into the depths of his own private compulsion let alone into those of life or into the world at large, but had stood high and dry on the sterile banks, thicketed around with his own secrecy and . . . prejudice" (J 159). Form for them takes the place of genuine concern, and they remain alienated from India. Daphne calls them "predictable people. . . . What the robot said they would also say, what the robot did they would do, and what the robot believed was what they believed" (J 460).

Faith in the holiness of established custom, of class and race superiority, of past mores, or "patterns" of any kind is their illusion. They mistake for arrogance and unfeeling in Indians what is really a refusal to assume a role. Merrick is certain that Kumar is guilty of raping Daphne because he would not humble himself when Merrick first interrogated him. And Mildred considers the behavior of Aziz disgraceful because, mourning privately for his mistress, Mabel Layton, he disappears for a few days and will not explain his behavior when he returns. Men and women of form subscribe to a code by which servants can be considered children but never people with the same feelings and rights as themselves.

Adhering to established behavior is a corollary in *The Raj Quartet* of a sense of bewilderment and an inner emptiness. Daphne speaks of the hollowness of life at the club, and of the essential deadness of people who, allowing themselves to feel only what the robot system dictates, lack an "originating passion" (J 460). These are people, the reader decides, like Brigadier-General Reid, Susan Layton and her mother Mildred, Ronald Merrick, and his fellow officer, Teddie Bingham.

Brigadier-General Reid's illusion is shared with his namesake, Brigadier-General Dyer. The man who mowed down hundreds of unarmed demonstrators at Amritsar in 1919, as the child Mohammed Ali Kasim is told by his father, sincerely "believed [that] God had charged him with a duty to save the empire . . . [and] that in Amritsar . . . was to be found an insidious threat to that empire" (S 70). Like Dyer, Reid is under the impression that his forceful repression of the unrest following the 1942 incarceration of Congress Party leaders will benefit England and India. He cannot understand that repression is likely to create more rather than less insurrection and is at a loss to comprehend the forces that are combining to overwhelm the British. And like his namesake, Reid seems to have a military genius for aggravating sensitive issues and causing preventable deaths. District Commissioner White holds that "if the Indians didn't start a rebellion Reid would be forced to invent one just so that by suppressing it he would feel he'd done his whole duty" (J 338). Despite Reid's pigheadedness, he is presented with objectivity and great empathy, as a devoted husband who remains very much in control of himself though torn by the loss of his wife, who dies of cancer, and of his son, who loses his life at forced labor in a prisoner-of-war camp. His mistake is to systematize all of reality; believing that one cannot be true to a code all one's life and then fail it at a difficult moment, Reid leaves his dying wife to go off to do his "duty" in Mayapore. The rigid pattern of his thoughts is also found in his sincere belief in Indian wrongdoing whenever Indians and British are in conflict. In cases of official and civilian disagreements, he assumes the official view is the correct one.

The brigadier-general does not think so much as believe what he is conditioned to believe; he is unable to conceive of a culpable or even a mistaken policeman, and where Indians are concerned, it is a question of punishment rather than fairness. Reid never questions Merrick's hypothesis about Hari Kumar's guilt, despite the oddity of Daphne's bicycle being conveniently discovered outside of Hari's house (where Merrick had it planted). "I congratulated him [Merrick] on his prompt action" (J 309) is his response. Though he denies it, his system presupposes the transgression of the six Bibighar suspects; symptomatically, he thinks how lucky the men are (if guilty) to be punished by mere imprisonment and forgets how unfortunate they must be (if innocent) to be punished at all. His defenses distort reality; he sees people and events not as they are or occur but as they conform to his set of rules. His entire organizational approach, his irritating eagerness for challenges over which he can assert his masculine force, his love of clarity at the expense of thought, must be seen as defensive, an unconscious way of never being caught facing that most frightening entity, the uncontrollable unknown.

Susan Layton, another hollow character for whom we feel a great deal of sympathy, is in her relations with her elder sister an antagonist: self-absorbed, selfish, ungrateful, and secretive. Above all, she is a girl of form, consciously dramatizing herself. In *A Division of the Spoils* Sarah speaks of "Susan's . . . continuing and frightening attempts to reduce reality to the manageable proportions of a series of tableaux which illustrated the particular crisis through which she was passing" (136). When she first appears in *The Day of the*

Scorpion, she has an image of herself as a young girl appropriately dressed (as the daughter of a lieutenant-colonel destined for promotion) for "a romantic encounter in an outpost of empire" (90). Later, she concentrates on giving herself the appropriate flushed and disheveled air (though not a hair is out of place) for one engaged to be married, and spends half an hour perfecting a suitable, enhancing pallor for the bride-to-be of an officer soon to be away at war. When Sarah, amazed, is led to ask whether Susan thought that "making love was just something you had to let Teddie do," Susan replies, "I don't know. I didn't think about it much. All that was on the other side." "The other side? The other side of what?" (S 351) is the startled response of Sarah, who, like Daphne, is always attempting a wholeness, and it calls attention to Susan's inability to see beyond the role. Getting married has a fairy-tale appeal for the girl whose main concern is to close her eyes to illusion-shattering reality (S 183). Merrick observes that she is happy the way a little girl is happy, and Sarah worries because she cannot remember Susan's ever having hurt herself badly enough to leave a scar.

When Teddie is killed, leaving Susan pregnant, her defenses collapse, and she feels like an exposed insect hurrying to get away after someone has picked up the stone. She can no longer play at being Susan; there is not much pleasure in a widowed mother's part. With Teddie dead, there is no one to give the baby to, no way of finding security through the roles of motherhood and wifehood. Susan's defensive supports are indicative of an ego too weak to stand alone, and when they are forcibly removed, she goes mad and tries to kill the baby in a symbolic sequence by substituting him for the scorpion in a circle of fire. With the help of a psychiatrist, she partly recovers but remains uncertain of herself, hysterical in temperament, and unable to see things as they are.

Ronald Merrick, the primary antagonist, whose philosophical creed is that "there is no love, only power and fear," is also a man deceived by form. He believes that "colour . . . [is] basic" (J 417) and proudly admits to attempting to stop Daphne from "crossing the road" (S 224). For Merrick, as in another way for Susan, all middle-class distinctions are an ideal. A newspaper announcement of the birth of Daphne's illegitimate, mixed-race baby is "a direct challenge to everything sane and decent that we try to do out here" (S 202). His worship of conventions is also seen in his old-fashioned belief in sexual propriety, an interesting credence in the light of his own perverted sexuality and one that reflects his immaturity. To Perron's amused astonishment, Ronald finds it incredible that a man should refer to the rape of Daphne Manners in front of a woman. He abuses Hari Kumar and Havildar Muzzafir Khan because he truly believes all Indians contemptible; any Indian who does not behave in the acceptable fawning manner must eventually be guilty of something obscene. On a deeper level he is abusive toward people who awaken in him homosexual impulses, which a man with his reverence for middle-class ideals would have to find humiliating.

Though Ronald Merrick is the primary antagonist, we retain a sense of sympathy for him, as for all of Scott's antagonists. He provides his wife with the psychological stability she needs and is, in Rowan's opinion, an excellent father to her son. Moreover, Merrick is the victim of a lower-middle-class background in class-conscious England ("I doubt there's a more unattractive sight than that of a schoolmaster currying class favour by making fun of the boy in his form whose background is different from the others" [T 160]). Like so many of the characters, he is the dupe of his own illusions. Merrick aspires to power and social distinction, and his marriage to Susan Layton Bingham after Teddie's death is his attempt to enter upper-class society in Anglo-India. He cannot bring himself to sneer at the simplistic notion of *man-bap* because he loves its ego-swelling legends and would prefer to believe them. Despite a confident manner, Ronald is not inwardly secure, and, like his wife, spends his life trying to fight the feeling of being an outsider. His unconscious sense of inferiority leads him to overcompensate by abusing those in subordinate positions, convinced of their inferiority. He finds his self-respect in the prejudicial laws of white society, which put him in the position of master. That is why he insists on the importance of maintaining a line between the races, which he feels give life form and purpose, and which people need "like a blind man with a white stick need[s] the edge of the pavement" (S 223–224).

Like so many of Scott's characters, Merrick encounters a situation which profoundly disillusions him and threatens his sense of identity. Prior to his murder at the end of the *Quartet*, Merrick becomes involved in a homosexual liaison with an Indian, which must have revealed to him some of his own twisted psychology and given him, Bronowsky speculates, "a moment of profound peace, but in the next the kind he knew he couldn't bear . . . because to admit this peace meant discarding every belief he had" (D 571). Mentally anguished, Merrick beats Aziz badly, hoping to be murdered in a grand "Wagnerian climax, the *raj* emerging from the twilight and sweeping down the hills with flaming swords" (D 571). The form and purpose of his life now uncertain, Merrick needs the drama to shut out an engulfing sense of meaninglessness.

Mildred Layton replaces Ronald Merrick as antagonist in the third novel, *The Towers of Silence*. When Mabel dies, Mildred throws lower-middle-class Barbie out of Rose Cottage and responds to pleas for her companion's proper burial by throwing a glass of cold water in the old missionary's face. A cold, vindictive personality, Mildred is concerned to get through the day with the least amount of trouble to herself, and uses her daughter Sarah to take much of the load of family responsibility off her own shoulders when her husband is a prisoner of war. She considers deference her due as the wife of the commander of the First Pankots and deference she receives; in a society where a woman's virtue is dependent on her husband's military rank people feel their sympathies owed to Mildred in the quarrel between her and Barbie, "anything else being unthinkable if the order of things were to be preserved" (T 256). After Sarah's abortion Mildred writes her off; subtly, she prevents one of Sarah's suitors from proposing to her and tries to get him to propose to her favorite, Susan; she also tries to get Sarah to bring home Nigel Rowan so that, her elder daughter thinks bitterly, "Susan can take one look at him and decide he's for her" (D 382). Mildred pretends the pregnancy and abortion never happened and to Sarah preserves the mask of perfect form and perfect cruelty—"silence, endless . . . as punishment . . . part of the code, the standard: the angel's face in the dark. Or was it a demon's?" (D 131).

With icy stoicism Mildred substitutes a traditional pattern of behavior for compassion. While holding Indians in contempt, she goes off to dispense the semblance of comfort to the wives of the soldiers in her husband's regiment, an act which the British community admires but finds a bit theatrical. Captain Coley lets it become known that "Mildred had gallantly drunk cup after cup of syrupy tea, eaten piping hot chappattis, a bowl of vegetable curry, been soaked in a sudden shower between villages, held squealing black babies, patted the shoulder of an ill-favoured looking woman who was weeping because since her husband went away she had grown old and fat; discussed the crops with village elders, more intimate problems with the wives and mothers, the hope of recruitment with shy striplings pushed forward by their old male relative to salaam Colonel Memsahib, and returned exhausted but upright" (T 258). As Mildred is true to the code rather than to any feelings for the people, her function is of limited value in the opinion of the narrator, who asks whether her exhaustion was due to her "suddenly becom[ing] conscious of acting out a charade which neither she nor the women she comforted believed in for a minute" [T 43]. She sheds her role like a skin when she returns to the bungalow and calls for gin. Her role-playing, alcoholism, dependence on Sarah, and adultery with Kevin Coley evidence insufficient inner resources in a time of stress. When Barbie accidentally discovers the adultery of Mildred and Kevin, the adjutant in charge of the First Pankot Rifles in the absence of Colonel Layton, she is "filled . . . with horror . . . [at] the absence of love and tenderness: the emotional inertia and mechanical pumping of the man, the cries coming from the woman who seemed driven by despair rather than by longing or even lust. It was as though the world outside the subterranean room was dying or extinct and the joyless coupling was a bitter hopeless expression of the will of the woman for the species to survive" (T 308). Mildred's depletion is accompanied by a fierce determination to preserve tradition and the crumbling edifice of the Raj.

The belief in forms is an illusion through which the antagonists cannot and do not wish to see. The most poignant example, perhaps, is that of Teddie Bingham, whose misguided courage and sudden reversal into protagonist makes criticism of him difficult. But he too exemplifies the man of form and, as such, stands opposed to the values of the novels. He is a likeable enough fellow, but one agrees with Sarah that there is not very much to him somehow. Cheerfully vacuous, he is able to court Susan only a few days after Sarah has turned him down and, we are told, he is not even alive to the fact that everything he does is "according to the rules laid down for what a man of his class and calling should do and for how and why he should do it" (T 109). Possessing neither much imagination nor much intelligence, he is dominated by a simplistic faith in the old world—in regimental honor and the *man-bap* role of savior and father to his Indian soldier-children. With a touching naiveté, he believes the myth and cannot give credence to the idea of a man of his own regiment becoming a turncoat. When Merrick questions their Indian National Army prisoner and discovers beyond a doubt that Baksh had been a Muzzy Guide, Teddie "stared at [Merrick], as if we'd uncovered something terribly sinister, so sinister it was unbelievable" (S 393–394). Ronald's description of Baksh falling at Teddie's feet is particularly revealing:

> Now, he said, he would be shot, and knew he deserved death for being
> disloyal to the uniform of his father and fathers before him. . . . He
> broke down and wept and begged Teddie to shoot him then and there.
> That young IO was terribly embarrassed. Oddly enough Teddie wasn't.
> He held the man's shoulder and shook him a bit and said, "You're still a
> soldier. Act like one. You've done very wrong, but I am still your father
> and mother." The old formula. But Teddie . . . really meant it. . . . It was
> a ridiculous scene in its way. It seemed to me to have nothing to do with

the reality of what was actually happening. He knelt and put his head on Teddie's boots, and that didn't embarrass Teddie either. I think it moved him. Very deeply. As it something he'd always believed in and put his trust in had been proved. (S 397–398)

When Baksh said there were two other ex–Muzzy Guides looking for a chance to give themselves up, Teddie took Baksh with him and went after them. In an area infested with Japanese, Teddie stood up in his truck, calling their names at the top of his voice, and was shot down. Scott knew the power of reversal in dramatic fiction, momentarily transforming an antagonist into a protagonist. What Teddie shares with the protagonists is both the courage to enact his conviction and consequent destruction at the moment of actualization. His belief in *man-bap*, however, is misguided; there is no "reality behind [that] illusion," (to borrow Sister Ludmila's words), and the reader feels on balance that his courage is foolhardy.

Both protagonists and antagonists are in a sense victimized by the times, and Scott's objectivity, controlled distance, and full definition of character are such that it is not always easy to distinguish one from the other. Where, for example, does one place Susan, or Rowan, or Teddie Bingham? They may be considered antagonists not because they play important negative roles in the dramatic action, as do Mildred and Merrick, but because they are opposed to the novels' values. But "antagonists" is not a completely accurate term for characters whose aggressions do not dominate their lives. The sympathy we feel is too intense. For Scott people are not the enemy so much as their defenses, their illusions of power and privilege, the forms under which they hide themselves. This is especially apparent in the case of the aristocratic Rowan, a quintessential Englishman of "remote and uncommitted" manner (D 263) who, in his capacity as governor's aide, interviews his former wasted schoolmate in prison and comes to the conclusion that "it wasn't Coomer [Kumar] who was being examined, so much as a system that had ostensibly given us equal opportunities" (D 391). Yet this same Rowan is made so uncomfortable by Guy Perron's egalitarian challenge on the governor's special coach to Pankot that he finds his belief in Kumar's victimization wavering and, despite the fact that Merrick represents everything he detests, feels relief in encountering him on the train; he even has an odd urge to forget what he knows about him. Rowan is a man of Jamesian sensibility made uncomfortable by anything not proper, not only by Perron's egalitarian talk but by Kumar's accusations of brutality against Merrick and by Merrick's homosexuality. He wants to marry Sarah Layton, but his sensibility—requiring the convergence of "the moral" and the "aesthetic"—holds him back, mainly because Merrick would be a brother-in-law. He feels this sense of contamination even though he knows Sarah shares his feelings about Merrick.

In Paul Scott's novels both antagonists and protagonists are overwhelmed by destructive forces which destroy their illusions and their lives. The difference between them seems to lie chiefly in the quality of these illusions and aspirations, and also in the fact that the protagonists share a telepathic or mystical vision which is not delusion but is vastly more important than the socially acceptable views of the antagonists. While understanding the British presence as a charade, the protagonists work to overcome the feeling of alienation from India, and are marked by an extraordinarily egalitarian sense of love and society. They refuse to partake in the collective British identity and even the sublest forms of race prejudice. Communion or love between equals is the goal, and they see and treat Indians as people. The Indian lawyer Srinivasan presents Scott's notion of the proconsular ideal when he says that Robin White gets a clear impression of the servants as men and does not feel superior to them, only more responsible for them: "It was his sense of responsibility that enabled him to accept his privileged position with dignity. . . . In one dazzling moment . . . I really felt I understood what it was the English always imagined lay but only rarely succeeded in showing *did* lie behind all the flummery of their power and influence" (J 202). Unlike Mildred, Reid, Merrick, or even Teddie Bingham (who is vexed because his servant is not available to tie his shoes), Mabel, Barbie, Edwina, Lady Manners, and Daphne have an especially sensitive relationship with their servants. In contrast to the antagonists, the protagonists, frequently at considerable risk to themselves, struggle to break through the system of defenses that bar communion and inner joy. Sarah "had spent most of her adult years fighting to dispel . . . the terrible enchantment of inherited identity . . . fighting as hard as Susan had fought to feel herself . . . drawn into it" (D 132). Sarah recognizes in herself and Ahmed Kasim "the compulsion to break away from . . . a *received* life" (D 592). Edwina Crane instinctively attempts to exceed her role as memsahib to reach her colleague Chaudhuri. Daphne and Hari struggle to break through society's barriers and their own psychological problems in trying not to be conscious of the fact that he is a black Indian and she a white English girl. In loving an Indian, Daphne becomes an outcast of British society (the one unforgivable sin, we are told, is betrayal of the group). Lady Manners shocks the British community by printing a notice of Parvati's birth in the *Times of India*.

Robin White brings three Indians to the club who are not evicted, only because he is the district commissioner. Sarah, to Dicky Beauvais' disturbance, speaks frankly of Indian National Army problems in front of an Indian driver and, to her Aunt Fenny's horror, visits Daphne's aunt when it is the intention of the family to snub her. Early in the relationship with Ahmed Kasim, Sarah's spontaneity and compulsion to go beyond the artificiality of convention makes her surprise him in the act of being very properly Indian and staying a few paces behind her during their early morning ride:

> Suddenly she wheeled the horse round in the same kind of tight circle Mr. Kasim had described before they set off on their gallop. She caught him before he had time to hang back and so confronted him in the act of reining in, but having done so she could not find an acceptable way of explaining her impulsive action, either to him or to herself. Curiously, though, in the moment before being embarrassed at finding herself at a loss, she thought that the world might be a more interesting and useful place to live in if there were more such . . . gestures as the one she had apparently made. (S 128)

The importance of the image is evident from its recurrent mention in the *Quartet*. At one point Bronowsky explains to Sarah that afterwards Ahmed would occasionally go off riding by himself, trying to recapture "some moment he missed, or did not seize, and only understood later was significant" (T 468).

Unlike the antagonists, the protagonists are able to learn to see beyond or reject the form of *man-bap*, "the combination of hardness and sentimentality from which Mabel had turned her face" (T 275). Edwina Crane had always been of two minds about "The Jewel in Her Crown," the semi-allegorical picture presented to her by the children of Muzzafirabad after she had braved the mob and saved the schoolroom from being burned down. The picture, an idealistic portrayal of British crown rule, showed Victoria seated on a golden throne, attended by her British advisors, surrounded by representative figures of her Indian empire (including remarkably clean beggars), and receiving, from a native prince, a gorgeous jewel, India itself. Miss Crane, who chose to leave Muzzafirabad rather than be put in what she considered an artificial and embarrassing position induced by her heroism, had always known that "the India of the picture had never existed outside its gilt frame, and the emotions the picture was made to conjure up were not much more than smugly pious" (J 30). When Clancey comes to offer comfort after Chaudhuri is killed trying to save her and ignores old Joseph, the servant who is devoted to him, she comments on the idealistic fraud of the picture by taking it down and locking it in the chest. What is missing from the artificial pomp and ceremony is "the unknown Indian" (T 388), as Barbara Batchelor, who comes into possession of the picture, realizes. The alleviation of the Indian's suffering, in Scott's view, is the substance that should have been the justification for the British presence in India.

How much has been lost by the substitution of the form for the substance of caring is touchingly evident where love has succeeded. Repeatedly, Indians respond with great warmth to kindness. There is the subdivisional officer who leaves White with tears in his eyes at not being blamed for riots that he was unable to control; there are Sister Ludmila's poor, illiterate boys whom she employs and who pay a scribe to write to her after they leave her service; there is Daphne Manners, for whom the servant Bhalu cuts flowers after she tries to control her instinctive fear of his dark skin on the night she has been raped. And when old Mabel Layton meets her former servant Ghulam Mohammed, he salutes, offers his arm, and takes her hand. Barbara Batchelor loves the unknown Indian in the person of the ragged little chokra Ashok, who runs errands for her. "Tu es mon petit Hindou inconnu," she whispers (T 364). Sadly, she distinguishes between *man-bap* and a more genuine emotion when she tells Ashok:

"Come . . . I am your father and your mother."
He came. She clasped his thin shoulders.
"You don't understand," she said in English. . . . "The world you and I live in is corrupt. I clasp you to my breast but you conceive of this in terms of an authority unbending. I offer my love. You accept it as a sign of fortune smiling. Your heart beats with gratitude, excitement, expectation of rupees. And mine scarcely beats at all." (T 364)

But the orphan shows, eventually, that he does understand; he refuses payment for some flowers he gets for Barbie to put on Mabel's grave, and brings tears to her eyes because, he says, he will only go to Rajputana if she goes too. It is clear, also, that Barbie recognizes the difference between love and its appearance when Sarah asks her whether Miss Crane's sitting at the side of the road holding the dead Chaudhuri's hand was *man-bap*, as Ronald thought: "No," she explains with quiet conviction; it was "Despair" (T 276).

Man-bap is not the only form the protagonists transcend. Sister Ludmila is to the world "the mad Russian woman who collects dead bodies and isn't a nun at all, but just dresses like one" (J 407)—a person of insignificance. In her childhood something had happened to Ludmila Smith which probably changed the course of her life. At that time she first saw beyond the shallow forms of the Sisters of Charity. The Sisters, with a false stamp of holiness upon them, had refused money for the poor from Ludmila's mother because she was a prostitute. The child Ludmila at first believes that God has spoken through the Sisters and feels "tainted."

> Ah, but then suddenly I saw the truth! . . . How angry He would be with them for refusing the money my mother had offered. . . . The money was to help people God said should be helped. . . . And how poor, how hungry such people must be if they were poorer than us and hungry all the time! . . . We went past a beggar woman. I hung back. We must give her some of the barley sugar, I said. My mother laughed. She gave me a coin instead. I put it in the old woman's dirty hand. She said God bless you. I was afraid, but we had good shoes and gloves and warm coats and God's blessing, and had made up to Him for what the Sisters had done wrong. . . .
> . . . For the first time I felt that I knew what [my mother] meant by luck. It was a warmth in the heart. Without realising it you found that you were smiling and could not remember what had made you smile. Often on my mother's lips I had seen this kind of smile. (J 131–132)

In contrast to the bitter feeling the Sisters left her with, the child Ludmila's act led to a further communion with the beggar woman and a "warmth in the heart." Physically blind when the narrator speaks with her in 1964, she does not mistake, as so many of the characters do, the illusion or the form for the reality of love. The values of love are stronger to her than the world's reality, and that is why she refers to "the world of legend and fantasy, the reality behind the illusion" (J 132), and thanks God for her blindness.

If the essential antagonists of *The Raj Quartet* are insular forms that include the desire for power and mastery, the authentic hero is the egalitarian love which includes more than "a spark of tenderness, an instinct for self-denial" (J 31), by which Edwina Crane was first drawn to Clancey. This protagonist has something in common with the creative, consecrated love of the *Bhagavadgita;* in other words, the elevation of love above self-interest leads to "a further union, a deeper communion" between people and nations and therefore to joy. The soul in the *Bhagavadgita* and the individual in the *Quartet,* free from constraints of selfishness, can break through the bonds of habit to act freely and creatively. Escaping from the artificiality of club life, yet oppressed by English society in India for her love of Hari Kumar, Daphne, speaking for many of Scott's protagonists, is "imprisoned but free, diminished by everything that loomed from outside, *but not diminished from the inside;* and . . . that's why I speak of joy" (J 405). But T. S. Eliot writes, "Between the idea/And the reality/Between the motion/And the act/Falls the Shadow." Tragically often, defensive and aggressive forms hinder the implementation of love, which remains, like that of the British presence in India generally, a *"love never made manifest"* (J 147).[4]

10. Psychological Defenses and Thwarted Union

The India of microscopic detail that Scott portrayed is ultimately a country of the mind. If Scott equated an idealized image of the Raj with paradise, an image that he is at pains to portray as illusory, then he saw actual British rule in India as an opportunity wasted, one that in a sense would always be wasted. It is easy to see that *The Raj Quartet* identifies loss of India with moral and psychological loss. Daphne Manners' thought that "It's all going, going away before I've touched any of it or understood any of it" (J 431) is echoed by historian Guy Perron as he watches "the villages of India—the India his countrymen were leaving, the India that was being given up" and wonders, "Along with what else?" (D 598). The images of loss and imprisonment that crowd Scott's fiction demonstrate not only the helplessness of the individual caught in cultural confrontation but, on another level, the repression of instinct and its unavoidable consequences for civilized men and women.

As early as his second novel, *The Alien Sky*, Scott saw India as a symbol. The fears of the main character, MacKendrick, impoverish his life, preventing his eloping with the woman he loves and immersing himself in India. The novel ends with his departure and his impotent desire for a richer life: "Now it was going. Oh, hold it, his heart cried, oh, enter it; dig deeply with the hands into it and raise out of it all the love and pity and compassion the music sings of. But now it is going. The light in the sky is going. The singing is fading. And the train is moving into the plain where night holds and the deep silence is broken only by the muffled drumming of the wheels and the distant cries of jackals" (208). There is somehow more real

This chapter is a revised version of an article that was previously published in *Literature and Psychology* 31 (1981): 75–87.

life in India, and although expressed in traditional terms, the alien sky is symbolically the inner freedom people desire and fear.

Scott shares an Indian fascination with Carl Jung, who wrote: "It is quite possible that India is the real world, and that the white man lives in a madhouse of abstractions. To be born, to die, to be sick, greedy, dirty, childish, ridiculously vain, miserable, hungry, vicious: to be manifestly stuck in illiterate unconsciousness, to be suspended in a narrow universe of good and evil gods and to be protected by charms and helpful mantras, that is perhaps the real life, life as it was meant to be, the life of the earth. Life in India has not yet withdrawn into the capsule of the head. It is still the whole body that lives."[1] India recaptures an earlier experience that has been lost, a more meaningful experience as it involves relative freedom from instinctual repression. The stimulation of repressed forces in the unconscious that intrigued Jung terrified Forster. For him, India represents a "primal" experience lost in the timelessness of the Marabar Caves, one that is not less meaningful but so meaningful that it takes the meaning out of existence. Whatever is "unspeakable" about Marabar makes "poor little talkative Christianity . . . only amount . . . to 'Boum,'" and identifies "pathos, piety, courage . . . [with] filth."[2] The touch of a baby's foot, which horrifies Mrs. Moore in the caves, can be seen as her and Forster's apprehension of the human being as animal, an apprehension that leaves them both devastated, revealing on Forster's part an instinctual terror and, at the heart of his metaphysical doubt, an intense spirit-body dualism that is emphasized rather than transcended in his art.

Clearly, Jung, Forster, and, as I shall demonstrate, Scott have intuited in India something representative of the life of the human body as opposed to the mind or spirit or soul. It has been said that the idea of thwarted union in *The Raj Quartet* is presented on three interrelated levels, historical, social, and psychological. Scott's symbolism describing the thwarted union of England and India, Daphne Manners and Hari Kumar, is explicit. Of primary concern in this chapter, however, is his unconscious association of India with the human body, England with the soul, as part of a description of the thwarted union of individuals, a state some psychoanalytic thinkers regard as characteristic of civilized men and women. Through its recapturing of the dirt and smells of India and the defensive English reaction to them, *The Raj Quartet* demonstrates, as does Orwell's *Burmese Days*, that civilization's repressed state explains at least partly why the majority of the English fail to achieve a sympathetic identification with Indian life. This condition bears significant responsibility as well for the defensive racist reactions and the consequent personal and historical tragedies.

To say that Scott's subject is a paradise lost is to speak, symbolically, of the civilized state, where soul is divorced from body. Paradise would be a pre-Oedipal body-ego, an ego before it is diluted and desexualized by the processes of instinctual repression and negation, a Dionysian ego, unselfconscious, overflowing and instinctual. Paradise, in short, would be a time of early childhood before the pleasure principle has been partially transformed by the castration complex into the reality principle. Freud theorized that the eternal aim of men and women is the recapturing of their childhood, and Scott's lost Anglo-Indian paradise is, psychoanalytically, representative of the adult's lost erotic exuberance and polymorphous perversity.[3] The idea of childhood as representing somehow a more idyllic state goes at least as far back as the creation myth, where loss of paradise for the human race is symbolic of the loss of the state of bliss in individual development. Wordsworth in the "Intimations" ode suggested that "Trailing clouds of glory do we come / From God, who is our home." And in the passage from "East Coker" that Scott liked to quote, Eliot wrote: "Home is where one starts from. As we grow older / The world becomes stranger, the pattern more complicated / Of dead and living" (IPF 132). For Scott there is frequently an identification between the moral and the relatively unrepressed. This chapter traces racism to the part repression plays in the Anglo-Indian character, follows the division of body and soul as revealed in character and symbol, and studies their symbolic unification.

Unlike Conrad, who writes of the isolation and the horror within, there is for Scott a sense of good, of tremendous capacity for love and life at the deepest core of human nature. Even the antagonist Merrick, who represents the "dark" and "arcane" side of us and whom the protagonists instinctively distrust, is yet, in Daphne's words, "fundamentally kind" (J 111). "Perhaps in his bones, in his soul" Sister Ludmila intuits, he understands the consecration of the room reserved for the dignity of dying (J 142). But fulfillment and communion are thwarted by individual and collective psychological defenses against forbidden fears and desires.

It is easy enough to see that a fundamental racial distrust and fear of the alien runs through the novels and that, with a few notable exceptions, the British behave coldly and self-righteously toward the natives. To use just one of several instances of studied insult, the Englishwomen at Gulab Singh's pharmacy interrupt Hari Kumar's conversation with the shop clerk as though he did not exist. Their racial distrust stems from an unfortunate propensity to chase imaginary villains, figures of the unconscious mind.⁴ This is why most of the men share a collectively protective attitude, which, in the opinion of independent-minded Sarah Layton, makes women feel that danger exists even when they know it does not. The tendency also explains why the Englishwomen must repress their attraction for Kumar, why Ronald Merrick to the end of his life remains convinced of Hari's guilt, and why Brigadier-General Reid can fire into a line of Indian demonstrators without qualms of conscience.

The more sympathetic characters, too, are not free of apprehension. Even the conscientious governor's assistant, Nigel Rowan, is unable to rid himself of a worrisome prejudice against former Chillingborough classmate Kumar. Indian lawyer Srinivasan tells the narrator, "Even when [British and Indians] most loved, there was the fear" (J 204). And for one confused moment after she has been raped, Daphne herself thinks that Hari was one of her attackers (J 434). But the characters we are led to admire refuse to indulge the impulse and, perhaps consequently, come to love India. The tale District Commissioner White relates is particularly revealing. When he first arrived in India, he hated the dirt and the smell and, typically, had bowel problems. He was lying on a charpoy, utterly miserable, when an Indian woman he didn't know came up and quietly but insistently waved away his protestations and fed him curds. He fell asleep and, waking, thought he had dreamt it all, except that the unfinished curds were on a brass tray next to him, together with a flower. He tells the narrator, "I felt that I had been given back my humanity, by a nondescript middle-aged Indian woman. I felt that the curds and the flowers were for affection, not tribute, affection big enough to include a dash of well-meant motherly criticism, the suggestion that my indisposition could be overcome easily enough *once I'd learned I had no real enemies*" (J 347; italics mine). Care and affection from an Indian enabled him to distinguish between the real situation and his unconscious fantasies.

If elemental fears, of whose unconscious origin most of the characters are unaware, are a primary source of English racism, what is also apparent, on closer inspection, is that the fears stem from repressed desire and that they are both genital and anal in character. The familiar sexual association is apparent when the British community find "the Bibighar Gardens affair . . . to be the *key* to the whole situation they presently found themselves in, the sharpest warning of . . . danger . . . to the women" (J 70; italics mine). The connection is evident too when Daphne cannot help feeling uneasy about the servant Raju's seeing her in an off-the-shoulder dress (J 116). And immediately after returning from the Bibighar, she is unable to suppress an instinctive cry of fear when the black servants advance to help her; she is ashamed, she says, "because this proved that in spite of loving Hari I'd not exorcised that stupid primitive fear" (J 439).

It seems scarcely an accident that the pivotal incident in *A Passage to India* is the supposed rape of Adela Quested or that the focal point of *The Raj Quartet* is based on sexual relations between the races—the rape of an English girl after her symbolic marriage to an Indian. In the case of Adela Quested, the projection of her own repressed desires evoked by the featureless Marabar Caves made her truly believe that Aziz had attempted to rape her. In both works the sexual relations that are feared are also at a deeper level wanted. Even Daphne speaks of the complication in her relationship with Hari "of the curious, almost titillating fear of his colour" (J 398). Earlier, when her instinctive fears are already aroused by the servant, she half expects to find at the top of the stairs "our resident ghost Janet MacGregor (the first occupant of MacGregor House, attacked by blacks during the Sepoy Mutiny). But there wasn't anything. I've not seen her *yet*. I felt relieved, but also cheated" (J 116).

The instinctive British revulsion is on the deepest level a reaction-formation to things anal as well as genital. The English are disgusted by the smell of the river, which permeates *The Jewel in the Crown*, and by the related acrid smell of the land. Hari Kumar, British in everything but skin color, speaks of "my own revulsion, my horror of the dirt and squalor and stink" (J 278). In a letter that he would have liked to compose for his English friend Colin Lindsey, he describes Chillianwallah Bagh, where he lives with his Aunt Shalini:

There is nothing that isn't ugly. Houses, town, river, landscape. . . . The whole place stinks of drains. . . . My trunk and suitcases are mildewed. There's a fan in the middle of the ceiling. More often than not it stops working during the night and you wake up suffocating . . . . From their point of view I'm unclean. They want me to drink cow-piss to purify myself of the stain of living abroad, crossing the forbidden water. Purify! I have seen men and women defaecate in the open, in some wasteland near the river. At night the smell of the river comes into my bedroom. In my bathroom, in one corner, there is a hole in the floor and two sole-shaped ledges to put your feet on before you squat. There are always flies in the bathroom. And cockroaches. You get used to them, but only by debasing your own civilized instincts. At first they fill you with horror. Even terror. It is purgatory, at first, to empty the bowels. (J 241)

Clearly, Hari has an overpowering disgust for India, which he identifies with the bowels. Yet, interestingly, he is discovered by Sister
Ludmila face down, drunk after Lindsey's failure to recognize him,
in the mire where the untouchables defecate each morning. Aside
from his drastic social and economic change, living in India is a continual torment because of the filth, poverty, squalor, and smell. He
becomes a man without a country, partly because he possesses the
strong British distaste for the overtly anal without having access to
the relief afforded by the club.

There is no shortage of examples in the *Quartet* of English disgust
for the products of excretion and the association of these products
with India and Indians (or those linked with them). The dark skin of
the people, together with the stink of the river, makes it easier for
the British to associate the Indian with feces. In *A Division of the
Spoils*, Guy Perron is told about an English officer excreting into a
Gandhi cap and floating it in the club swimming pool (presumably
already contaminated by the presence of Indians), and later passing
wind when the chief minister of Mirat comes into the room. In two
distinct incidents (in *The Jewel in the Crown* and in *A Division of
the Spoils*) drunken British Club members empty the chamber pots
into the swimming pool after Indians have used it. And a fear of contamination motivates the Englishwoman at Gulab Singh's pharmacy, who, while selecting powders and lotions for her white skin,
manages to talk to the store attendant "without once looking at him
or letting her hands come within touching distance of his" (J 161).

From a psychoanalytic point of view, this pattern of behavior is
similar to the one involving relationships between the races. What
is repressed is at a deeper level desired. The obsessive distaste the
British show for the overtly anal is a reaction-formation against the
coprophilic instinct. Children take a great interest and pride in excrement, which they, in the nature of Swift's Yahoos, would enjoy
moulding and smearing if they were permitted to do so. Moreover, at
one stage in the child's development, the anal and genital zones or
functions are confused, and in adults the separation between the two
impulses is not complete.[5] Daphne writes to her Aunt Ethel, "You
took that dirt and poverty and squalor in your stride, as if it didn't
exist, although I knew that's not what you actually felt about it,"
and then adds, "But this is why I snatched the blouse from Hussein.
I couldn't bear to see him holding it up; examining it, *touch[ing] it
with his black fingers*" (J 114). The same revulsion is present in Hari
Kumar, who associates Aunt Shalini's husband dying of syphilis in a
brothel with his own hope at the dining table that "she won't touch
anything but the outer rim of the plate" (J 242). The anal-erotic

confusion is also apparent in one Englishwoman's strong reaction to Daphne's refusal to abort her fetus; the contemptuous Englishwoman would have considered it "a duty . . . an obligation even . . . to tear the disgusting embryo out of the womb and throw it to the pidogs" (J 161). The love of power and destructiveness implicit in anal-erotic impulses implies a sexual violation; thus the community's obsession with the idea of black-white rape and innocence betrayed. The only genital contact such a woman can imagine with a man whose skin is brown is based on an anal sadomasochistic fantasy which combines destructiveness with filth, a fantasy she cannot help but fear or, at a deeper level, desire.

Having seen the Indian as essentially evil or degraded in the unconscious projections of their own minds, the British band together for protection. The idea of "Turtonism" as defensive and protective is used repeatedly in the *Quartet*. District Commissioner White notices in India, along with the dirt and the smell, "the conscious air of superiority that one couldn't get through the day without putting on like a sort of protective purdah" (J 346). There are references to "that old privileged circle that surrounded and protected the white community" (J 44) and to "that old instinct to stay within the harbour of the charmed circle" (J 33). As pro-Indian as she is, Edwina Crane finds it a relief to know that she can always fall back on its protection. And Daphne, before she sees what a spiritually deadening, boring business it is, finds so much security in being with her own kind at the club that she does not at first notice how much the women dislike her.

The circle that protects, however, also imprisons. The British pay for their defense with a deterioration of the quality of life in moral and intellectual terms. The worst elements in the group surface; stagnation, hostility, or just plain bitchiness prevail. And the club as a kind of womb is noticeable in the imagery. The Mayapore English are "blanketed . . . in the colonial warmth of their racial indestructibility" (J 268–269). Daphne soon comes to identify such clinging together for protection as imprisonment, "a sort of creeping boredom, like a paralysis . . . [which people] probably all hate . . . but daren't let go of" (J 385). At the same time that Turtonism is defense against instinctive fears and desires, it is insulation against experience. Disliking its stifling effect, Daphne leaves the club to go to Hari, a move which is at once an effort to touch a human being of another race and to reach her own inner being. Both contacts permit the unfolding of love and joy—a sense of individuality and the feeling of being undiminished from the inside.

The rejection of group values accompanied by an attempt to break

through unconscious barriers is shared by many of Scott's protagonists, most notably Daphne's subsequent replacement in the novels,
Sarah Layton. The distinction is not absolute, but characters like
Sarah or Daphne who incorporate the novels' values (as opposed to
those like missionaries Barbara Batchelor or Edwina Crane, who are
searching for them) have more than most of the English in India reconciled themselves to their subconscious fears and desires. More
truly in touch with others and with their own inner selves, they consider the fulfillment of physical needs of particular importance.
Sarah Layton's intense sexual needs are shared by Daphne, who is
"attempting always a wholeness" (J 152). We are told that Daphne's
liking for Hari is hopelessly mixed up with the physical effect he has
on her, which turns liking into love (J 413). After Bibighar, when she
has nightmares of being raped by a many-lingamed Siva, the dream
ends when she is "no longer blind and see[s] the expression on his
face which is one of absolution and invitation" (J 434); the dream
ends on a note of forgiveness for the contamination of the rape and
of renewal of physical desire.

Characters who embody the values of the novels generally suffer
an instinctual repression less severe and are consequently more
open to an undiluted experience of India. Several develop a liking for
the acrid smell of India, a smell which "perhaps . . . [Daphne] had
learned to accept or not to notice, if not to love, to need" (J 209). Guy
Perron, "for all his doubts about its present source . . . had long since
learned to appreciate the sensuousness of the warm smell of the East
and how it could set mind and body at ease" (D 36). Daphne and later
the narrator chose to "risk all" when they visit the temple barefoot;
their feet feel "gritty" (J 205, 423). Dowager Mabel Layton bends on
her knees in the garden to "grub out weeds with her bare hands"
(T 20). Sarah, to her surprise, finds that she prefers the "dung-
smoked countryside" to the city; she goes down "on her knees in
the filth and the muck, her skirt wet through" (D 587), getting water
for the wounded in the communal train murder. And Barbara
Batchelor reminds the reader that it was against the background of
"suffering, sweating, stinking, violent humanity . . . [that] you had
to visualize Jesus working" (T 80). Symptomatically, Scott gives a
detailed description of Daphne's MacGregor House toilet, literally
enthroned:

> Returning to the other end, literally ascending the throne which is
> mounted on a broad dais anciently carpeted in the deep blue red of
> mouldy cherries, the splendour of the paperholder fixes the attention.
> Here are lions, gilt-maned, gilt-faced, each holding in its gilt jaws an end
> of the bracket which supports the roll of buff, wood-chip austerity paper.

The jaw of the nearer lion (and presumably that of its mate on the other side) adequately receives the ball of the little finger. Its head is as large as a clenched fist, so large that its cheek rests almost upon the cheek of its gilded counterpart. The effect is of two big cats grinning over the simple duty they have to hold, in readiness, something that is required for a cat-like but, because of the paper, ridiculous human function.
(J 102)

The implication is that a richer life accompanies a more natural atti-tude toward the bowels.[6] Such an attitude also produces a character of greater individuality and maturity. The symbolism is apparent when Daphne rides in a tonga and, unlike the other English, prefers to sit face forward, braving the horses' posteriors. Turtonism must be seen as a kind of regression; by a harsh flight from the anal and genital impulses, people regress (into club life) and cannot move for-ward into maturity.

In "East Coker" Eliot implies that life springs from dung and death. Not unexpectedly, Scott's protagonists have, comparatively, mastered their fear of dying. For one thing, they are willing to leap, to risk all for a cause. Daphne might well have been saved if she had not risked her life to have her baby "properly." Ahmed Kasim goes to his death at the hands of the communal mob rather than risk the safety of his English friends. While Susan Layton screams hys-terically at the first sign of danger and the Turtonish Peabodys try to fortify themselves with malted milk, Sarah Layton and Guy Perron refuse to indulge their fears, doing what they can to help the wounded. When Sarah discovers that she cannot bear to bind the horrible-looking wounds, she busies herself at the pump. The reader feels gently guided to the admiration of characters who have come to terms with their instinctual fears—not to Lili Chatterjee's horror of death and consequent defensive indifference to India's suffering multitudes but rather to Sister Ludmila's fearlessness in defying the curfew to pick up the destitute dying in the no man's land which serves as a public toilet for the untouchables.

Sister Ludmila, who, like Daphne, is not afraid to dirty her hands (there is an unconscious relationship between fear of dirt and fear of death), makes a life out of giving dignity to the dying. Ascetically and symbolically, she atones for and transforms her feelings of worthlessness into divine love by embracing death (the dying). She gives again and again the love she would have liked to have given to her mother, a prostitute, who died destitute and alone. Significantly, the only decorative object in Sister Ludmila's room is a statue of dancing Siva, "the destroyer and the restorer, the great ascetic and the symbol of sensuality."[7] Confining herself to a cloistered situation where she devotes herself to the dying rather than, like Daphne, to the world at large, she finds in the statue the symbolic fullness of body and spirit for which she is looking: "The dance of creation, preservation and destruction. A complete cycle. A wholeness" (J 152). What she understands, perhaps unconsciously, is that acceptance of death and sensuality leads to full life and joy.

Perron's stream-of-consciousness reflections in his room one hot day are of interest in a similar connection:

> Rain. Geckos. Clack-clack-clack. On the walls. Heraldic lizard shapes, pale yellow on the grey-white wash. Chasing one another, intent on copulation. He had woken erect himself—and, half asleep, smiled, reassured both by this and the realization that the faint discomfort in his bowels had gone, that he was acclimatized. He peered at his wristwatch. It was only half-past four. He had slept for two hours, after a lunch of chicken pulao, mutton curry lightly spiced in the northern Indian style, and Murree beer. Somewhere a gutter was overflowing. . . .
>
> But, returning, he paused on the threshold of the bedroom, alert. There was a smell he hadn't noticed before. A foul, sweet smell. He glanced around. In a moment or two the smell seemed to have gone. He sat down and poured tea. He glanced up at the sloping rafters; then lit a cigarette, smoked the recollection of the smell away. The shrouded bed looked like a catafalque. There was a sudden flash of lightning that lit the bathroom and momentarily distorted the shape of the bed. After that, the thunder. And then the humdrum sound of continuing but gradually diminishing rain.
>
> As he finished his tea the bathroom was flooded in sunshine.
> (D 500–501)

In symbolic terms Scott's associations are of more importance than Perron's. In the reaching into the unconscious that must be part of every creative writer's talents, Scott as Perron comes up with associations of copulation, excretion, and death, which end in a sunshine symbolic of life or joy.

Here Norman O. Brown's modification of Freud's ontology in *Life Against Death* is helpful because it offers an analytic explanation of the same psychocultural questions, including the significance of excrement, that Scott presents in fictional terms. Brown writes that the degree to which people embrace the death instinct largely determines the quality of life they will enjoy. Those parts of people's lives that are typically repressed are their rude instincts, genital and anal, which are in the child confused, stemming from an early fear and repression of the fact of death. Fear of death begins with "the human infant's incapacity to accept separation from the mother, that separation which confers individual life on all living organisms" (284).

Fear of death leads to fear of life, that erotic, exuberant, polymorphously perverse full life of the body, and fear of the body which dies. Ironically, only an ego strong enough to die is strong enough to live. In flight from death, then, human beings deny that they are bodies and acquire souls. They sublimate and civilization is born; all civilization is built on a division of body and soul which has its start in the child's denial of death and separateness.

To recapitulate, *The Raj Quartet* demonstrates in the minds of colonial Europeans an association of India with forbidden feces and licentious sex. The image of the unconscious that is projected onto the Indian inspires unconscious desire and defensive disgust in the European. The less harsh repression of the instincts shared by Scott's protagonists leads them to desire not so much sexual relations with Indians as to glimpse the unrepressed full life of the body of which they are symbolic.

In his intuitive exploration of the defenses against our inner fears and desires, Scott laments the lost union not only of England and India, white and black, but, however unconsciously, soul and body, and the instincts of life and death. At the heart of civilized society's neurosis is the division of body and soul that is reflected in the *Quartet*'s imagery. Life and death, in Brown's terms, are not in conflict at the biological level but exist in some kind of dialectical unity. The closer people come to acceptance of their instincts, the closer to peace, because the death and life instincts no longer battle as they do in Perron's ambivalent feeling about the Arabian Sea: "Disgusting. Peaceful" (D 467). One part of him swears he will never leave, while the other screams to be let go.

As portrayed in *The Raj Quartet* (and in a significant number of the novels that have been written about India), the British find the body debasing and are repelled by India, which they associate with the sexual and anal functions. The symbolism of body/India and soul/England,[8] reflected in the difference between Harry Coomer's school in England, Chillingborough, and Hari Kumar's home in India, Chillianwallah, is also apparent in the following description of Kumar's memories of England and feelings about India:

> His sharpest memories were of piles of leaves, wet and still to the touch, as if in early morning after a late October frost. To Hari, England was sweet cold and crisp clean pungent scent; air that moved, crowding hollows and sweeping hill-tops; not stagnant, heavy, a conducting medium for stench. And England was the park and pasture-land behind the house in Sidcot, the gables of the house, the leaded diamond-pane windows, and the benevolent wistaria.
> Waking in the middle of the night on the narrow stringbed in his

room at Number 12 Chillianwallah Bagh he beat at the mosquitoes, fisted his ears against the sawing of the frogs and the chopping squawk of the lizards in heat on the walls and ceiling. He entered the mornings from tossing dreams of home and slipped at once into the waking night-mare, his repugnance for everything the alien country offered: the screeching crows outside and the fat amber-coloured cockroaches that lumbered heavy-backed but light-headed with waving feathery antennae from the bedroom to an adjoining bathroom where there was no bath— instead a tap, a bucket, a copper scoop, a cemented floor to stand on and a slimy runnel for taking the dirty water out through a hole in the wall from which it fell and splattered the caked mud of the compound. (J 238–239)

Images suggesting soul are cool, fresh, airy, even rarified and spa-cious, and Perron refers to the status-conscious being "born only to breathe that rarified, oxygen-starved air of the upper slopes and peaks" (D 17). Those images suggesting body are hot, heavy, stag-nant, insect-and-animal peopled, and Perron thinks to himself that though English soldiers know nothing of India, "yet India was there, in the skull, and the bones of the body. Its possession had helped nourish the flesh, warm the blood of every man in the room, sleep-ing and waking" (D 103).[9]

Lili Chatterjee criticizes the British for their division of body and soul when she discusses the English view of a saint: "An English person automatically thinks of a saint as someone who is going to be martyred, a man whose logic isn't going to work in a final show-down with the severely practical world, a man in fact who is a saint *per se.* Apart from occasional temptations (for which they prescribe hairshirts) they expect these saints of theirs to be so *un*-earth-bound that they have one foot in heaven already. And of course by heaven they mean the opposite of earth. They divide the material from the spiritual with their usual passion for tidiness and for people being orderly and knowing their place" (J 77). The division is emphasized when the psychiatrist Captain Samuels shocks the prudish Pankot community by his direct reference to "the human orgasm [as] a major contributory factor to physical and mental health" (T 356). Likewise, the community pictures Daphne as "frail, ethereal and beautiful in victim's white" (T 80), but she turns out to be "rather large and ungainly and in need of spectacles . . . in a rather grubby dress" (T 79–80).

Edwina Crane, Lili Chatterjee perceives, is a woman who sepa-rates material and spiritual things. Not really aware of what is hap-pening around her, she lives very much in her own thoughts. Thus all her good works, Lili says, have been going on in a vacuum. Significantly, she has her first genuine communication with an Indian when she feels the barriers between them torn down in the *physical* exhilaration of shared danger. The lack of lower range in Edwina is apparent in the tinny missionary song which seems so out of place both for the hungry Indian children who sing it and as protection against the rioters who attack her and kill the Indian who comes to her defense:

> There's a Friend for little children
>   Above the bright blue sky
> A Friend Who never changes,
>   Whose love will never die;
> Our earthly friends may fail us,
>   And change with changing years,
> This Friend is always worthy,
>   Of that dear Name He bears.
>
> There's a rest for little children
>   Above the bright blue sky,
> Who love the Blessed Saviour
>   And to the Father cry;
> A rest from every turmoil,
>   From sin and sorrow free,
> Where every little pilgrim
>   Shall rest eternally. (J 24)

Juxtaposed with the song is this sentence: "Ahead of them the rioters were spread out across the road" (J 65). It is significant as a symbol of the ineffectiveness of spirit without body that Crane and Chaudhuri are singing the song when they have their fatal encounter with the rioters.

Barbara Batchelor, in *The Towers of Silence,* represents the spiritual England that had good intentions toward India. She too is ineffectual; she too shows a divided self—we are told that love of Barbie's kind "did not extend to flesh" (74) and that she feels a faint revulsion for the throbbing motion of her Waterman's fountain pen. As the novel progresses, the separation in Barbie becomes more pronounced until it finally ends in madness. As a kind of disembodied spirit she thinks, "God . . . had waited a long time for her . . . consciously to enter the private realm of inner silence and begin to learn how to inhabit it even while her body went its customary bustling way and her tongue clacked endlessly on" (T 191).

But the most significant imagery describing the division is that of Mayapore's black town and white cantonment, so carefully mapped out by the narrator in *The Jewel in the Crown.* They meet physically on the ground between the Bibighar Gardens and the MacGregor House. On one level, racial barriers are crossed by moving symbolically, as Daphne did, from the leaping point for whites, the MacGregor House where she lives with Lili Chatterjee, into the Bibighar Gardens, which witness the consummation of her love with Hari Kumar. As the ghost of Janet MacGregor warns, her house, the last point before Bibighar, is a dangerous place for people with white skins (J 150). By crossing over into the Bibighar, Daphne displays what Sister Ludmila calls the courage to leap; she leaves once and for all the safety of the group and enters fully the Indian world; there is danger in so doing, but there is also more real life there. Sister Ludmila tells the narrator:

> It is curious. But there has always been this special connexion between the house of the singer and the house of the courtesans. Between the MacGregor House and the Bibighar. It is as though across the mile that separates them there have flowed the dark currents of a human conflict, even after Bibighar was destroyed, a current whose direction might be traced by following the route taken by the girl running in darkness from one to the other. A current. The flow of an invisible river. No bridge was ever thrown across it and stood. You understand what I am telling you? That MacGregor and Bibighar are the place of the white and the place of the black? To get from one to the other you could not cross by a bridge but had to take your courage in your hands and enter the flood and let yourself be taken with it, lead where it may. (J 150–151)

Between Bibighar and MacGregor flow the metaphorical currents of British-Indian history, and of life and death. To enter them means at the same time to unite English with Indian and, by overcoming instinctual fears, soul and body. Though Mayapore's Indian town and English cantonment meet physically in the ground *between* the Bibighar Gardens and the MacGregor House, Bibighar itself appropriately remains the thematic center of the *Quartet*. On one level the novels demonstrate that it was up to the British, who had alienated themselves from the country they ruled, to truly cross over into that country by becoming part of it. Psychoanalytically, the movement is the same. In the individual's repressed state, object has been displaced upward, and spirit must descend to body again if they are to be united. It is necessary to cross over from the MacGregor House to the Bibighar Gardens, where Daphne and Hari meet and, also appropriately, make love.

Green, wild, and overgrown, Bibighar, originally built by a prince, a voluptuary, for his courtesans (J 75), is a sexual image, suggesting passion. Associated with the rains, it is also a symbol of fertility and rebirth. Daphne says,

> I'm glad I came before and not in the middle of the rains. It's best to undergo the exhaustion of that heat, the heat of April and May that brings out the scarlet flowers of the gol mohurs, the "flames of the forest" (such a dead, dry, lifeless-looking tree before the blossoms burst) the better to know the joy of the wild storms and lashing rains of the first downpours that turn everything green. That is *my* India. The India of the rains.
>
> There's another name besides Hari's that we never mention. Bibighar. So although you were in Mayapore once, and may have visited the gardens, I don't know whether you have a picture of them in your mind or not. There it is all greenness. Even in the hottest months, before the rains, there is a feeling of greenness, a bit faded and tired, but still green—wild and overgrown, a walled enclosure of trees and undergrowth, with pathways and sudden open spaces where a hundred years ago there were probably formal gardens and fountains. (J 391)

Bibighar is the fount of life. To cross over onto Indian land is to come to terms with instinctual fears and therefore to enter a fuller life of the body. This kind of courage leads to a creative individuality and to a joy which is Dionysian in the unrepressed state. Significantly, Daphne juxtaposes her increasing but socially restricted sense of joy with an extension to the Indian side of the river: "And you see for me there was a growing sense of joy, whatever there was for the people who watched and waited. It was now that Mayapore seemed to change for me. It was no longer just the house, the road to the cantonment bazaar, the road to the hospital, the hospital, the maidan, the club. It extended to the other side of the river" (J 404).

Fittingly, there are no barriers in the Bibighar, and yet people do not enter. "At the back of the grounds the wall is crumbled and broken and gives on to waste ground. At the front of the garden there is an open archway on to the road but no gate. So the garden is never closed. But few people go in. Children think it is haunted" (J 392). The barriers are self-imposed; the associations of danger are there because of instinctual repression. That is in part why Daphne says, "Going in there, through the archway, or standing up and getting ready to go back into the cantonment—those were the moments when this feeling of being about to hide or about to come out of hiding to face things was strongest" (J 392). Outside, there is comparative deadness, for people are cut off, as it were, from the fount and from each other's individuality. When Daphne observes that Poulson has never been in the Bibighar, Scott is saying that White's assistant has never left the safety of his own community; he has not led the life of loving commitment, which for Scott is also the life of joy.

While Scott's conception of love is on the one hand traditional and moral in its emphasis on human tenderness, on another it approaches the Dionysian in its advocacy of physical joy.[10] Love, when it unites spiritual with physical, achieves a kind of consecration in the *Quartet*. Even after Jimmy Clark seduces Sarah Layton, she sees herself as having entered "her body's grace" (S 454). A person who is forever trying to fill other people's needs, she is herself completed by physical love. The ever-perceptive wazir, Count Bronowsky, notes the change, though he does not know its impetus. Sarah, after Clark and despite her perception of his disreputable example, reflects Daphne's wholeness.

It is appropriate that Sarah's strong physical need in part finds fulfillment in her love of the land, India. Unwed Sarah, Perron discovers on his return to India, has found happiness because she is "in love with the land itself" (D 496). Love of the land is able, at least temporarily, to replace love of a man for Sarah because the land, with its smell and its peace, symbolizes the body and the instincts, which, unrepressed, bring joy. The strong emphasis on physical need in the novels may be seen as unconscious yearning for an earlier stage in human development, a desire which must be at the root of the Westerner's fascination with the East. Because the child enjoys polymorphous perversity, the impact of the sounds, sights, and smells of the East on Westerners enable them to remember the ineffable of their own childhoods.

In the last part of *A Division of the Spoils*, Scott gives us glimpses of actions that symbolize the erotic exuberance in all of life that civilized beings have lost and that the protagonists momentarily approximate. Dionysian joy for Scott appears to be connected with selflessness. When Perron asks Sarah what made her give so much time to the nawab's daughter, Shiraz, she replies eloquently:

> "Her unhappiness." Then she cantered away, towards the open ground beyond the military tents and horse lines.
> Suddenly she cries out and thrashes her reins, left, right, and gallops off, making for the distant city wall, or what is left of it. The gateway alone is intact. I try to catch up but she is by far the better and more confident horseman, and she knows the lie of the nullahs, which I don't. But, behind her as I am, we seem to career together towards that implacable pink stone. Then she suddenly veers and shouts again, loudly, savagely, and races her horse back at a pace I really can't match: thrashing

the reins in that way, left, right, as if charging cannon in some desperate enterprise. And there is nothing there except the pale blue sky, the green of the shade trees, the tawny strain of the scrubby earth. I let her go, ease my own horse's pace, watch her; small white-shirted figure, going like a little demon into the distance, leaping the nullahs. I think it was her way of saying goodbye to a place where she had been free and happy. (D 552–553)

The symbolism is even more apparent in Sarah's watching Ahmed hawking. Ahmed and the hawk, Perron observes, are engaged in something very much like "a game of love" (D 517). Ahmed's flight-ing movement

cit[es] the hawk at its prey—a movement that produced in the bird ap-parent momentary lack of co-ordination, quickly righted, and develop-ing into a powerful and breath-taking ascent, a great arc, the beginning of a spiral of such formal beauty that Perron caught his breath and held it until he discerned in the empty heavens, through the planned geome-try of the hawk's attack, the objective, the intended point of killing con-tact: a dark speck intent on escape. . . . The hawk plummeted. Its shape merged with the speck. Sarah cried out, with pleasure and pain. He looked at her. All he could see was her hand gripping the binoculars, her slightly open mouth, the brave little thrust of chin and the tautened throat. (D 516)

The *Quartet* attempts to recapture symbolically civilization's lost Dionysian joy in Sarah's joyous frenzy and in the orgastic movement of the swooping hawk (though its glimpse of bliss is not free of civi-lization's sadomasochistic anal-eroticism which identifies sex with death in the female). In the descent to body, symbolized by the land India, Scott seems to have intuited something approaching poly-morphously perverse erotic exuberance and found in it, as in ordi-nary sexual joy, a partial answer to, or at least compensation for, the tragedy of thwarted love.

11. Symbol, Structure, and Texture

Ben Jonson paid Shakespeare the highest compliment when he said that the writer was not only of an age but for all time. In a similar fashion, we have seen that *The Raj Quartet* appears to go beyond the appeal of its history to a more universal importance. When Scott's work transcends the immediate picture to represent a cosmic view of broad human significance, it is appropriately further enlarged by symbol, which has a structural as well as textural function. From this cosmography evolves the warp and woof of the fabric of the novel, the interweaving of its longitudinal microcosmic and macrocosmic (and psychocosmic) symbolism in which people and events depict the experiences of the English in India, and its latitudinal (linear) symbolism, created by the progressive repetition in varying contexts of dramatic events and tableaux. Superimposing the vertical and horizontal lines of this symbolic fabric on the circular narration, we gain the structural and textural sense of totality characteristic of *The Raj Quartet*.

Creating a sense of totality is a primary temptation of the historical novelist,[1] though the books are not historical novels in the usual sense. They are, of course, memorable for their ability to recapture the shock of history on individual lives, to transform abstract historical fact into a rounded representation of human experience. But Scott's characters function symbolically as well as dramatically. It is not just that fictional characters living at the time give expression to the impact of history upon individual lives so that history becomes more immediate, but that there are emotional and symbolic correspondences between individual lives and the fate of nations. It is not just that characters are, as the narrator observes, "caught up [and overwhelmed] by his own people's history and the thrust of a current that simply would not wait for them wholly to comprehend its force" (J 171). Scott reminds us continually that his people must be seen not only in their historical context but as illustrative of it. This purpose involves a continual movement from microcosm to macrocosm that makes the use of the extended metaphor or analogy, which functions as symbol, a matter of course and adds greatly to the internal cohesiveness, textural richness, and expanded but controlled scope of the novels.

At any moment in the novels, the life of a character can zoom into focus as the life of England in India. After seeing Mabel Layton, on Mildred's instructions, buried in the wrong place, Barbara Batchelor thinks, "There . . . went the *raj*, supported by the unassailable criteria of necessity, devoutness, even of self-sacrifice because Mildred had snatched half-an-hour from her vigil [over Susan's labor] to see the coffin into the hole she had ordered dug. . . . But what was being perpetrated was an act of callousness: the sin of collectively not caring a damn about a desire or an expectation or the fulfilment of a promise so long as personal dignity was preserved and at a cost that could be borne without too great an effort" (T 245). And Perron, disturbed by a memory of Coomer (Kumar) playing cricket, sees in Hari's face his own historical awareness "that to misjudge, to mistime, would lead to destruction" (D 107). Kite hawks then circle around Perron's head, waiting for him to fall asleep and bringing to mind the vultures that hover outside Barbie's mission hospital room, waiting for the death of the Raj. Not a fixed but a shifting symbolical relation comes into focus, whose chief function is the same as that of the lengthy historical views and capsule family histories which remind and persuade the reader through the lives of individual Indian and English characters of what should have been and what is not.

Despite Scott's early view that literary symbols should be spelled out,[2] his analogues frequently cease their one-to-one correspondence to become more traditional symbols. At the end of *A Division of the Spoils,* the diminution of Hari Kumar ("the leftover, the loose end of our reign, the kind of person we created—I suppose with the best intentions" [J 475]) represents not only what the English have done to India but the abandoned hopes and possibilities they feel themselves. And the unknown Indian, in Barbara Batchelor's fantasy, crying out silently on the road from Dibrapur, can turn into Daphne, "the girl in white . . . running in the dark from a martyrdom, or from something unimaginable, which might even have been love" (T 304). Because Scott's characters are not arbitrary but have a "real" existence and because his images frequently suggest more than one meaning, I have chosen to incorporate all of Scott's imagery in the larger term *symbol* rather than *extended metaphor* or *synechdoche, allegory* or *allegorical fantasy* (Edward Thornhill uses the term *allegorical fantasy* in *The Corrida at San Feliu* [203]).

The *Quartet* contains innumerable texturally enriching correspondences between microcosm and macrocosm, but two are more
extended than the others and of more importance. The first is the
thwarted union of Daphne and Hari, or England *and* India; the second is the life of Barbara Batchelor, or England *in* India. Symbolically, once the union between the countries is thwarted in *The
Jewel in the Crown*, England must leave India, as it does in *The Towers of Silence* and in *A Division of the Spoils*. The primary motif of
Daphne's rape is an analogue for the rape of India by the British—
"there has been more than one rape" (J 462), Daphne writes, and in-
timates that the other is what has been done to Lili Chatterjee's
country: "I don't mean done in malice. Perhaps there was love, Oh,
somewhere in the past, and now, in the future, love as there was between me and Hari. But the spoilers are always there aren't they. . . .
The Ronald Merricks. The silly little man who summed up his own
silly little island history when he whistled and said, 'some wog con-
tractor is making a packet'" (J 462). Perhaps because only a suggestion of what could have been has come out of the British-Indian relationship, the offspring of Hari and Daphne, Parvati, is presented
briefly as a shy, retiring female.

In the relationship of Hari and Daphne and in their characters as
well, Scott would seem to be demonstrating an ideal blending of the
races. Daphne is an English girl who is far more Indian in her love of
the country and the people than is Hari, who detests both and whose
upper-class manner and perfectly accented English make it clear
that he is an Indian only in skin color. Nonetheless, why the rape of
an English girl, done in malice and desire for revenge, should parallel
the rape of India is at first puzzling. Salman Rushdie was highly
critical of the connection when he wrote:

> Where Forster's scene in the Marabar Caves retains its ambiguity and
> mystery, Scott gives us not one rape but a gang assault, and one perpe-
> trated, what is more, by peasants—smelly persons of the worst sort. It is
> useless, I'm sure, to suggest that if a rape must be used as the metaphor
> of the Indo-British connection, then surely, in the interests of accuracy,
> it should be the rape of an Indian woman by one or more Englishmen of
> whatever class—not even Forster dared write about such a crime. So
> much more evocative to conjure up white society's fear of the darkie, of
> big brown cocks.[3]

His unfortunate comment plays to a racial gallery[4] and ignores the
emphasis of the *Quartet*, which is not the rape of an English girl by a
gang of unknown Indian hooligans but on the victimization of that
English girl and her Indian lover by "the glittering insufferable *raj*"

(D 33). Like another reviewer who faulted Scott for not dealing with the sexuality of Indian women,[5] Rushdie does not allow Scott his donnée. Scott's subject is not British villains and Indian victims, or the other way around, and the historical dimension of his novels, however admired by historians, is secondary to his transcendent vision of the forces that thwart union. The rapes are linked by the love of power and destructiveness, the desire for mastery common to all races.[6] Bibighar is the creative center of the *Quartet*; character, plot, tension, everything flows in and out of the image of the girl running that, we recall, began *The Jewel in the Crown* in Scott's imagination. It is also the mystical and moral core of the novels, incorporating the forces of life and death as well as the union of body and soul; Bibighar is more important even than Sister Ludmila's Sanctuary for the destitute dying. For the narrator, it has a tragic beauty: "Bibighar. After a time even the most tragic name acquires a kind of beauty" (209). To see only the crude rape is to ignore the more important marriage. Bibighar is the place where Daphne and Hari were united in physical love and paid the tragic price of their courage. As it grows into symbol, Bibighar stands not so much for rape as for what could have been had the world been other than it is. Bibighar is the center of *The Raj Quartet* just as Marabar is the center of *A Passage to India*. What is comparable to the strength of Marabar in Scott's *Quartet* is not the rape of Daphne Manners, however, but the subtler, three-tiered symbolic structure, historical, social, and psychological, pointing to images of thwarted or aborted union.

The theme is woven into the texture of the novels, and there are reverberations of the doomed union of India and England, as represented by Hari and Daphne, in the sensitive relationships between sympathetic English female characters and their male Indian servants or assistants. Such relationships can be observed between Edwina Crane and Joseph; Mabel Layton and Ghulam Mohammed; Mabel, Barbie Batchelor, and Aziz; Sister Ludmila and Mr. de Souza; Lady Manners and Suleiman. The most notable example is the relationship between Sarah Layton and Ahmed Kasim. Kasim is not a servant but in self-mocking deprecation insists on behaving like one by riding a few paces behind Sarah. Unlike the other English who can relate to their servants only in the position of master, the characters we admire see them with feelings like their own and are repaid with admiration and respect. In Scott's view these women, so unlike those who unsex themselves by considering themselves superior to Indian men, have the sort of relationship with Indians that justified England's presence in India.

Most of the English do not consider Indians to be their equals, however. Barbie gives Merrick the picture that inspired the ironic title of the first novel of the *Quartet*, insisting that he hold it in his artificial hand. She says that they have had plenty of "the pomp" and "the obeisance," but that the picture represents an unfulfilled hope because "the unknown Indian . . . isn't *there*" (T 388). The unknown Indian has been left out of England's pretentious conception of its role. The measure of the failure of the British in India is in the plight of this Indian, who appears in various real and phantasmagoric guises—as, among others, Hari Kumar; his grieving Aunt Shalini prostrate before Merrick at the train station; Ahmed Kasim; the silently reproving children Barbie has presumed to bring to God; the Indian bride smiling bravely while her white satin gown is spotted red by the prick of the seamstress; Barbie's orphan, Ashok, who makes her weep because he would give up his dream of elephants to follow her anywhere; the dead Chaudhuri, who, blinded by cataracts in Barbie's dream, appropriately howls, duplicating India's symbolic castration, as does Hari Kumar when, bound and gagged, he weeps in frustration, powerless to save from rape the girl to whom he has just made love.

Kumar's fate and Kasim's—abandonment and its consequence, diminution and death—are minitypes of what England has, however unintentionally, allowed to happen to India during partition. In both cases Scott traces the evasion of responsibility. Though individuals try with limited success to rectify the wrong committed against Kumar, publicly the British in India do not acknowledge Merrick's mistake and are glad to have his military heroism provide an excuse for quietly shelving the affair. The parallel for Kasim is explicitly stated. As soon as the narrator re-creates for himself and for us the scene of Ahmed's murder on the train to Premanagar, his train begins to move, and it is almost as though there were something "greasy and evasive" on the tracks, almost as though, by not seeing the body fall, the English were able to pretend to themselves that it did not. He says, "Increasing speed, the train puts distance between itself and the falling body and between one time and another so that in the mind of the traveller the body never quite achieves its final crumpled position on the ground at the feet of the attackers" (D 112). Scott further implies that the tragedy of partition began with the rape of India when he ties Ahmed's murder, which is obviously identified with the destruction of a united India, with the Bibighar tragedy— "when the body falls it . . . will not fall to the ground so much as out of a history which began with a girl stumbling on steps at the end of a long journey through the dark" (D 113).

If *The Jewel in the Crown* is concerned with the marriage that was prevented by the rape, *The Towers of Silence* is a working out of the British-Indian relationship in deliberately sustained symbolical terms. The reader who sees mere repetition in this novel misses its evocative and delicately woven fabric. Scott is fond of giving clues to his intention: "There is one mind common to all individual men" (D 277). "If the whole of history is one man . . . it is all to be explained from individual experience. There is a relation between the hours of our life and the centuries of time" (T 77). So writes Emerson, and retired missionary Barbara Batchelor is fascinated by his essays, which she tries unsuccessfully to understand. What Emerson is saying and Scott emphasizing in his classic realist text[7] is that history can be seen as a projection of the psychology of men and women, or even of a single person, the same forces that become manifest in history being present in varying degrees in all of us. Additionally, if each new law or political movement is one manifestation of our protean nature, then the study of history, the *Quartet's* objective, reveals not only conflicting historical forces but opposing forces in human nature.

The events of Barbie's life, together with her feelings and dreams, symbolize the novels' "truths" about England in India. Barbie is their unseeing instrument, and through her unfulfilled yearnings and psychological revelations the reader is guided to a sense of regret for the frustration of an ideal as well as to Scott's view of the causes of British failure in India. There are symbolic portrayals of England's lost moral purpose, longing for the past and tardy realization of an authentic function; there are pictures of England's good intentions and delusions and a final realization of the substance of the failure: the inconsistent policies dictated by different ruling interests, the omissions and forgotten principles, the alienation and selfishness of the British, together with the weight of past mistakes, however well intentioned. Also presented is the longing of the British to resurrect the principles of the old Raj, the clear impossibility of doing so, and the death and anticipated burial of the Raj.

The marriage of England to India was unsuccessful partly because of inconsistencies in policy caused by different ruling interests. That Barbie is divided against herself is apparent when she thinks, "My life . . . has become extraordinarily complicated. There is more than one of me and one, I'm not sure which, has a serious duty to perform" (T 79). Later, feeling the pull of madness, she retches as she catches sight of infinite retreating reflections in the double mirror. Barbie's parents—her mother a prude, her father a gay blade who loved life and knew how to enjoy it—might well represent the eighteenth-century merchant adventurers and the nineteenth-century self-righteous English in India, together creating a twentieth-century representative of a well-meaning but bungling British Empire. Anxiety-ridden and compulsive, Barbie is caught between the dying or withdrawing forces of selfless purpose and those of selfish insularity. Though possessing the good intentions of Mabel and Sarah Layton, Barbie does not for a long time understand the egalitarian love for which they stand and which should have prevailed in India. She is a believer in the benevolence of established authority and accepts the community view of things at face value until, as Mabel's companion, she clashes with Mildred's harsh and condescending spirit.

In her disappointment about her missionary work and in her feeling that God "no longer . . . believed in her or listened to her, [as] . . . if she had spent her life doing something of which He disapproved" (T 12), Barbie is representative of the British in India yearning for the moral certainty and sense of purpose of the past. Her search for meaning and continual perusal of Emerson is England's bewildered quest for an explanation of what has gone wrong in India. Her belief that God no longer listens to her parallels the sense the British have of the meaninglessness of their unappreciated sacrifice. For purpose and meaning, lower-middle-class Barbie turns to her friend and social superior, Mabel Layton, who has taken her into Rose Cottage as a companion to keep daughter-in-law Mildred out. At varying times Mabel is for Barbie the best of the old Raj, her means of serving God, and God or Love Himself. In her (and to a lesser extent in Ethel Manners) Scott's identification of idealistic England with moral purpose, egalitarian love, and the divine is apparent. Mabel seems ponderous and detached, stony-faced and numbed, because she must defend herself against the pain of unfulfilled love. Wishing to preserve what is left of past ideals, she cuts herself off from communication with the present; she is an anachronism, like her roses (and the dead, stuffed birds of paradise in the novel of the same name). "The gods once loved [the roses] but forgot [they] should die young" (T 30), and ideals die as ideals when they are actualized. She is the spirit of loss and of mourning, the England that sees the opportunity missed, the guardian of the lost ideals. Her sense of hopelessness gives her a look of the profoundest resignation Barbie has ever seen.

Only in the rose garden does Mabel achieve tranquillity. She spends her time not participating in the artificial social life of the memsahibs but in tending the flowers of her rose garden, which represents, at various times, India, the work the British should have done in India, the past, the Raj incorporating the imperial ideal in its beauty. In the creative devotion of tending flowers, Mabel demonstrates the attitude the British should have had toward India. The tying of the ideal of love to nature lends the ideal power and meaning. Of Mabel Barbie says, "Her days are spent in celebration of the natural cycle of seed, growth, flower, decay, seed" (T 207); her roses attest to careful tending and kneeling "to grub out weeds." Mabel has no sense of false dignity and appears to lack an awareness of the imperial glory Barbie senses to be irrelevant to the work the British had to do in India. The novels suggest that the British, like Mabel, could have harvested the roses of their ideal (Aziz and Mabel know exactly how to cut the blossoms without weakening the bush or spoiling its shape) had they tended them with care and without fear of involving themselves or dirtying their hands. But the ideal is destroyed and Mabel imprisoned, like the butterflies which cannot fly out of the prison of the exquisite old lace christening gown and make love in the sunshine. Stolidly, hopelessly resigned, Mabel, like God, seems deaf and does not even attempt to protect Barbie from Mildred, suggesting the apparent indifference of God or the inability of past idealistic England to protect present England when confronted by the embodiment of narrow interest.

In Barbie Scott captures Britain's genuine bewilderment about the means of helping India. This too is why Mabel is deaf and why Barbie thinks, "I have lost her . . . but come to that I have never really found her" (T 201). For the most part, England sees India through a veil of its own needs and illusions. This myopia causes Barbie initially to mistake the meaning of her friend Edwina's guarding of Chaudhuri's body as an act of pure devotion rather than bleak despair, and to attempt the conversion of Indian children to narrow Christianity—symbolically, to the British way of life. Often England was tormenting India when it was trying to help. The truth is revealed in dreams. Barbie dreams of the little girl whose blue crayon she took away in the mission school because she had colored God blue, like Krishna. She dreams that she could not remember the little girl's name when she called the roll. The girl could not remember it either and silently accused her of depriving her of both name and crayon, and would not go away until her name was called. The name is the identity the British have taken away from the Indians, the message that Krishna as well as Jesus must be accepted; Indians are to be treated as equals. Though Barbie learns to go beyond her fundamentalist Christianity and afterwards pictures Parvati worshipping both Jesus and Krishna, her attempt at friendship is mistimed. When she wants to shake hands, the little girl keeps hers behind her back. The message is the same when Barbie pictures to herself the scene of Miss Crane's holding the dead Chaudhuri's hand with the caption "Too late" written under the illustration. She realizes that all along she has not understood the meaning of love. The well-intentioned British learned too late that alienation caused the distress, an illumination Barbie muses on when she compares Mabel's transplanted English roses, which had flourished in Indian soil because they accepted what was offered, with the English, whose God did not follow them to India because they had remained aliens: "You are now native roses. . . . Of the country. The garden is a native garden. We are only visitors. That has been our mistake. That is why God has not followed us here" (T 283).

Barbie has sporadic realizations, increasingly frequent as the novel progresses, of what tasks she has omitted performing despite her good intentions. She shows her tardy understanding of what British purpose should have been when she writes to the current mission administrator asking her whether the mission ever brought the children of India love, "not pity, compassion or instruction but love" (T 203). She tells her replacement that, despite her chatter and confident stride, she is beginning to suspect that she has never known what love is. The egalitarian relationship is also stressed in the symbolism of the apostles' spoons. Commenting on British social and racial prejudice, she thinks the apostles, these "simple, hard-working men, good with nets and boats, swarthy-skinned, smelling of sweat, of fish, of the timberyard; men who worked with their hands . . . [would] get short shrift in Pankot" (T 298). In presenting her wedding gift of apostles' spoons to Susan Layton, Barbie delivers a message of egalitarian love to the insular English, and this is symbolically why Mildred cruelly returns them. The frustration of English love for India is again apparent when Barbie is thwarted in her desire to give the spoons to Lady Manners as a present for Parvati (T 343).

The sporadic realization of her omissions terrifies Barbie. One day, while reading Emerson, she comes across the same passage that Guy Perron is to point out to Nigel Rowan, "Nothing can bring you peace but yourself. Nothing can bring you peace but the triumph of principles" (T 202). She cries out in fear because she cannot remember what her principles are. Barbie's search for God, it is clear, is England's for its principles. She is alarmed when she realizes that the unknown Indian should have provided the authentic purpose for her life. While her great desire had always been for useful service performed in love, she had never thought of the Indian as an equal. When she glimpses him in an "I-Thou" relationship, she understands the suffering of India and, like Mabel, the caretaker of the British ideal, is tormented by it.

Because England's ideal should have ended in the egalitarian union of England and India instead of the suffering of the unknown Indian, Barbie dreams of Mabel (whom she knows to be tormented by nightmares of Gillian Waller) "turn[ing] into the pillow, crushing and splintering the lenses, cutting herself, bleeding slowly from closed eyelids so that she appears to be crying blood" (T 207). Mabel's death signals the demise of the Raj, its ideals unfulfilled. Barbie receives news of her death while helping Mr. Maybrick gather and organize the pages of his Bach. It is symbolic of the thwarted union of independent India that there is not time to put on the binding. Similarly symbolic of England's principles laid to rest, or the Raj buried without the promised union, is the burial of Mabel's body against her wishes—in the convenient place instead of the promised place next to her dead husband. Emphasizing the enduring character of the misfortune, Barbie envisions her in anguish for all eternity. When she manages to get into the mortuary, she sees a ghastly sight—Mabel's partially pigmented body, open staring eyes, and a mouth from which "a wail of pain and terror was emitting" (T 238). Barbie attempts to rectify the wrong by trying compulsively to bring her back; so well does Barbie make her need known that the townspeople have a comic vision of her transporting a statue of Mabel piece by piece in her suitcase to the town square and rebuilding her there. But Mabel cannot be reconstructed, and once the moral purpose of the Raj is dead, Barbie begins to anticipate her own death. Bereft of Mabel, she is thrown out of Rose Cottage by Mildred; the spirit of insular selfishness has thrown England out of India and, in cementing over the rose garden, has destroyed its ideals. Paralleling the British sense of diminution in the final days of the Raj, Barbie feels that "when she left the cottage forever she would enter an arena of defeat from which she could see no exit" (T 270).

The immediate cause of the accident which leads to her death is the trunk which, too heavy for the tonga, throws it off balance on the steep road down from Rose Cottage. Barbie says that the trunk is her history and, for that matter, Sarah's and Mabel's too. Without it, according to Emerson, none of them is explained. But there is no room for her trunk at Clarissa Peplow's, where she is moving, no room for her explanation. Though the narrator tells us that Sarah's brow had become creased, and Barbie is not sure she understands the complicated situation herself, the symbolism is clear enough for readers who add the historical dimension to their analysis. Mabel, Sarah, and Barbie share a spirit of good intentions. If the trunk represents the history of all of them, it is the history of all the good the British did and tried to do in India, together with the illusions ("The

Jewel in Her Crown" is in the trunk until Barbie gives it to Merrick) and the mistakes. Barbie's thought that Sarah, being young, "would not have learned as yet to understand the grave impediment to free movement which luggage represented in one's affairs" (T 279) indicates that her luggage symbolizes the weight of the past exerting a controlling influence on the present, a theme also indicated when Barbie thinks at one point, "the trunk was all that God need ever notice or take into account; . . . she herself had become unreal and unimportant" (T 272).

Barbie wants to leave the trunk in Rose Cottage because England wants evidence of its presence and good intentions to remain in India. The trunk, however, is discarded by Mildred's mali. Symbolically, then, the history of the good intentions of the British in India is in the hands of the spirit of narrow selfishness, which, in discarding it, destroys the British and their history. On the way downhill in a tonga too light for the heavy trunk, Barbie feels "the weight of the trunk at her back: her years pressing on her, pushing her forward, pushing her downward" (T 390). Instinctively, she tries to stop, her feet pressing hard against the footboard, but she has little strength; the horse does its best but the tonga goes out of control. The weight of the past overwhelms all the good the British tried to accomplish in India. Her desire to have back "The Jewel in Her Crown" emphasizes the part illusions played in the disaster. Her head, covered by the beautiful lace veil, becomes a "nest of butterflies . . . caught in the lank grey hair" (T 390). Just before the crash these imprisoned ideals assume the form of a "monstrous membrane" (T 392) that blinds her and the driver. Once the tonga crashes, she is conscious of the rain falling on the dead butterflies on her face. Like an England that would pride itself on the fulfillment of a promise, Barbie does not understand what has happened; for her the accident that would end in her madness and death has been an apotheosis in which "God had shone his light on her at last by casting first the shadow of the prince of darkness across her feet" (T 392). She marches into Clarissa Peplow's bungalow telling her she has seen the devil and asking for a spade with which to resurrect Mabel.

As the tonga gained speed, Barbie saw an apparition of Mildred's face, "eyes hooded, mouth turned down, quirked at the corners; glass held under chin in droop-wristed hands" (T 390), which then dissolved and reformed as Merrick's. Clearly, Merrick and Mildred are representative of the forces that destroy England in India. Barbie identifies Merrick as the devil because he is the aggressive, manipulative element that exploited India in the process of asserting its own superiority. He is "the dark side of their history . . . inseparable from the image of the woman in white [Hari's Aunt Shalini] . . . plead[ing] with him for an alleviation of suffering of which . . . he had been the cause" (S 359). Barbie, the Raj, fearing death by strangulation, gasps at the sight of him suggestively looking toward the verandah where Mabel had died and "at the noxious emanation that lay like an almost visible miasma around the plants along the balustrade which had grown dense and begun to trail tendrils" (T 375). The alienation of the British from India is suggested by his unapproachability ("there was no way into him at all" [T 409]), and the moral corruption of the self-righteous by his sadistic homosexuality and by Mildred's drunkenness and adultery with her husband's vacuous adjutant, Coley.

Finally, Barbie, as England in India, lies dying in the Hospital of the Samaritan Mission of the Sisters of Our Lady of Mercy. Powerless to save India from disaster, she has castration dreams (she cannot hold the pencil because both her hands have been severed). Previously an incessant chatterer, she is now struck speechless; promises are meaningless when Britain permits the subdivision of the subcontinent.

Barbie's wits were scattered at the beginning of the novel and at the end she is quite mad, yet there is sense in her madness, and Scott continues to use her as an instrument of truth. When Sarah comes to visit, Barbie tells her she has nothing to give her for her kindness, "Not even a rose," since the ideals of the old order have been destroyed. Deluded, she calls her Gillian Waller because it was the massacre of unarmed Indians at Jallianwallah Bagh that signaled the end of the British in India. She is obsessed with "birds," which turn out to be the vultures that eat the dead bodies of the Parsees atop the towers of silence where they have been placed. The symbolic beginning of the longed-for burial of Barbie, the Raj, is evident when she is no longer able to tell Sarah what it was she remembered because "the birds had picked the words clean" (T 396).

It is clear too that Scott is describing a Raj whose structure had been fundamentally sound (D 134–135) when the narrator tells us, as Barbie approaches death, "Asleep, Barbie no longer dreamed. Her dreams were all in daylight. Do not pity her. She has had a good life. It had its comic elements. Its scattered relics had not been and now can never all be retrieved; but some of them were blessed by the good intentions that created them" (T 396). Her dreams were all in daylight because, to the end, England is deluded by its unfulfilled aspirations. This is made additionally clear by her last hoarsely whispered words, "I am not ill, Thou art not ill, He, She, or It is not ill. We are not ill. You are not ill, They are all well. Therefore . . ."

(T 397). The novels demonstrate that to the end England as a whole refused to admit, even to itself, responsibility for the disaster in India but claimed a moral victory in Indian independence. Barbie's death "in sudden sunshine, her shadow burnt into the wall behind her as if by some distant but terrible fire" suggests the demise of England in India, signaled by the atomic bomb ending World War II.

The *Quartet* is detailed in its evocation through symbol of Scott's feelings about the British in India. But the work is not just a series of apparently objective novels in which people and events symbolize history; the books transcend the immediate scene to serve as a metaphor for a profound philosophical view, supported by the reflective style of the narrative and its balancing, often starkly dramatic prose. ("There is no God," missionary Edwina Crane cries in despair, "not even on the road from Dibrapur" [T 386].) The *Quartet* is a historical lament, a vast panorama of amazing verisimilitude and internal correspondences, of such broad human appeal and controlled expansive virtuosity as to be called a symphony in four movements in and transcending the immediate limits of time and space.

A single theme, that of the unachieved unity of love and joy, occurs in various guises in all four movements. The work is cyclic in nature; each movement retains the original thematic material while making its own variations and additions. Beginning and ending with the same image, the novels develop the theme of lost unity harmonically and contrapuntally. Throughout, there is the three-note chord already examined in the chapters of this text. Counterpoint is apparent in the interweaving of individual tragedies which all point in terms of individual psychologies to the ultimate failure of their striving after unity. Tableaux, landmarks, and the smells of India arise as motifs which are sounded throughout the *Quartet*, acting as unifying forces and growing into symbol. Modulation is achieved through the repetition of the same events from differing points of view and through the slightly different focus of the central theme in each of the four movements.

The narrator's temporal and spatial peregrinations act at the same time as a device for achieving verisimilitude and as a means of expanding scope and intensifying effect. The dimension of time, of history, is frequently superimposed on the one of space as the narrator re-creates for the reader his travels along the same routes and to the same places that his characters frequented as he tries to imagine what they must have thought, how they must have felt, even what they must have smelt. This juxtaposition is explicitly stated when the narrator, entering the MacGregor House, a place containing its own and Daphne's tragic history, relates, "It is in going upstairs that the feeling of mounting into the past first comes and ever afterwards persists, no matter how many times the routine journey is undertaken" (J 95). Other, more implicit instances of superimposition are plentiful. Taking a bath in the MacGregor House tub, the narrator shuts his eyes against the difference in sex, to better imagine himself as Daphne. On the train to Ranpur, he will muse over how surprisingly undramatic the scenery seems in view of the horror executed in the place where Ahmed's body fell. Or traveling with Srinivasan in the Studebaker past the Bibighar and "the smoky metallic railway smell that is the same anywhere in the world, and was certainly no different twenty-two years ago, [he will] . . . breathe in sharply and think: This is what she smelt as she cycled back from Sister Ludmila's Sanctuary" (J 209).

Sister Ludmila gives the reason for the superimposition when she tells the narrator:

"Your voice is that of a man to whom the word Bibighar is not an end in itself or descriptive of a case that can be opened as at such and such an hour and closed on such and such a day. . . . Given the material evidence there is also in you an understanding that a specific historical event has no definite beginning, no satisfactory end? It is as if time were telescoped . . . and space dovetailed? As if Bibighar almost had not happened yet, and has happened, so that at once past, present and future are contained in your cupped palm." (J 133)

Telescoping time means transcending it or creating a timeless significance for historical events. Time telescoped and space dovetailed add poetic texture to that density already created by macrocosmic/microcosmic/psychocosmic correspondence, bring the past alive, and point to the continuing influence of the past on the present. Superimposition of past on present is one way of showing through structure that errors of the past are continued into the present, certainly in terms of the division of the country and alienation of the British from India, which is as evident in 1964 as it was in 1942.

Telescoped time, together with dovetailed space and telepathic insight, makes people and events larger than life, of epic proportions and cosmic significance. Through repetition they grow into symbol, which also serves as a device for expansion of scope and internal unification. Superimposed on the circular narration, symbol ties together levels of meaning longitudinally, or harmonically, and latitudinally (the repetition of place, smell, tableaux, and narrative from shifting points of view is necessarily progressive[8]). So the *Quartet* seems a world unto itself with its own dynamic.

Not all the landmarks that tie the stories together are repeated often or emphatically enough to grow into symbols; but of those that do, there is the leper at the entrance to the Chillianwallah Bazaar or the Tirupati Temple, who appears to grow into a minor symbol of the pain and horror of India as the characters react to him in the same way that they react to that horror. Hari, who tries to pretend that his own nightmare world is not real, looks away in case he should meet the leper's eyes, while Sister Ludmila, who works with the suffering, sees him more positively, "with his limbs cut back, like those of a bush that had to be pruned in order to ensure the bloom" (J 155). And the smell of the river, which disgusts the English in general but which the protagonists seem to learn to need or to miss, becomes a symbol of alienation and of India and the desire to return to a full life of the body. Even a little item like a raincape (rain appears always to accompany crisis) can strike a familiar chord in the reader and so texturally tie together incidents through the common idea of disaster. The raincape appears to signify ineffectual or illusory shelter; there is a raincape left in the back of the burning car so that Miss Crane has nothing with which to cover Mr. Chaudhuri. The men who rape Daphne cover her head with her own raincape. Barbara loses her sou'wester at Kevin Coley's house where the adjutant and Mildred are engaging in adulterous sexual relations; in her terror at the possibility of discovery, she runs from the house, slips, and twists her ankle in the rain, eventually catching the pneumonia that is the beginning of her decline. At the end of *The Towers of Silence*, the raincape becomes the lace shawl whose dead butterflies cover Barbie's face after the tonga crash.

The novels are replete with tableaux that operate as motifs, symbols of overwhelming forces. In addition to the several illustrations of Barbie's awakening too late to help the unknown Indian, there is Edwina Crane, sitting by the roadside in the pouring rain holding the dead Chaudhuri and crying, "I'm sorry. Sorry it's too late. . . . There's nothing I can do" (J 429–430), and there is Daphne Manners, repeating Edwina's words when she fears for Hari's safety and wondering where she had heard them before. The dominant tableau is, of course, Daphne running alone from the Bibighar to the MacGregor House after the rape. Because Scott captures the image of the girl running in the night in various situations, with various shadings, the effect is at once integral and modulating both to the image and to its context. By means of repetition and variation, the image is slowly constructed as a symbol. In the following passage, note how the last line superimposes the 1942 past on the more distant nineteenth-century past, both of which are described from the perspective of a

1964 present. The method is texturally enriching and the symbol is
enlarged in time, adding dimension and meaning:

> Ask to go to the room at the top of the old tower [of the Purdah Hospi-
> tal]. From there you can see over the roofs of the black town across the
> river and make out the roof of the MacGregor House. I wonder how
> often the prince who loved the singer climbed the steps of the tower to
> look at it? And I wonder whether his son also climbed the tower to look
> across the river at the Bibighar. From the Bibighar also it must have
> been possible in those days to see the house of the singer. They are only
> one mile distant. Not far, but far enough for a girl running at night.
> (J 147)

The image which begins the *Quartet* also ends it:

> Fleeting moments: these are held a long time in the eye,
> The blind eye of the ageing poet,
> So that even you, Gaffur, can imagine
> In this darkening landscape
> The bowman lovingly choosing his arrow,
> The hawk outpacing the cheetah,
> (The fountain splashing lazily in the courtyard),
> The girl running with the deer. (D 598)

The lines "The girl running with the deer," "The bowman lovingly
choosing his arrow," and "The hawk outpacing the cheetah" symbolize at once the overwhelming forces against her—against the
good and the beautiful and the loving—and the nostalgic, gentle
mood of acceptance in which the poet Gaffur, like the anglicized
Hari Kumar, and I think we must say, the novelist Scott submit to
the inevitable. Here the final tableau renders the image timeless, in
a Keatsian fashion catches a sightless vision (the poet is blind),
a soundless splash (of the fountain in the courtyard), a frozen motion; or the imagination's concept of beauty which is not visible,
sound which is not audible, and motion which does not contain
movement.

Scott has intimated from the very first sentence of the *Quartet*
that he means to use elements of telescoped time and dovetailed
space to develop into symbol the pivotal theme of the *Quartet*,
Bibighar, a name which after a time, the narrator informs us, acquires a kind of tragic beauty: "Imagine, then, a flat landscape, dark
for the moment, but even so conveying to a girl running in the still
deeper shadow cast by the wall of the Bibighar Gardens an idea of
immensity, of distance, such as years before Miss Crane had been

conscious of standing where a lane ended and cultivation began: a
different landscape but also in the alluvial plain between the mountains of the north and the plateau of the south" (J 9). The distance or
immensity alluded to begins the spatial expansion Scott incorporates into his novels. Such expansion is evident from the frequent
use of the panoramic view, whether the aerial metaphor Sister Ludmila uses to describe the races uniting toward evening on the
maidan (J 282), or the narrator's godlike aerial view of Mayapore at
the end of *The Jewel in the Crown*. This is a metaphor for Scott's
inquiry into the truth—historical, sociological, metaphysical, psychological: "The plane banks, nosing east, almost taking the course
of the river that leads to Miss Crane's unimaginable coast. With this
God's-eye view of the created world she never had to cope, which
perhaps was a pity, because the topography she found so inhibiting
from ground-level reveals itself from this height, and at this speed,
as random and unplanned, with designs hacked into it by people
who only worked things out as they went along" (J 478). This spatial
expansion, incorporating Scott's view of our metaphysical vulnera-
bility, is also evident when a terrified Daphne runs home to "safety
that wasn't safety because beyond it there were the plains and the
openness that made it seem that if I ran long enough I would run
clear off the rim of the world" (J 436).

The vastness of the Indian plain, which "blankets the mind with
an idea of scope so limitless that it is deadening" (J 208), is a multi-
faceted symbol. There is a Forsterian sense of nature as hostile in its
indifference. Like the historically rich fort where Kasim had spent
his imprisonment, people are also diminished in relation to the juxtaposed infinity of the Indian plain (D 397, 111). Sarah thinks of the
plain, which shows the curious phenomenon of the disappearance of
the horizon as the morning progresses, as "always retreating . . . always making off, getting farther and farther away and leaving people
and what people have built stranded" (S 127). Miss Crane is oppressed by a god whose burdensome indifference is symbolized by
the plain: "She felt dwarfed, famished in the spirit, pressed down by
a tremendous weight of land, and of air and incomprehensible space
that even the flapping, wheeling crows had difficulty keeping up in.
And she thought for a moment that she was being touched by the
heavy finger of a god; not the familiar uplifting all-forgiving God she
went through the motions of praying to, but one neither benign nor
malign, neither creating nor destroying, sleeping nor waking, but
existing, and leaning his weight upon the world" (J 18). In dwarfing
humanity and rendering the individual insignificant, the plain be-

comes a symbol of overwhelming metaphysical and psychological forces indifferent to the lives people try to carve out for themselves.

But we cannot forget that in these novels India is also a symbol of the unconscious mind, and that the limitlessness of the unconscious is also suggested in the vast extent of the Indian plain. This link is apparent when Daphne, watching the dancing Siva, suddenly finds she cannot watch the statue any longer because she is being drained of her mobility, "becoming lost in it" (J 431); or when she is awed by the larger-than-life reclining Vishnu "that overpowered you with a sense of greater strength in sleep than in wakefulness" (J 422).

If the Indian plain appears to represent the indifference of nature to the fate of humanity, the land India also and paradoxically represents for Scott both those destructive defense mechanisms that form part of the malign spirit and those forces in the unconscious that must be relatively unrepressed if people are to live full lives. We must remember that Scott, like his narrator and many of his protagonists, was deeply attracted by the land at the same time that he was repelled by it. His love of India is apparent in Daphne's words: "Behind all the chatter and violence of India—what a deep, lingering silence. Siva dances in it. Vishnu sleeps in it. Even their music is silence. It's the only music I know that sounds conscious of *breaking* silence, of going back into it when it's finished, as if to prove that every man-made sound is an illusion" (J 468). The silence is that of the eternal or the preverbal unconscious and is representative of a preambivalent stage of development. The implication is that the Indian world is closer to the unconscious than the English, less repressed. Perhaps this is why the Indian god is sensual, "smooth and naked, with square shoulders and full lips that curve at the corners into a smile. The eyelids are shut but seem always to be on the point of fluttering voluptuously open" (J 206).

In using the sheer vastness of the Indian plain, then, Scott is at once symbolizing the immensity of the psyche and the enormity of his undertaking, which gives the impression of containing all points of view and is, like Tolstoy's *War and Peace,* a world unto itself, a totality. The sense of immensity involving an "absence of orientating features" (J 208) lends itself to symbolism and the view that Forster and Scott share, that in India is contained all things. It suggests an attempt to see things in their totality, whether in the form of clashing Mosque, Caves, and Temple, or in contrasting views of historical, sociological, and psychological unities.

12. Staying On after the Raj

In the very first sentence of Paul Scott's last completed novel, *Staying On*, Tusker Smalley dies of a massive coronary at the very moment that his wife, Lucy, is going under the dryer and having her white hair blue-rinsed and set in the Seraglio Room of Pankot's Shiraz Hotel. Disposing of one of his two main characters at the outset might present an impediment for a lesser technician. Scott, however, holds his reader's interest through the slow unveiling of a situation and a relationship, establishing from the beginning a backward-looking motion of gentle regret for a British couple who "hung on" in India long after everyone else went home following partition in 1947. *Staying On* is not a story of plot but of character, a gentle afterthought to *The Raj Quartet* which mocks human foibles and quietly laughs at human aspirations. Though lacking the scope and complexity of Scott's major work, the novel contains an intriguing narrative method and the same Jamesian subtlety of thought and feeling in human relations. A "sad comedy" like the 1963 novel set in London, *The Bender*,[1] *Staying On* will be remembered for its presentation of the theater of ordinary life and its dramatic juxtaposition of the comic and the heartbreaking.

For followers of *The Raj Quartet*, *Staying On* provides an opportunity to see some of the same people and places twenty-five years later. The setting is the hill station of Pankot, almost exclusively divided between Smith's Hotel and St. John's Church. Lucy and Tusker Smalley, the last of the British in Pankot, are a socially dull but dependable couple who were briefly encountered previously in the *Quartet*. The Smalleys, whose name suggests their diminished circumstances as well as Britain's diminished position as a world

This chapter is a revised version of an article that was published previously in *Journal of South Asian Literature* 17 (1982): 225–229.

power, are living a life of genteel poverty that contrasts sharply with the gaiety and wealth of their Indian friends. Ashok, the orphan boy of *The Towers of Silence,* who would have given up his dream of working with elephants in Rajputana to stay with retired missionary Barbara Batchelor, has been taken up by an Indian businessman and become an excellent photographer. Mahmud's niece, Minnie, the shy little "Ayah" who saved baby Teddie Bingham's life when his deranged mother, Susan, placed him in the center of a circle of fire, is now grown plump and grumpy as gigantic Lila Bhoolabhoy's servant. And there is a long letter from Colonel Layton's daughter, Sarah, who has long since married and borne the children of Guy Perron of *A Division of the Spoils.*

Setting and character are not all that tie *Staying On* to Scott's magnum opus. The thematic unifier, the "protagonist" of *The Raj Quartet,* is the idea of thwarted or aborted love. In so many of his novels Scott writes of love which remains unfulfilled, whether because of psychological defenses or external circumstances. In the *Quartet,* many well-meaning English are prevented by insular forces from expressing their feelings for Indians. In *Staying On,* Tusker and Lucy Smalley do not communicate with each other and have not done so for years. If *The Raj Quartet* shows aspirations to "a further union, a deeper communion" tragically betrayed, *Staying On* portrays the same aspirations on a smaller scale sadly and comically reversed. The tone of the novel suggests a resignation at injustice longstanding enough to elicit the humor from almost every situation.

The apparent theme is one of comic reversal—things are not what they should be in a world where "a fat money-grubbing Punjabi woman can cause a Christian Sahib a moment's disquiet" (21–22) as well as a fatal heart attack[2] (and where a barking, snapping fool of a dog is terrified into submission not from Tusker's masterful "Heel, sir" but from mali's gentle "Bless you.") After the dramatic announcement of Tusker's death in the first sentence, the reader's interest is held with the piquant comedy of the Punjabi hotel owner, sixteen-stone Mrs. Lila Bhoolabhoy, and the manager, Mr. Frank Bhoolabhoy, less amply endowed.

The reader will not miss the wordplay on diminished circumstances. Lucy's mother's name was Large; her maiden name, Little; her married name, Smalley. What is great is falsely great. Mrs. Large neglected and used her daughter, and made it plain that she preferred her strapping sons; gross Mrs. Bhoolabhoy's view of the world is limited to her own self-interest; the Shiraz, that "modern monstrosity" with its appeal for the influential and the well-to-do, has diminished the old-world charm of Smith's and taken its customers. (In its turn the Lodge, where the Smalleys live, is diminutive in relation to Smith's.) The Shiraz is to Smith's what the Bhoolabhoys are to the Smalleys—their more expensive but devalued replacements. In the Bhoolabhoy connection, the reader's sympathies are with the smaller of the two, Francis; in the Smalley relationship, with petite Lucy rather than heavy-set Tusker.

In *Staying On*, smaller is aesthetically and morally better, and the often incongruous juxtaposition of great and small creates much of the humor. There is Bhoolabhoy, who must extricate himself before the morning storm after waking "to find himself in bed with Lila, stark naked, his mouth and nose half smothered in her immense breasts, his shoulders clamped in the iron embrace of her arms and his legs pinioned between hers. She seemed to be playfully blowing on the top of his head. . . . He unstuck his perspiring face from her bosom and squinted upward . . . [to see] the morning light already filtering through the curtains and illuminating the fine hairs on her upper lip" (98–99). Much of the delight of *Staying On* is in the unexpected and rather ludicrous point of view, provoked not only by the contrast between great and small but by the juxtaposition of material and spiritual. Bhoolabhoy's Christianity contrasts with his wife's materialism: "Francis [Frank] Bhoolabhoy was a cradle Christian. What Mrs. Bhoolabhoy was no one knew. She had been married so many times that her original family name seemed lost in antiquity. She showed no interest in any religion, in any kind of hereafter, only in the here and now and in how this might be arranged to her advantage" (19).

Sometimes the humor is dependent on cultural misunderstanding. In the opinion of the Smalleys' servant Ibrahim, "when flush toilets were installed in the hotel, they should have been put in at the Lodge as well. Flush toilets were part of the Christian religion, like sitting in your own dirty bath water" (36). In *The Raj Quartet* Edwina Crane, tormented to suicidal depression by the murder of her Indian companion during the August 1942 riots, writes in despair, "There is no God. Not even on the road from Dibrapur" (T 386); in *Staying On* Ibrahim assures mali Joseph of the sacredness of Tusker's "very old English phrase[s], 'bugger-off' and 'piss-off'" (52).

Scott's handling of similar material is indicative of a fundamental shift in the tone of the two works. A small change in empty St. John's center of gravity "created an illusion of echo without traceable source" in *The Raj Quartet*, leading Barbara Batchelor to feel that "the church's guardian angel had half-opened and then closed one of his gigantic wings" (T 271). In *Staying On* the Shiraz Hotel seems to shudder and shift as that principle of gross selfishness, Lila

Bhoolabhoy, sits down. *Staying On* bears the same relationship to *The Raj Quartet* that Melville's resigned *Billy Budd* does to his anguished *Moby Dick*. While an agonized religious principle underlies the *Quartet, Staying On*, on the contrary, is not a working out of anguish at injustice but a starting from and playing with that activating principle. Thus, its form is tighter and more controlled, and it is tempting if not entirely accurate to say that the primary difference between these two realistic works is one of romantic expansion versus classical control.

As in the *Quartet*, Scott shows himself a master of character. Although there are gaps in our knowledge of the characters, we become convinced that we know everything about them essential to know—where they are, what they are saying and doing, how other characters react to them, their thoughts, their misinterpretations, and subtle changes in their expressions. Often their gestures or expressions reveal what they are thinking—for example, Lucy putting her hand to her lined cheek and smiling uncertainly as Bhoolabhoy assures her that Ashok is an excellent photographer who makes every detail show.

One does not feel in *Staying On*, as one sometimes does in *The Raj Quartet*, that Scott articulates too much; more is left to inference. In the *Quartet* the question of role-playing, the "charade" of British life in India, is enunciated at length by various characters. In *Staying On* the unwillingness of the British to extend themselves, to have anyone step out of one's "proper place," is handled briefly and ironically:

> Ibrahim regretted the passing of the days of the *raj* which he remembered as days when the servants were treated as members of the family, entitled to their good humours and bad humours, their sulks, their outbursts of temper, their right to show who was really boss, and their right to their discreetly appropriated perks, the feathers they had to provide for the nest when the nest they presently inhabited was abandoned by homeward-bound employers. Ibrahim had been brought up in such a nest. He still possessed the chits his father had been given by Colonel Moxon-Griefe and a photograph of Colonel and Mrs. Moxon-Greife with garlands round their necks, Going Home, in 1947. He had also inherited and preserved the two letters which Colonel Moxon-Greife had written to his father from England. Finally he had inherited the silence that greeted his father's two letters to Colonel Moxon-Greife inquiring about the possibilities of work in England for young Ibrahim, now going on twenty. (22)

One felt in *The Raj Quartet* that Scott could impose a mystical vision of thwarted love that appeared realistic rather than sentimental because it was solidly grounded in myriad details. Similarly, in *Staying On*, Scott prevents the touching from sinking to the sentimental by juxtaposing it with small details of impersonal or unpleasant reality. In the churchyard, for example, toiling Joseph asks Lucy to read gravestones for him so that he can recite a prayer for the dead. She begins reading and is uncomfortably made aware that the grave before them is that of a five-year-old child. The tableau is immediately tempered by the click of the camera, their sudden awareness of Ashok taking pictures of them. We see in another example Lucy's unfulfilled sexual longings contrasted with Tusker's brief, weekly heaving of himself onto her. His heart attacks are also attacks on his dignity. At the Desais' Holi party, he collapses spread-eagled and painted as a clown; at home, Lucy and Ibrahim find him half on, half off the toilet, legs spread, pajama bottoms down round his ankles.[3] At the novel's end, Lucy's plea to Tusker to take her "home" with him is a toilet reverie.

Though the plot hinges on the Bhoolabhoy-Smalley connection, Lucy's unfulfilled relationship with Tusker is at the emotional center of the novel; the Bhoolabhoy-Smalley relation can be seen as a vehicle for bringing out the story of two frustrated, unfulfilled lives. Yet, even in this, Scott does not lose the comic touch. There are whole days of silence between Tusker and Lucy when Ibrahim cannot talk to them, no matter how important his message, because no one is communicating with anyone, not even with the dog. The social system appears to be at the heart of their communication problems. British India had a social structure almost as rigid as the Hindu class and caste system. Apparently unambitious, Tusker was content to do the paperwork that got other people promoted and did not get the colonel's position that Lucy had coveted until shortly before partition. When independence came, he was too young to retire and too old, in his view, to begin somewhere else. In the new India, the impoverished Smalleys feel "almost as far down in the social scale as the Eurasians were in the days of the *raj*" (181).

The elaborate pecking order in British India could be very trying to junior wives, and Lucy, reflecting Scott's concern with the destructiveness of social form, resented the system which kept her in place and "brainwashed" her into believing that her prime concern was to be "a perfectly complementary image of Tusker and his position" (142). Constricted by the society, they withdrew from and turned on each other, Tusker becoming the irascible buffoon, raging inwardly at his helplessness and diminished position. Lucy never understood the fundamental inability to communicate: "Tusker and I do not truly communicate with one another any more. . . . His si-

lence is his silence and my loquacity is my loquacity but they
amount to the same thing. I can't hear what he is thinking and he
does not hear what I'm saying" (78); she feels that after forty years of
marriage they should understand each other at the deepest level
(142).

Like many in Scott's novels who find joy eluding them, Lucy
senses that the sadness of her life is in its unfulfilled promise: "A
life like a flower that has never really bloomed" (67). The lack of love
in her childhood has not been compensated by a happy marriage, but
its effect is magnified by Tusker's insensitivity to her needs. Echoing
George Spruce in *The Bender*, she says, "I [have] had a sad life" (67),
and continues, "It seems that my love, my life, has never had its face
to me and that I have always been following behind, or so dazzled by
sunlight that I could not see the face when it once turned to me"
(208).

In keeping with Scott's pattern of establishing a tenuous communion just before the onset of disaster, Lucy receives the night before
Tusker dies "the only love letter she has had in all the years she had
lived" (197). *Staying On* establishes the poignance of having out-
lived one's usefulness and been left behind while the shoddy and the
vulgar triumph. Scott, who was long in coming into literary recognition, dedicated the novel to his publisher and thirty-year friend
Roland Gant with the comment that they had both, in a sense,
"stayed on."

13. Paul Scott and His Fiction

In "Unity Identity Text Self," Norman N. Holland puts into textual context Lichtenstein's theory of the mother's imprint on the child of "'a primary identity' itself irreversible but capable of infinite variation." In Holland's equation, identity is to the self what unity is to a text; identity and unity are the invariables, self and text the variables. "Identity is the unity I find in a self if I look at it as though it were a text," he writes.[1] A developed adult's (invariant) "identity theme," if that person is a writer, can be discovered by an analysis of that author's (variable) texts. The identity theme, then, permits the grasping of the writer's "character" or "personality" or "unchanging essence" (as influenced by the interpreter's own identity theme). With the object of discovering Scott's identity theme, the sameness of which is synchronically carried through the variables of his experience, let us turn to his texts.

To read the pre-*Quartet* novels is to see that, one and all, they are stories of psychological imprisonment. Whether repressed, depressed, or inadequate, Scott's early protagonists are all wounded in some fashion. There is the inability of MacKendrick in *The Alien Sky* to experience love and life, the imprisonment by the extended self through love in *A Male Child* and through aggression in *The Mark of the Warrior,* the imprisonment by a life of consumption rather than dedication in *The Birds of Paradise* and by another sort of meaningless life in *The Bender.* There is also a helplessness to prevent the tragedy in *The Chinese Love Pavilion* that would be repeated on an individual and national scale in *The Raj Quartet.* Scott's vision of the artist as wounded, Edward Thornhill and his deformed Duende in *The Corrida at San Feliu,* brings to mind Edmund Wilson's classic text, *The Wound and the Bow,* which uses the myth of the Greek hero Philoctetes to relate the artist's gift to a childhood wound to the psyche; there is a relation, he claims, between "the incurable wound and [the] invincible bow" (225).

It appears likely that Scott's fiction sprang not only from his many different "faces,"[2] as his daughter Sally theorizes, but from an attempt to overcome the loss of the self. For the search for a true and acceptable self is the identity theme that ties together the early and later fiction. It is not insignificant that in Scott's first novel, *Johnnie Sahib*, the reader is left with an ambivalent view of the title character and wonders who the real Johnnie Brown is. Or that Thornhill laments that he never found his "still centre, except in each book as I write it" (CSF 96). Or that Kram, in the unfinished manuscript "The Appointment," feels that "hundreds of parts . . . are open to me to play, and unless I play one of them I feel nothing."[3] From Jim Taylor's sense of futility in *Johnnie Sahib* and Joe MacKendrick's inability to grasp his deeper self in *The Alien Sky* to George Spruce of *The Bender*, living in a sheltered cocoon of thought and unable to communicate except in correspondence or on the telephone, and Thornhill's inability in *The Corrida at San Feliu* to understand his own behavior after a lifetime studying other people's, Scott's earlier protagonists suffer an impairment of the ability to experience true emotions and seem suspended, as it were, in a "state of noncommunication."[4]

All of the early and middle protagonists appear to suffer characteristics of narcissism or the loss of self—anxiety, depression, emotional dependence, an exacting inner censor, a strong sense of unreality, a sense of disunity of body and soul, feelings of emptiness and imprisonment, as though in childhood they had been forced to develop a "false self." Loss of the self is described in Alice Miller's *Drama of the Gifted Child* as a failure to develop one's own personality in favor of a false grandiose or depressive self imposed by a seriously flawed parental self.[5] It is not insignificant that *I, Gerontius*, Scott's first published poem, is grandiose and bombastic: "I shall not pass unheard. / . . . / They shall say of me / 'That stone the corner one / he touched it as he passed along this way.'"[6] And not accidentally, the mothers (but not the aunts) portrayed in Scott's novels are unattractive figures. In *The Alien Sky* there is the "vicious, controlled anger" (25) Joe MacKendrick knows so well, the spiteful maliciousness of pitiable Marion Hurst in *A Male Child*, the vindictive pretentiousness of *The Bender*'s Violet Spruce, and the mother of whom protagonist David Chalmers in the unfinished fragment "Mango Rain" has been ashamed since childhood.

These early and middle novels are illustrative of another characteristic of the loss of the self—a split often between its affectionate and assertive components.[7] Caring in the early novels goes along with a certain weakness, conscientiousness, and lack of vitality on the part of the protagonists. The books are expressive of the tension between the impulses toward love and aggression, values Scott is attempting to integrate in his pre-*Quartet* novels. There is always a contrast presented in a symbiotic or rival relationship between two men, a freer and a more repressed character lacking will and, occasionally, moral courage. In the attempts of some of the early, caring, dependent introverts to carve out their own identities by incorporating something of the personality of the more unrepressed, often amoral, aggressive characters, we see this polarity—Jim Taylor and Johnnie Brown of *Johnnie Sahib*, Joe and deceased Dwight MacKendrick of *The Alien Sky*, Colin Craig and the Ramsays of *The Mark of the Warrior*, Tom Brent and Brian Saxby of *The Chinese Love Pavilion*. The depressive introvert-protagonist-observer, who lacks the sexual energy of the heroic or grandiose observed, admires, envies, and fears him or fears for him. He desires to rid himself of feelings of emptiness, generally and perhaps unconsciously, by introjecting some aspect of the personality of the extrovert. However, reminiscent of Conrad's Marlow, he usually watches the observed enter psychological territory onto which he dare not or cannot follow and develops ambivalent feelings about him. With the notable exception of their integration in *A Male Child*, the values of assertion and affection remain polarized in pre-*Quartet* novels.

The theme of psychic impotence in the earlier novels culminates in the image of the aging writer as cornered bull in *The Corrida at San Feliu*. From there it is a quantum leap to *The Raj Quartet* and the imprisonment of the protagonists not so much by psychological as by historical and social forces. Where the earlier novels are concerned with the largely unsuccessful quest for a definition of self, the later ones are written from the perspective of one who has found it in his art and projected his findings onto the world.[8] After his return to India in 1964 Scott discovered a metaphor of "cultural confrontation" which projected onto British India of the 1940s patterns already existing in his mind. Scott wrote to his daughter Sally in 1966 that since he published his second novel as his first, he had been working within the limitations demonstrated in that novel, "getting nearer and nearer to the ideas that belong, in a sense, to my youthful attitudes."[9] The themes perfected in *The Raj Quartet* are present in rudimentary form in the early novels, even in those set in contemporary London. The largely unsuccessful quest in the earlier novels for meaning, more abstractly for truth and a definition of self, becomes in *The Raj Quartet* a search for the psychological truth responsible for the related tragedies of British abandonment and division of India and the separation and sufferings of the English girl Daphne Manners and her anglicized Indian lover Hari Kumar.

The punitive voice of conscience which plagues a number of the earlier protagonists, most notably Thornhill, would become a nation's conscience or, rather, criticism of the lack of it. The neurotic preoccupation of Marion Hurst with a more ideal, illusory past, developed in *A Male Child,* set in London, would become the refusal of the British community to separate itself from the dead, idealized Raj. Scott's recognition in *The Birds of Paradise* that, despite attempts to bury it, the unhappiness of the present grew out of the past, would become an attempt to demonstrate as a novelist-historian that British policy was largely responsible for the abandonment of India and the consequent division of the subcontinent. The "too late" theme poorly used in *Johnnie Sahib* and revived in *The Chinese Love Pavilion* would be poignantly stated in the relationship of Edwina Crane to her murdered Indian colleague and would symbolize England's relationship with India.

A sense of unreality, in one form or another, pervades all of Scott's fiction and is related to his fascination with characters caught between two worlds. It is expressed, for example, in George Spruce's feelings about his childhood, where reality and illusion seem reversed, or in Tom Gower's feeling of "formlessness, an almost negative despair which was at once part of him and outside him, sustaining and suspending him between two worlds" (AS 140). In Scott's short story "After the Funeral,"[10] Cinderella is as good and selfless as she can be in taking care of her self-centered father and selfish sisters after her mother's death. Her reward is not marriage to the prince, however, but the *dream* of dancing with him as she listens in bed to the strains of music coming from the palace where her sisters are dancing.[11] The story ends here, with devastating irony, reminding us of Edward Hurst's, George Spruce's, Hari Kumar's, and Paul Scott's own unfulfilled aspirations to attend the university and have the kind of career and privilege to which it would lead. In Scott's fiction aspirations for happiness and fulfillment prove to be unattainable or ephemeral and therefore appear illusory, as one critic also noted when he described the writer's subject as the loss of an illusory paradise.[12] In *The Raj Quartet* the confusion of reality and illusion is experienced by a British community caught between two worlds, one dying and illusory, the other struggling to be born. Emphasizing the indifference of the fates to what men and women most want for themselves, the sense of unreality experienced by protagonists and antagonists in the later novels is present mainly in times of stress, a development which gained Scott dramatic impact and his reader's empathy.

If the early books are concerned with the search for identity, the later ones, from the writer's point of view, find the self in the true values of love shared by the protagonists and the nonself in the false values of power and privilege shared by the antagonists. The later novels show no such dimension as the dangerous hidden aggression of some of the earlier protagonists who espouse more humanitarian values. The most notable example is that of the would-be selfless Thornhill, whose creative unconscious drives him to take his own life together with that of his unfaithful wife. If the early novels are characterized by a yearning of the protagonists to incorporate the strength of the antagonists and occasionally see love as weakness, the later novels have no such dimension. Thornhill laments, even in himself, the subordination of love to the desire for power, and, like his character Thompson, he considers love the mere staunching of wounds. In the *Quartet*, however, Scott was able to give love un-equivocally the highest value, expelling aggression onto the nonself in the form of Ronald Merrick, "the dark side of us"[13] and the only character with any significant role in all four novels. We have met a variation of Merrick before; he is, for example, the embodiment of the power and mastery that Joe MacKendrick (himself yearning for the love he sees as weakness) longed to incorporate from his dead brother, Dwight.

The emotionally wounded, easily put-upon protagonists of the early novels stand in contrast to the strong-willed, life-affirming heroines and heroes of *The Raj Quartet* who, so far from suffering the feelings of emptiness common to their predecessors, remain un-diminished from within, regardless of harsh fates imposed by the outside world. It is not so much qualities that are lacking in the pro-tagonists but outside cruelty and social convention that imprison them and make illusions of their aspirations. In the later novels, feelings of emptiness are projected onto antagonists devoted to the sustaining of an illusion—of superiority, privilege, and permanence in India—and onto a universe indifferent to people's needs and de-sires. Where sexual energy (libido) in the earlier protagonists is im-prisoned inside the self, in *The Raj Quartet* love is strong in itself but often powerless in the external world, a life-affirming dynamic that incorporates the idea of tragedy.

Scott's mature philosophy concentrates on love and union as ele-ments of paradise, something suggested in *A Male Child* and touched on in *The Chinese Love Pavilion*. The impulse toward union, which exists on three levels and provides the structural strength of *The Raj Quartet*, is a result of the strengthening of the controlling sense of self expressed in the novels. We can see the change if we compare MacKendrick's search in the Indian bazaar in

The Alien Sky ("Somewhere . . . was understanding and love. Somewhere in the street there was himself to be found" [113]) and Thornhill's unsuccessful longing for "a glimpse of the reality behind the
illusion that man can care for someone other than himself" (CSF 213)
to Sister Ludmila's appreciation of the blindness that better enables
her to see "the reality behind the illusion" (J 132).

The Raj Quartet represents a defining of the self through the
strength of creative egalitarian love. "Creativity" and "vitality,"
"the freedom to experience spontaneous feelings,"[14] the idealization
of the natural and the instinctual that we saw in Daintree in *The
Birds of Paradise*, an objection (shared by Sarah Layton and Ahmed
Kasim) to "a *received* life" (D 592), these values are what Scott cele-
brates in the *Quartet*. They are opposed to the deadness of the false
self, which is projected in those novels in the conventions and in
feelings of racial and psychological superiority, of power and mastery.

Like Edwina Crane, Scott must have been looking for an image of
himself which would not diminish him, an image which allowed
him to live deeply, fully, which fused the libidinal and aggressive
sides of his being into one strong, loving, masculine self; the paradise of an integrated self is one definition of what had been lost. His
striving against forms or conventions as an impediment against
union, his admiration of Daphne's wholeness, expressed through
Sister Ludmila, can be seen as his desire to overcome the compart-
mentalization of self, to integrate the two selves expressed in *The
Alien Sky* or the several selves expressed in *The Bender* as Tim,
George, and Guy Spruce.[15] "Towards a more perfect union, a deeper
communion" represents for Scott not only a desire to communicate
with others but to unify his various compartmentalized selves into
one cohesive whole.

It also represents, however unconsciously, an attempt to unify
body and soul. Edward Thornhill and Thornhill's artist, Bruce Craddock, complain that they live too much in their heads, that art is
only a game. We think of Tom Brent in *The Chinese Love Pavilion*,
who found so much satisfaction in physical labor on the farm, when
Thornhill asks, "Isn't it better to have built one good strong bridge
or ploughed one straight furrow than to have scribbled away for years
trying to create order out of chaos"? (102–103). *The Raj Quartet*
demonstrates an increased capacity to open up to the full range of
experience, reflected in Daphne's insistence on living deeply by
crossing to the other side of the river, the Indian side, and emphasized in the contrast with MacKendrick's inability in *The Alien Sky*
to experience India and the full life of the body.

From the beginning, Scott was fascinated, even obsessed, by an India that Nigel Craddock in *The Corrida at San Feliu* saw as a cross between reality and fantasy, and this obsession had to have come before any historical interest.[16] If Scott saw India as what David Rubin calls "the source of light,"[17] it represents for him and in general for Western men and women the key to repressed sexuality. This is why the dominant imagery of the *Quartet* suggests imprisonment. In India, as Ernest Jones said years ago, the whole body lives. Heinz Kohut has used the term "tragic man" to describe a disunity of body and soul typical of our culture. This disunity is experienced intensely by characters who suffer a loss of the self. Kohut's theory is summarized below:

> At the "lower" level, it is an experience of wholeness in the body, groundedness in one's reality, continuity over time, and cohesiveness. At the "higher" level, it is the experience of integrity, meaningfulness, and purpose in the context of a lifetime. . . . the *experience* of self in its most complete form is not dualistic, but unitary.
>
>   . . . The tragedy of Kohut's "tragic man" is the conscious experience of the lack of wholeness and unity, indeed the experience of fragmentation, enfeeblement, and unrealized potential. The depression of tragic man is the awareness of *what could have been* with the achievement of wholeness compared with *what is* in the reality of his experience of fragmentation and enfeeblement.[18]

It is this experience, this sense of mourning an integrated self, that Scott projects onto the world of his fiction.

Scott had, we recall, returned from World War II cynical and disillusioned. He wrote, "My interest in the closing years of the British power in India is probably due to my feeling that, in India, the British came to the end of themselves as they were and have not yet emerged from the shock of their own liberation."[19] The liberation was, in part, from their illusions of grandeur. The false, idealized Raj must be seen psychoanalytically as a projection of the false grandiose self. British *"love"* for India *"never made manifest"* (J 147) is a projection of libidinal repression, also evident in the communication problems of (among others) Ed and Myra Thornhill and of Tusker and Lucy Smalley. Remembering Brent's and Scott's misplaced admiration of grandiose Saxby in *The Chinese Love Pavilion* (by the time Scott wrote *Staying On* what is great or large is falsely so), we can see by way of contrast in the elegiac tone of *The Birds of Paradise* and *The Raj Quartet* Scott's projected mourning over his true self, of what could have been, and—in his dismissal of the false grandeur of the Raj—a healthy embracing of its ordinariness.

Notes

Preface

1. Paul Scott to author, January 4, 1976 [1977], Paul Scott Collection, Special Collections, University of Tulsa McFarlin Library, Tulsa, Oklahoma (cited hereafter as Scott Collection).

2. Paul Scott, interview with author, New York, December 1977.

3. Patrick Swinden, *Paul Scott: Images of India*, p. 6.

4. M. M. Mahood, "Paul Scott's Guardians," *Yearbook of English Studies* 13 (1983): 253.

5. David Rubin, *After the Raj: British Novels of India Since 1947*, p. 151.

6. Roland Gant, "Paul Scott Remembered 1," in *The Making of "The Jewel in the Crown,"* pp. 116, 115. "To most discussion Paul brought a kind of lugubrious gaiety that was composed of mocking cynicism, hilarity in the contemplation of human vanity, trendiness and pomposity and a loathing of the phoney" (115).

7. Paul Scott called Bronowsky "a man of many personalities." Paul Scott, interview with author, Urbana, September 1975.

8. James Leasor, quoted in Gant, "Paul Scott Remembered 1," p. 112.

9. Hilary Spurling and Sally Scott, interviews with author, London, July 1988.

10. Thomas F. Staley confirms this impression in "The Meeting," in *After Paul: Paul Scott's Tulsa Years*, ed. Alice Lindsay Price, p. 2.

1. Paul Scott: A Biographical Sketch

1. Paul Scott, autobiographical sketch, 1965, Scott Collection. Much of the material in this chapter is taken from several additional unpublished and untitled autobiographical pieces available in the Scott Collection.

2. We are reminded of the enormous sensitivity with which Scott would portray unmarried elderly women. The aunts, not the mothers, are positive figures.

3. Peter Bewick Scott, interview with author, London, July 1988.

4. Hilary Spurling, *Paul Scott: A Life*, pp. 5, 13. Scott describes himself

as "impulsive, impatient, but a hard worker. Head in the clouds. Feet on the ground. Sometimes. A practical dreamer" (SR 4).

5. Paul Scott, autobiographical sketch, 1960, Scott Collection.

6. Ibid.

7. Also see Spurling, *Paul Scott*, pp. 9, 19.

8. Spurling, p. 71; Gant, "Paul Scott Remembered 1," pp. 114–115.

9. Peter Bewick Scott, interview with author, London, July 1988.

10. Nancy Edith Avery-Scott, interview with author, London, July 1988.

11. Hilary Spurling, interview with author, London, July 1988; Sally Scott identifies his age as fifteen (Sally Scott to author, April 1, 1989).

12. Spurling describes Paul Scott's father as distant, indifferent, and absent-minded, a man who lived in the past (*Paul Scott*, pp. 31–32, 50).

13. Ibid., p. 47.

14. Paul Scott, autobiographical sketch, 1965, Scott Collection.

15. Spurling, *Paul Scott*, pp. 53–66.

16. Ibid., pp. 70, 122.

17. Paul Scott to author, April 3, 1975, Scott Collection.

18. Spurling, *Paul Scott*, p. 94.

19. Ibid., p. 99.

20. Scott quoted these words from the *Kirkus* review in an April 2, 1966, letter to Dorothy Ganapathy, Scott Collection.

21. Carol Scott, interview with author, London, July 1979; Nancy Edith Avery-Scott, interview with author, London, July 1988.

22. Peter Bewick Scott, interview with author, London, July 1988.

23. He held five different titles: bookkeeper, accountant, chief accountant, finance manager, and company secretary, without appropriate increases in salary, and at all stages, he was the only person in the accounts department (WS 205).

24. Charles Pick, interview with author, London, July 1988.

25. Roland Gant, interview with author, London, July 1979; Spurling, *Paul Scott*, p. 176.

26. Sally Dennison, "Course Notes," in *After Paul: Paul Scott's Tulsa Years*, ed. Alice Lindsey Price, p. 26.

27. Paul Scott to Roland Gant, June 30, 1975, Scott Collection.

28. Gant, "Paul Scott Remembered 1," p. 112; Penny, as Elizabeth Avery, wrote English country childhood novels, among them *The Margaret Days* and *The Marigold Summer*.

29. Scott had reservations about the change, which was due to the Communist scare (Paul Scott to Adele Dogan [Horwitz], February 1, 1960, Scott Collection). Among his unpublished writings in the Scott Collection were an original radio comedy, "Sahibs and Memsahibs" ("The Colonel's Lady"), performed by leading lady Valerie White, and several drafts of an unperformed stage play, "The Situation," based on Kumar's prison interrogation.

30. Spurling, *Paul Scott*, p. 238; Dorothy Olding, interview with author, New York, April 1988. Scott had come to Harold Ober after using the Ann Watkins and William Morris agencies. Beginning with *The Chinese Love Pavilion*, Morrow's sales of the early novels came to roughly 3,000 copies of

each novel in Scott's lifetime, which represented an increase over sales of *A Male Child* (1,050) and *The Mark of the Warrior* (2,056).

31. Scott got half of the $17,000 (Spurling, *Paul Scott*, p. 237).

32. Scott had at one point turned down an offer of chief editor at Collins (Paul Scott to John Willey, August 28, 1957, Scott Collection).

33. *The Birds of Paradise* was a Book Society choice, but it sold one-half to two-thirds as many copies as *The Chinese Love Pavilion* (Spurling, *Paul Scott*, pp. 258–259).

34. *The Bender* was performed on television in 1964; see Robin Moore, *Paul Scott's Raj*, p. 205.

35. Spurling, *Paul Scott*, pp. 133, 128.

36. Driving sober, Scott would wobble down the middle of the road; drunk, he drove "straight and true" (Carol Scott, interview with author, London, July 1979).

37. Spurling, *Paul Scott*, pp. 251, 227–228.

38. Gant, "Paul Scott Remembered 1," p. 115.

39. Paul Scott to author, July 19, 1975.

40. Spurling, *Paul Scott*, p. 272.

41. Roland Gant, interview with author, London, July 1979.

42. Spurling, *Paul Scott*, p. 205.

43. Gant, "Paul Scott Remembered 1," p. 113.

44. Paul Scott to Dorothy Olding, July 6, 1965, Scott Collection.

45. Paul Scott to Tim Manderson, April 9, 1972, Scott Collection.

46. Paul Scott to Roland Gant, October 11, 1966, Scott Collection.

47. Dorothy Olding, interview with author, New York, April 1988.

48. Ibid. Bruce Hunter, Scott's literary agent and director of David Higham Associates, roughly estimates hardback sales of each of Scott's novels in his lifetime at between five and ten thousand (Bruce Hunter to author, December 8, 1988).

49. Roughly one hundred of the eight hundred-odd fiction and nonfiction books he reviewed between 1960 and 1977 were about India (Robin Moore, *Paul Scott's Raj*, p. 43). He reviewed for the *New Statesman, Books and Bookmen,* the *Times,* and the *Times Literary Supplement.* Additionally, he wrote on a regular basis a fortnightly review column in *Country Life* when reviewer Richard Church died in 1972. He had to read six new books and then write a two-thousand-word review of three or four (Paul Scott to author, November 19, 1974). Scott's novels did not lend themselves to serialization; unfortunately, attempts to serialize them were unsuccessful (Dorothy Olding, interview with author, New York, April 1988).

50. The New York figures are as follows by the time of his death in 1978: 10,554 copies of *The Jewel in the Crown;* 6,369 of *The Day of the Scorpion;* 4,451 of *The Towers of Silence;* and 3,781 of *A Division of the Spoils. Staying On* sold 8,733 copies (Dorothy Olding, interview with author, New York, April 1988).

51. Charles Pick, interview with author, London, July 1988.

52. Paul Scott to Charles Pick, July 11, 1972, Scott Collection.

53. Paul Scott to Roland Gant, February 15, 1976, Scott Collection.

54. Thomas F. Staley, "The Meeting," pp. 1–2.

55. Robin Moore, "The Historian's Novelist: Paul Scott and the Raj," audiotape of a lecture, November 19, 1987, Scott Collection. Also see Paul Scott, autobiographical sketch, 1965, Scott Collection.

56. Heinemann's distribution was delayed until spring of 1977; the publication was reissued in November 1984 (Charles Pick, interview with author, London, July 1988).

57. Thomas Staley, telephone interview with author, November 1977.

58. Paul Scott, interview with author, New York, December 1977.

2. The Early Novels

1. Patrick Swinden, *Paul Scott: Images of India*, p. 12.

2. Quoted in K. Bhaskara Rao, *Paul Scott*, p. 24.

3. See the untitled autobiographical sketch that Scott wrote for his Eyre and Spottiswoode publisher, Maurice Temple-Smith, on the occasion of the publication of *The Birds of Paradise*, pp. 1–2, Scott Collection. Scott uses his concern with the importance of work in people's lives to distinguish his characters from Forster's in "India: A Post-Forsterian View," pp. 118–119. He also claims elsewhere that a person's work is tied to a particular sense of deprivation.

4. See Scott's autobiographical sketch for Maurice Temple-Smith, Scott Collection.

5. For a discussion of this unconscious need, see Alice Miller, *The Drama of the Gifted Child: A Search for the True Self.* Scott's Edward Thornhill in *The Corrida at San Feliu* shares this need as the young man described in "The First Betrayal."

6. In Marion Hurst, Scott portrayed his own mother Frances, "mourning her lost poet." Spurling, *Paul Scott*, p. 170.

7. The parallels with Scott's life are striking. Not only had Edward's poems been published in a wartime series, but "The poor boy had wanted so desperately to go to University, but at 18 he had to go into an office, shipping at first, then . . . had to forego reading English literature" (74). The similarities suggest in Edward a view Scott may have had of himself; "[Edward] was treated . . . as if the sun rose and sank in him, but he knew it didn't. He knew he was a deceitful, lying little prig when he was a child" (176).

8. Paul Scott to Dorothy Ganapathy, February 20, 1965, Scott Collection.

9. Quoted in Paul Scott to Roland Gant, September 22, 1966, Scott Collection.

10. The setting was inspired by Scott's Officers Training School in Belgium.

11. Baksh bears a situational resemblance to the captured Indian National Army soldier Mohammed Baksh, who gets Teddie Bingham killed and Ronald Merrick wounded in *The Day of the Scorpion.*

12. Thayer Hobson to Paul Scott, June 27, 1957, Scott Collection.

13. Muriel Spark to Paul Scott, August 5, 1958, Scott Collection.

14. "For myself, the act of writing a novel is an act of asking questions, not answering them, My curiosity is more valuable to me than are my transient assumptions" (Paul Scott, autobiographical sketch, 1965, Scott Collection.

3. The Middle Novels I

1. Paul Scott to author, July 19, 1975, Scott Collection.

2. Peter Green to Paul Scott, July 16, 1958, Scott Collection. The letter, written before the novel was in its final form, is interesting for its encouragement and constructive criticism.

3. Paul Scott "Biographical note: Paul Scott, for J. B-H.," p. 2, Scott Collection.

4. Creepers were for Scott an image of suffocation and imprisonment. In one version of Colin Craig's recurrent nightmare, "The fat leaves and creepers had to be thrust aside, but every so often he was imprisoned by them and had to struggle to free himself" (MW 32). Barbara Batchelor, going mad in *The Towers of Silence*, is threatened by a thickening miasma of plants.

5. The character of Dora, who grew up in India and whose father was an officer in the Indian army, may have been inspired by M. M. Kaye.

6. David Rubin, *After The Raj: British Novels of India since 1947*, p. 114.

7. Rubin says, referring to a passage in Iris Murdoch's "The Sublime and the Beautiful," that the sensibility William exhibits in the *machan* is indicative of "the tolerance and objectivity of the great novelist" (ibid., p. 114).

8. C. Wrey Gardiner, *The Flowering Moment*, quoted in *The Birds of Paradise*, p. 10.

4. The Middle Novels II

1. *The Bender* was inspired by one of Scott's own benders that, unknown to his wife, ended in an impulsive and not very serious attempt at suicide. He claimed he did not want to write the novel but had to (Paul Scott to Muriel Spark, November 9, 1961, Scott Collection).

2. Swinden makes this claim but finds it grounds for dismissing the novel as one lacking in "moral seriousness and psychological density" (*Paul Scott: Images of India*, p. 17).

3. Additionally, Scott here borrows from the facts of his brother's life and his father's. Unlike George, he was himself the favored son and, like George, his father was often in difficulty with the bank manager. Scott's great aunt, Ada Lindsey, gave the suggestion of her name to George's aunt, Ada Lisle, who was probably inspired by his mother's sister Ruth. Spurling confirms that Frances Scott provided the model for Vi Spruce (*Paul Scott*, p. 247).

4. Paul Scott, interview with author, Urbana, September 1975.

5. This was the same assignment Scott later gave to his creative writing students at Tulsa (Sally Dennison, "Course Notes," p. 23).

6. Scott may have been thinking of Roland Gant, who reports that they used to write comic obituaries of one another ("Paul Scott Remembered 1," p. 115).

7. Scott detested his great uncle, Mark Scott, a wealthy Yorkshire mill owner (Spurling, *Paul Scott*, pp. 3, 26). Mark Scott probably inspired Thornhill's Uncle James.

8. Scott felt that literature was "not a fit subject for academic study" because it meant studying "an illusion under the illusion that it is reality" (Paul Scott to Sally Scott, February 18, 1969, Scott Collection).

9. "Paul spoke about the difficulty of writing, about his *duende*, a Spanish demon, who constantly hissed at him that he was no good, that he didn't have it in him to write anything worthwhile. It was only by taming this *duende* that he could then go on and write the next novel" (Dennison, "Course Notes," p. 25).

5. Origins of *The Raj Quartet*

1. "Writing is a criticism of life with a point of view attached. It's an ordering of chaos," Paul Scott told his creative writing class at the University of Tulsa (Dennison, "Course Notes," p. 24). Nearing the completion of *The Jewel in the Crown*, he wrote to Dorothy Ganapathy that although the novel would be about 175,000 words, "I shall have written a quarter of a million, including discarded versions and sequences" (April 18, 1965, Scott Collection).

2. The correspondence shows an unintentionally humerous contrast between Narayanji's excitement at having his master at last come to visit his village, with its "modern" conveniences, and Scott's secretly appalled response to the devastatingly primitive conditions.

3. Paul Scott to Jean Leroy, April 9, 1966, Scott Collection. A variation of the quoted passage is found in "Method: The Mystery and the Mechanics," pp. 80–81.

4. Scott said that Daphne Manners was based on an Australian girl, Carolyn Davies, and Kumar on her boyfriend, Neil Ghosh, whose character he did not like as well as Kumar's. Paul Scott, interview with author, Urbana, September 1975.

5. Francine Ringold, "A Conversation with Paul Scott," *Nimrod* 21 (Fall/Winter 1976): 22.

6. Ibid., p. 31. In her memories of Paul Scott's creative writing classes at the University of Tulsa, Sally Dennison reports the same thought expressed in a slightly different order: "Begin with a central image. . . . You see the characters and the expressions on their faces. From that expression you see what situation they're in. These characters produce other characters. The characters produce tension, tension produces structure, structure produces words, and the words produce the total image" (Dennison, "Course Notes," p. 31).

7. Paul Sharrad, "The Books behind the Film: Paul Scott's *Raj Quartet*," *East-West Film Journal* 1 (1987): 82.

8. Paul Scott to Dorothy Ganapathy, July 6, 1966, July 29, 1966, and September 5, 1965, Scott Collection; see especially the last, with its description of Ganapathy's Heathrow airport departure for Bombay after a London visit.

9. See Scott's description in "Enoch Sahib: A Slight Case of Cultural Shock," in *On Writing and the Novel*, pp. 129–130. His experience with some English in the Juhu hotel lounge and their deliberate slight of his Indian companions is recaptured in "An Evening at the Club" in *The Jewel in the Crown*, pp. 169–209.

10. Paul Scott to Dorothy Ganapathy, July 20, 1966, Scott Collection. When I once suggested to Scott that he could have been the narrator, he wrote, "No, not quite. Nearly. But not. . . . Basically this writer/traveller/ stranger is a mechanism for achieving both detachment and involvement. In other words I can't easily think of me as me. There's always, in any novel, that invisible character, the person who is writing the book, the man who has to be *convinced* that it all happened, and so convinces you because he tells you it does" (Paul Scott to author, November 19, 1974, Scott Collection).

11. Paul Scott to Dorothy Olding, October 26, 1975, Scott Collection.

12. Ibid.

13. Nina Baym discussed this characteristic of Hawthorne's in "Hawthorne's *Scarlet Letter:* Producing and Maintaining an American Literary Classic," University of Illinois Twelfth Humanities Lecture, Urbana, April 13, 1988. And like Hawthorne, Scott sometimes uses a certain factual ambivalence in the creation of a legend, whether in the story of Lieutenant Hakinawa, the gentle Japanese officer in *The Chinese Love Pavilion* who is driven to suicide either by the ghosts of the pavilion's garden or his love for Teena Chang, or in the various versions of the story of MacGregor in *The Jewel in the Crown* and whether he burned the Bibighar because he considered it an abomination or because he lost the Indian girl he loved to an Indian boy.

14. Paul Scott to Dorothy Ganapathy, July 29, 1966; to B. V. V. Narayana Doss, January 14, 1964, Scott Collection.

15. This obsessive concentration led to a certain absentmindedness. See his description of the writer as "self-absorbed, living in his mind to an extent that often makes him personally rather difficult to live with" (FF 29).

16. Paul Scott to K. B. Rao, October 16, 1975, Scott Collection.

17. Roland Gant, interview with author, London, July 1979.

18. Ringold, "A Conversation with Paul Scott," p. 27; Paul Scott to David Higham, March 29, 1965; to M. M. Kaye, March 21, 1971, Scott Collection.

19. Paul Scott to Dorothy Ganapathy, April 18, 1965, Scott Collection.

20. James Leasor, quoted in Gant, "Paul Scott Remembered 1," p. 112.

21. Rubin has pointed out the similarity in *After the Raj*.

22. Paul Scott to author, February 9, 1975, Scott Collection.

23. There is a reference in *A Male Child* to John Steele of *The Alien Sky* doing "experimental farming in a place called Ooni, in India" (39).

24. He said this repeatedly to his students at the University of Tulsa. See Dennison, "Course Notes," p. 24; see also Paul Scott to Dorothy Ganapathy, July 22, 1965, Scott Collection.

25. Paul Scott to D. H. Burjorgee, January 25, 1976, Scott Collection.

26. Paul Scott, interview with author, September 1975, Urbana. Scott also told University of Maryland doctoral student "Bandy" Burjorjee, "People you meet in real life run through your mind, subsequently, like frames in a cinematograph film. Sometimes you freeze an image momentarily, and set them off on imaginary courses with different personalities and different backgrounds and histories, but somehow reassured by their actuality" (Paul Scott to D. M. Burjorjee, January 25, 1976, Scott Collection). He may have been blending and transforming the characters of his daughters to create an ideal daughter in Sarah and a difficult daughter in Susan. Certainly, they were mixed with other characters, as he wrote to Burjorjee, "Sarah and Susan bear some physical resemblance to two girls I met in the NWFP whose father (a brigadier) was a prisoner of war."

27. The woman who was the model for Daphne Manners suggested to Scott in Calcutta in 1964 that he meet "Sister" Teresa (Her "right . . . to be called Sister, let alone Mother, was being questioned in Calcutta"). He decided against it, however, because he had already imagined her character (Paul Scott to author, December 31, 1975, Scott Collection). Both the fictional Conway and the real Corfield had their own ideas for keeping princely power, opposed official policy, advised against signing the Instrument of Accession, and ended by delaying integration only to make the settlements more costly for the maharajahs; Scott suggested as much to Burjorjee, adding, "But MAK is a Muslim and did not quarrel" (Paul Scott to D. M. Burjorjee, June 7, 1976, Scott Collection).

6. Overview of *The Raj Quartet*

1. Compare Scott's use of the narrator with Thackeray's. His acknowledged influences are Eliot, Ibsen, Chekhov, and Thackeray (Paul Scott to author, August 15, 1974). Also note his unsentimental adaptation of *Vanity Fair*'s war-loss / pregnant wife / insanity theme in *The Day of the Scorpion*.

2. Nancy Wilson Ross presents this view of Scott's work as historical novel in this unusual sense; see "Unsung Singer of Hindustan," *Saturday Review*, June 24, 1972, p. 59.

3. For this reason, Scott did not believe he had written historical novels. In a WILL television interview with announcer Grace Babakhanian and history professor Blair Kling on September 15, 1975, at the University of Illinois, he claimed that he could not project himself back into the past because he did not have "that kind of gift."

4. Georg Lukacs, *The Historical Novel*, trans. Hannah Mitchell and Stanley Mitchell, p. 42.

5. George Orwell, *Burmese Days*, p. 247.

6. Shirley Hopkinson, review of *The Day of the Scorpion*, *Library Journal*, October 15, 1968, p. 3800.

7. Max Beloff, "The End of the Raj: Paul Scott's Novels as History," *Encounter* 272 (May 1976): 66.

8. Scott said that he was not representing a historian's view, that "the

images are those of one who was/is emotionally involved" (Paul Scott to author, October 26, 1975, Scott Collection).

9. Scott, taking this idea from critic Walter Allen, says, "The India in the novels I write about India is used as a metaphor [for my view of life]. If I write about Anglo-India in 1942 I do so not only because I find that period lively and dramatic but because it helps me to express the fullness of what I'm thinking and feeling about the world I live in" (IPF 116–117).

10. Benita Parry, "Paul Scott's Raj," *South Asian Review* 8 (July/October 1975): 359.

11. See, for example, Rao, *Paul Scott*, p. 128.

12. Paul Scott, interview with author, Urbana, September 1975; also see Paul Scott, draft blurb to *The Raj Quartet*, Scott Collection.

13. ". . . the last division of all, which has to be overcome, is that of the colour of the skin" (draft blurb to *The Raj Quartet*, Scott Collection).

7. The Illusion of Principle: British Policy in India

1. Sharrad, "The Books Behind the Film," p. 82.

2. "By liberal humanism I mean, broadly, the human consciousness of human dignity that began with the Renaissance and came to an end in the form we knew it in the Second World War and its aftermath. Our imperialism was as much an expression of it as our reforming zeal. We are still . . . bent on reforms . . . But the mind is detached. It is practical rather than inspired"; see Paul Scott, "Meet the Author: Manchester," in *On Writing and the Novel*, p. 70.

3. Scott said that it was the sense of alienation that caused the tragedy: "I think the promise was unfulfilled because the English never really identified with their colonies. . . . The administration always felt themselves in a sense in exile. I don't think you can successfully influence a country . . . if you feel constantly that you're abroad." (WILL television interview, University of Illinois, September 15, 1975).

4. Paul Scott to author, October 26, 1975, Scott Collection.

5. "India," said Scott, "has always been an enormous bore to the English people" (interview with author, Urbana, September 1975).

6. Paul Scott, "The Raj," in *John Kenneth Galbraith Introduces India*, ed. Frank Moraes and Edward Howe, p. 75.

7. Francis Hutchins, *The Illusion of Permanence: British Imperialism in India*.

8. Michael Edwardes, *The Last Years of British India*, pp. 47–48.

9. Ibid., p. 202.

10. Paul Scott to author, December 31, 1975, Scott Collection.

11. Scott himself wrote, "A novel that has any serious claim to be a work of art, will always, in its essence, defy the attempt to render it down to its chemical ingredients" (MM 76).

12. Parry, "Paul Scott's Raj," pp. 159–160. Scott would have agreed: "Nothing is worse for a novel than for the novelist to see all sides of a question and fail to support one. You must commit yourself," (MM 79).

13. Scott was surprised and amused to receive from General Mohan Singh (see Merrick's letter in "A Question of Loyalty" [TS 135–142] and "The Circuit House" [D 418–423]) a letter "saying how much he appreciated this English attempt to convey the INA situation fairly" (Paul Scott to author, April 14, 1976, Scott Collection).

14. Paul Scott, review of *The Closed Harbour* by James Hanley, *Times Literary Supplement*, November 11, 1971, p. 676.

15. Scott wrote that "for the majority of people the times are always out of joint. . . . there are areas of the world, times/places in history, when this disagreeable fact is especially dramatically worked out (conflicts between nations taking momentarily the place of conflicts between individuals)" (Paul Scott to author, October 26, 1975, Scott Collection).

16. Maxwell Geismar, Afterward to *The Scarlet Letter* by Nathaniel Hawthorne (New York: Washington Square Press, 1955), pp. 277–279.

8. The Tragic Pattern

1. Ringold, "A Conversation with Paul Scott," p. 22.

2. Paul Scott to author, October 29, 1975, Scott Collection. In the midst of his excitement about the rave reviews of *The Jewel in the Crown*, Scott wrote to Dorothy Ganapathy, "Today—as in all periods when personal happiness is at its height—have had the sad news that my elder brother is in hospital with a completely detached retina of the left eye. . . . Don't know how to break this news to my aged mother, who is virtually blind herself. How short-lived is personal happiness" (July 23, 1966, Scott Collection).

3. See Arthur Miller, "Tragedy and the Common Man," in *The Idea of Tragedy*," ed. Carl Benson and Taylor Littleton, p. 70.

4. As early as *The Mark of the Warrior*, the village of Khudabad, the "Place of God" (102), was empty. One meaning of Khudabad, in Urdu and Farsi, is the "Abode of God."

5. See Prosser Hall Frye, "Romance and Tragedy," and Joseph Wood Krutsch, "The Modern Temper," in *The Idea of Tragedy*, pp. 27, 65.

6. Sally Scott, interview with author, London, July 1988.

7. One wonders whether Duleep Singh lent his name to the creation of Duleep Kumar. Duleep Singh was a famous "English" Indian who converted to Christianity and was made wealthy by Queen Victoria but stripped of his riches when he recanted and died in poverty.

8. Miller describes this as the tragic flaw in "Tragedy and the Common Man," p. 69.

9. "Perhaps only people who sacrifice themselves are truly memorable. . . . Sometimes they are memorable as misguided fools (Paul Scott to author, October 26, 1975, Scott Collection).

10. The expression is Scott's, used in other contexts. Scott once said that in writing one should "*risk all!* Be willing to use people you know, but use literary tact" (Dennison, "Course Notes," p. 26); and also *The Jewel in the Crown*, pp. 205, 423.

11. Paul Scott to author, October 26, 1975, Scott Collection.

9. Antagonists and Protagonists: Insular Form against Union

1. Beloff, "The End of the Raj," p. 66.

2. "Man-bap. . . . It meant Mother-Father, the relationship of the *raj* to India, of a man like Colonel Layton to the men in his regiment, of a district officer to the people of his district, of Barbie herself to the children she had taught. Man-bap, I am your father and your mother" (T 275).

3. "You can't be English and alive without being sensitive to the class problem. . . . I don't think an English writer can write a novel without . . . class being in the background, even if it's not consciously written in; class can't be detached from the English novel" (Paul Scott, interview with author, Urbana, September 1975).

4. The phrase is used allegorically in *The Jewel in the Crown* (146–147) in a story of the Bibighar which describes the unconsummated love of a prince for a singer.

10. Psychological Defenses and Thwarted Union

1. Carl Jung, "The Dreamlike World of India," in *Civilization in Transition*, trans. R. F. C. Hull, p. 518.

2. E. M. Forster, *A Passage to India*, pp. 150, 149.

3. See Norman O. Brown, *Life against Death: The Psychoanalytical Meaning of History.*

4. Otare Mannoni, in *Prospero and Caliban: The Psychology of Colonization*, writes that Westerners attracted by the colonial situation are often immature personalities drawn to a world without people, the better to occupy it with figures from their unconscious minds (pp. 101–102). Philip Mason Woodruff, in his introduction, holds Mannoni's theory of the colonial situation on Madagascar valid for what he knew of India after many years spent in the Indian Civil Service.

5. Sigmund Freud, "On the Universal Tendency to Debasement in the Sphere of Love," in *The Standard Edition of the Complete Psychoanalytical Works of Sigmund Freud*, ed. and trans. James Strachey, 11:189.

6. Edwina Crane's thought (J 55) reflects Scott's comment: "The bowels play an important part in one's emotional life" (IPF 116).

7. *The New Encyclopaedia Britannica Micropaedia*, 15th ed., s.v. "Siva."

8. Scott was unaware of the association when he wrote the *Quartet* (interview with author, September 1975).

9. Scott was concerned that these lines were interpreted as sentimental (Parry, "Paul Scott's Raj," p. 363): "I was of course . . . thinking of them as young Englishmen who were better-nourished than they would have been if the empire had never existed. Physically—not spiritually." As a demonstration of his point, Scott mentions the "dialogue between Perron and Purvis, and . . . between Perron and Mr. Hapgood, the Banker in Bombay" in *A Division of the Spoils* (Paul Scott to author, November 22, 1975, Scott Collection). If there is a latent sense of India as psychically enriching (an unrecognized part of oneself) in the stylized language of these lines, it is solidly

grounded in the unconscious sense of India as body, a significance which excludes sentimentality.

10. "Dionysian" implies eroticism in all of life, not just the sexual function.

11. Symbol, Structure, and Texture

1. Georg Lukacs, *The Historical Novel*, p. 42.

2. "If the symbol can be justified it is best to use it for all it is worth, to be honest about it, to say: This is my symbol and this is what it means. I dislike symbols that remain obscure, I fancy my leg is being pulled or that the author isn't sure himself or his symbol. Either way his illusion suffers" (Paul Scott, "Imagination in the Novel," in *On Writing and the Novel*, p. 28).

3. Salman Rushdie, "Outside the Whale," *American Film* 10 (January 1985): 70.

4. See Christopher Hitchens's criticism of Rushdie's remarks in "A Sense of Mission: *The Raj Quartet, Grand Street* 4 (Winter 1985): 189–199. See also the comparison of Scott and Forster in Chapter 6.

5. Barbara Grizzuti Harrison, "Indian Chic: What They Didn't Tell You in *The Jewel in the Crown* and *"A Passage to India,"* Ms, March 1985, p. 30.

6. On another level, Daphne is a symbol of England or soul, and her rape symbolizes the body's vengeance on the mind for their separation.

7. See Catherine Belsey's discussion of the "classic realist" text in *Critical Practice*, pp. 67–84.

8. Scott's favorite definition of a book was borrowed from Bernard Bergonzi, professor of English at the University of Warwick: "A small, hard, rectangular object, whose pages are bound along one edge into fixed covers, and numbered consecutively" (FF 9).

12. Staying On after the Raj

1. Scott called *The Bender* "a sad comedy of London life" (IPF 120) and *Staying On* his "Indian *Bender*" (Paul Scott to author, July 19, 1975, and May 9, 1976, Scott Collection).

2. The circumstances of the death of Paul Scott's father may have provided some inspiration for Tusker Smalley's death. Whereas Tusker had a fatal heart attack, Mrs. Boolabhoy's eviction letter in his hand, Tom Scott died in his mid-eighties after bronchitis led to pneumonia, not long after learning he was to be evicted from his rented home.

3. The scene was probably inspired by his learning of the death in the water closet of Peter Goodbody, an acquaintance who had stayed on in India (Spurling, *Paul Scott*, p. 379). He had hoped the man would be a source of information (Paul Scott to author, July 19, 1975, Scott Collection).

13. Paul Scott and His Fiction

1. Norman N. Holland, "Unity Identity Text Self," *PMLA* 90 (1975): 814, 815.

2. Interview with Sally Scott, London, July 1988.

3. Kram with his existent and nonexistent brother is reminiscent of George Spruce and his brothers in *The Bender*. Also of interest is Scott's comment that "writing fiction is the act of an imposter (quoted in Spurling, *Paul Scott*, p. 151). According to Spurling, Scott could "call all his life on a capacious repertoire of character parts, or alter egos plucked out of the air to relieve his feelings" (ibid., p. 71).

4. Alice Miller, *The Drama of the Gifted Child*, p. 12. Miller is quoting D. W. Winnicott.

5. The term "false self" is Winnicott's. According to Miller, "Grandiosity is the defense against depression" and seeks to save the self-object (already lost in early childhood) "through the illusion of achievement . . ."; depression is the defense against the deep pain over the loss of the self" (ibid., pp. 38, 63). Furthermore, "the combination of alternating phases of grandiosity and depression . . . are two sides of . . . the 'false self' [Winnicott's term]" (43).

6. Paul Scott, *I, Gerontius: A Trilogy: The Creation—The Dream—The Cross*, Resurgam Younger Poets Series, No. 5, p. 2.

7. See Heinz Kohut and his discussion of the effect on the child of the "flawed parental self" ("Introspection, Empathy, and the Semi-Circle of Mental Health," *International Journal of Psycho-Analysis* 63 [1982]: 404).

8. Here the comment of his friend Ruth Sansom is of interest: "The only time Paul's two halves found unity was when he was writing." Quoted in Spurling, *Paul Scott*, p. 133.

9. Paul Scott to Sally Scott, February 18, 1966, Scott Collection. Art was an ideal perfection which could be approached but not attained. He says elsewhere: "A book contains one's limits imprisoned in text, never the perfection of fantasy for which one strives."

10. Dying, Scott knew the story would be published in hardcover after his death and, grinning wickedly, told Roland Gant, "I picked a good title, didn't I" (Preface to *After the Funeral*, p. xiii). It was first published in the London *Times* at Christmas 1977 (Dennison, "Course Notes," p. 27).

11. Scott wrote a preliminary version of the story for his students at Tulsa as an example of what he wanted them to do for an assignment that involved writing a fairy tale (Dennison, "Course Notes," p. 27). The published story is exquisitely illustrated by Sally Scott. For years her father had planned to do a series of fairy tales "without the magic" if she would illustrate them (Sally Scott to author, April 1, 1989).

12. Swinden, *Paul Scott*, p. 2.

13. In corroboration, James Leasor sees Scott during his army days as Ronald Merrick. See Spurling, *Paul Scott*, p. 366.

14. Miller, *The Drama of the Gifted Child*, pp. 56–57.

15. I am indebted to Hilary Spurling for the view of Tim Spruce as another side of Paul Scott.

16. In this opinion I differ from Robin Moore and the views expressed in the historical lecture on Scott, "The Historian's Novelist," Scott Collection.

17. Rubin, *After the Raj*, p. 50.

18. Stephen M. Johnson, *Humanizing the Narcissistic Style*, pp. 61–62.

19. Paul Scott, autobiographical sketch, 1965, Scott Collection.

Bibliography

Works by Paul Scott

After the Funeral. Preface by Roland Gant. Illustrations by Sally Scott. An-
  doversford, England: Whittington Press and William Heinemann, 1979.
The Alien Sky. 1953. Reprint. St. Albans, England: Panther, Granada, 1975.
  U.S. edition: *Six Days in Marapore.* New York: Doubleday, 1953.
"The Appointment." Draft opening to a novel. Scott Collection, McFarlin
  Library, University of Tulsa.
Autobiographical sketch, 1960. 6 pp. Scott Collection, McFarlin Library,
  University of Tulsa.
Autobiographical sketch, 1965. 3 pp. Scott Collection, McFarlin Library,
  University of Tulsa.
Autobiographical sketch, written for Maurice Temple-Smith, on the occa-
  sion of the publication of *The Birds of Paradise,* with a note to David
  Higham. 3 pp. Scott Collection, McFarlin Library, University of Tulsa.
The Bender. 1963. Reprint. St. Albans, England: Panther, Granada, 1975.
"Biographical Note: Paul Scott, for J. B-H [John Bright-Holmes]." 3 pp. Scott
  Collection, McFarlin Library, University of Tulsa.
The Birds of Paradise. 1962. Reprint. St. Albans, England: Panther, Granada,
  1975.
"The Careerist." Unfinished novel in several drafts. Scott Collection, Mc-
  Farlin Library, University of Tulsa.
The Chinese Love Pavilion. London: Eyre and Spottiswoode, 1960. U.S. edi-
  tion: *The Love Pavilion.* New York: William Morrow, 1960.
"The Colonel's Lady." Outline for television comedy. Scott Collection,
  McFarlin Library, University of Tulsa.
The Corrida at San Feliu. 1964. Reprint. St. Albans, England: Panther, Gra-
  nada, 1974.
The Day of the Scorpion. 1968. Reprint. London: Mayflower, 1970.
A Division of the Spoils. London: William Heinemann, 1975; New York:
  William Morrow, 1975.
Draft blurb for *The Raj Quartet.* 1976. 2 pp. Scott Collection, McFarlin Li-
  brary, University of Tulsa.

"The Form and Function of the Novel." 1973. Revision of "The Architecture of the Arts: The Novel." Scott Collection, McFarlin Library, University of Tulsa.

I, Gerontius: A Trilogy; The Creation—The Dream—The Cross. Resurgam Younger Poets, no. 5. London: Favil Press, 1941.

"India: A Post-Forsterian View." In *Essays by Divers Hands*, ed. Mary Stocks. New Series 36. London: Oxford University Press, 1970.

The Jewel in the Crown. 1966. Reprint. St. Albans, England: Panther, Granada, 1973.

Johnnie Sahib. 1952. Reprint. London: Mayflower, 1968.

A Male Child. 1956. Reprint. St. Albans, England: Panther, Granada, 1974.

"Mango Rain." Also entitled "Married with Two Children." Unfinished novel in several drafts. Scott Collection, McFarlin Library, University of Tulsa.

The Mark of the Warrior. 1958. Reprint. St. Albans, England: Panther, Granada, 1979.

"Mylor Creek." *Poetry Quarterly* 3 (Spring 1941): 24–25.

On Writing and the Novel. Ed. Shelley C. Reece. New York: William Morrow, 1987. Also published as *My Appointment with the Muse.* London: William Heinemann, 1986. Includes "Imagination in the Novel" (1961); "Aspects of Writing" (1965); "Meet the Author: Manchester" (1967); "Method: The Mystery and the Mechanics" (1967); "The Architecture of the Arts: The Novel" (1967); "Enoch Sahib: A Slight Case of Cultural Shock" (1969); " The Yorkshire Post Fiction Award" (1971); "After Marabar: Britain and India, A Post-Forsterian View" (1972); "Literature and the Social Conscience: The Novel" (1972); "A Writer Takes Stock" (1973); "Notes for Talk and Reading at Stamford Grammar School" (1975). These essays, often in several versions, are also available in the Scott Collection.

"Paul Scott—Biographical Details, Etc." ["after 1972"]. 2 pp. Scott Collection, McFarlin Library, University of Tulsa.

Pillars of Salt. In *Four Jewish Plays*, ed. H. R. Rubenstein. London and Southampton: Camelot Press, Victor Gollancz, 1948.

"The Raj." In *John Kenneth Galbraith Introduces India*, ed. Frank Moraes and Edward Howe. London: Andre Deutsch, 1974.

Review of *The Break-up of British India*, by B. N. Pandey, and *The Great Divide*, by H. V. Hodston. *Times Literary Supplement*, October 30, 1969, pp. 1257–1258.

Review of *The Closed Harbour*, by James Hanley. *Times Literary Supplement*, November 11, 1971, p. 675.

Review of Conrad Studies. *Times Literary Supplement*, December 26, 1968, p. 1450; and November 3, 1966, pp. 993–994.

Review of *The Continent of Circe*, by Nirad C. Chaudhuri. *Times Literary Supplement*, December 2, 1965, p. 1093.

Review of *Gandhi*, by Geoffrey Ashe. *Times Literary Supplement*, April 11, 1968, p. 368.

Review of *Servant of India*, by Martin Gilbert, and *Diaries of Sir James Dunlop Smith. Times Literary Supplement*, May 18, 1967, p. 418.

"A Small Hard Rectangular Object." 1976. Scott Collection, McFarlin Library, University of Tulsa.
"Scott's Raj—Or India Returned": Outline for a Possible TV Book Programme, For Melvyn Bragg." Autobiographical piece written for the publication of *A Division of the Spoils*, May 1975. Scott Collection, McFarlin Library, University of Tulsa.
Staying On. London: William Heinemann, 1976; New York: William Morrow, 1976.
"The Situation." Drafts of a stage play, c. 1969–1970. Scott Collection, McFarlin Library, University of Tulsa.
The Towers of Silence. 1971. Reprint. St. Albans, England: Panther, Granada, 1973.

Criticism, Commentaries, and Selected Reviews

Ableman, Paul. "Paul Scott: A Comic Vision?" *Books and Bookmen* 24 (November 1978): 48–49.
Appasamy, S. P. "The Withdrawal: A Survey of Paul Scott's Trilogy of Novels on India." In *Literary Studies: Homage to Dr. A. Sivaramasubramonia*, ed. K. P. K. Menon, M. Manuel, and K. Ayappa Paniker. Trivandrum, India: Aiyer Memorial Committee and St. Joseph's Press, 1973.
Banerjee, Jacqueline. "A Living Legacy: An Indian View of Paul Scott's India." *London Magazine* 20 (April/May 1980): 97–104.
Beloff, Max. "The End of the Raj: Paul Scott's Novels as History." *Encounter* 272 (May 1976): 65–70.
Boyer, Allen. "Love, Sex, and History in *The Raj Quartet*." *Modern Language Quarterly* 46 (March 1985): 64–80.
Burjorjee, D. M. "*The Raj Quartet*: A Literary Event." *New Quarterly* 2 (1977): 121–128.
Copley, Anthony. "The Politics of Illusion: Paul Scott's *The Raj Quartet*." *Indo-British Review* 11 (1984): 58–73.
Degi, Bruce J. "Paul Scott's Indian National Army: *The Mark of the Warrior* and *The Raj Quartet*." *CLIO: A Journal of Literature, History, and the Philosophy of History* 18 (Fall 1988): 41–54.
Dennison, Sally. "Course Notes." In *After Paul: Paul Scott's Tulsa Years*, ed. Alice Lindsay Price, pp. 20–33. Tulsa, Oklahoma: HCE Publications/ Riverrun Arts, 1988.
Farrell, J. G. "Indian Identities." Rev. of *A Division of the Spoils*. *Times Literary Supplement*, May 23, 1975, p. 555.
Gant, Roland. "Paul Scott." *Bookseller*, March 11, 1978.
Gant, Roland. "Paul Scott Remembered 1." In *The Making of "The Jewel in the Crown*," pp. 111–116. New York: St. Martin's Press, 1983.
Giles, Frank. "Real Rubies of the Raj." *Sunday Times*, December 4, 1977, p. 16.
Gooneratne, Yasmine. "Paul Scott's *Staying On:* Finale in a Minor Key." *Journal of Indian Writing in English* 9 (July 1981): 1–12.

Greenberger, Alan J. *The British Image of India: A Study in the Literature of Imperialism, 1880–1960.* London: Oxford University Press, 1969.

Green, Peter. "Casting Off the White Man's Burden." Review of *A Division of the Spoils* and *The Raj Quartet. Washington Post,* August 10, 1975.

Granada Television. *The Making of "The Jewel in the Crown."* New York: St. Martin's Press, 1983.

Hamilton, Iain. Review of *The Day of the Scorpion. Daily Telegraph,* September 12, 1968.

———. Review of *The Jewel in the Crown. Daily Telegraph,* July 28, 1966.

Harrison, Barbara Grizzuti. "Indian Chic: What They Didn't Tell You in *The Jewel in the Crown* and *A Passage to India." Ms,* March 1985, pp. 28, 30.

Hitchens, Christopher. "A Sense of Mission: *The Raj Quartet." Grand Street* 4 (Winter 1985): 180–199.

Hopkinson, Shirley. Review of *The Day of the Scorpion. Library Journal* 93 (October 1968): 3800.

James, Richard Rhodes. "In the Steps of Paul Scott." *Listener* 101 (March 1979): 359–361.

Johnson, Richard M. "Sayed's Trial in Paul Scott's *A Division of the Spoils:* The Interplay of History, Theme, and Purpose." *Library Chronicle of the University of Texas* 38 (1986): 76–91.

Kaye, M. M. "Paul Scott Remembered 2." In *The Making of "The Jewel in the Crown,"* pp. 116–118. New York: St. Martin's Press, 1983.

Keating, H. R. F. "Last Days of the Raj." Review of *A Division of the Spoils. Country Life,* May 1, 1975, pp. 1144–1145.

Khattak, Zahir Jang. "British Novelists Writing about India-Pakistan's Independence: Christine Weston, John Masters, Ruth Prawer Jhabvala, and Paul Scott." Ph.D. diss., Tufts University, 1987.

Knightly, Philip. Review of "Imperial Triumph." *The Raj Quartet. Sunday Times,* May 4, 1975.

Leonard, John. "Love and Death in India." Review of *Staying On. New York Times,* August 21, 1977.

Levin, Martin. Review of *The Towers of Silence. New York Times Book Review,* February 20, 1972.

Lister, Richard. Review of *The Jewel in the Crown. Evening Standard,* July 19, 1976.

Mahood, M. M. "Paul Scott's Guardians." *Yearbook of English Studies* 13 (1983): 244–258.

Mellors, John. "Raj Mahal: Paul Scott's Indian Quartet." *London Magazine* 15 (June/July 1975): 62–67.

McBratney, John. "East-West Meetings under the Raj: Rudyard Kipling, E. M. Forster, and Paul Scott." Ph.D. diss., University of California–Berkeley, 1987.

McBratney, John. "The Raj Is All the Rage: Paul Scott's *The Raj Quartet* and Colonial Nostalgia." *North Dakota Quarterly* 55 (Spring 1987): 204–209.

Moore, Robin. "The Historian's Novelist: Paul Scott and the Raj." Audiotape of lecture, November 19, 1987. Scott Collection, McFarlin Library, University of Tulsa.

————. *Paul Scott's Raj.* London: William Heinemann, 1990.

Moorhead, Caroline. "Getting Engrossed in the Death Throes of the Raj." *Times,* October 20, 1975.

Muggeridge, Malcolm. Review of *Staying On. New York Times,* August 21, 1977.

Nye, Robert. Review of *The Day of the Scorpion, Guardian,* September 12, 1968.

————. Review of *The Jewel in the Crown. Guardian,* July 22, 1966.

Parry, Benita. "Paul Scott's Raj." *South Asian Review* 8 (July/October 1975): 359–369.

Peterstone, Karina. "The Concept of History in Paul Scott's Tetralogy, *The Raj Quartet." Zeitschrift fur Anglistik und Amerikanistik* 37 (1989): 228–233.

Pollard, Arthur. "Twilight of Empire: Paul Scott's *Raj Quartet." In Individual and Community in Commonwealth Literature,* ed. Daniel Massa, pp. 169–176. Msida: University of Malta Press.

Popham, Janis, and Janet Tedesco. *An Introduction to the Raj Quartet.* Lanham, Maryland: University Press of America, 1985.

Prescott, Orville. Review of *The Jewel in the Crown. New York Times,* July 29, 1966.

Price, Alice Lindsay, ed. *After Paul: Paul Scott's Tulsa Years.* Tulsa, Oklahoma: HCE Publications/Riverrun Arts, 1988.

Price, R. G. G. "New Fiction." Review of *The Day of the Scorpion. Punch,* September 4, 1968, p. 21.

Pryce-Jones, David. Review of *A Division of the Spoils. Times,* May 8, 1975.

Rao, K. Bhaskara. *Paul Scott.* Ed. Kinley E. Roby. Twayne English Author Series. Boston: Twayne, 1980.

Ringold, Francine. "A Conversation with Paul Scott." *Nimrod* (University of Tulsa) 21 (Fall/Winter 1976): 16–32.

Ross, Nancy Wilson. "Unsung Singer of Hindustan." Review of *The Jewel in the Crown, The Day of the Scorpion,* and *The Towers of Silence. Saturday Review,* June 24, 1972, pp. 58–60.

Rubin, David. *After The Raj: British Novels of India since 1947.* Hanover and London: University Press of New England, 1986.

Rushdie, Salman. "Outside the Whale." Review of the television series "The Jewel in the Crown." *American Film* 10 (January 1985): 16, 70, 72–73.

Scanlan, Margaret. "The Disappearance of History: Paul Scott's *Raj Quartet." CLIO: A Journal of Literature, History, and the Philosophy of History* 15 (Winter 1986): 153–169.

Shahane, Vasant A. "Kipling, Forster, and Paul Scott: A Study in Sociological Imagination." In *The Twofold Voice: Essays in Honor of Ramesh Mohan,* ed. S. N. A. Rizvi, pp. 195–208. Salzburg: Institut fur Anglistik und Amerikanistik, University of Salzburg, 1982.

Sharrad, Paul. "The Books behind the Film: Paul Scott's *Raj Quartet." East-West Film Journal* 1 (1987): 78–90.

Spurling, Hilary. *Paul Scott: A Life.* London: Hutchinson, 1990.

Srivastava, Aruna. "The Pageant of Empire: Paul Scott's *The Raj Quartet* and Related Versions of Imperialism in the Anglo-Indian Novel." Ph.D. diss., McMaster University (Canada), 1989.

Staley, Thomas F. "The Meeting." In *After Paul: Paul Scott's Tulsa Years*, ed. Alice Lindsay Price, pp. 1–3. Tulsa, Oklahoma: HCE Publications/ Riverrun Arts, 1988.

Swinden, Patrick. *Paul Scott*. Writers and Their Works. Windsor, England: Profile, 1982.

———. *Paul Scott: Images of India*. London and Basingstoke: Macmillan, 1980.

Tedesco, Janis. "Staying On: The Final Connection." *Western Humanities Review* 39 (Autumn 1985): 195–211.

Weinbaum, Francine S. "Aspiration and Betrayal in Paul Scott's *The Raj Quartet*." Ph.D. diss., University of Illinois, 1976.

———. "Images of the British Raj in the Granada Television Film Serial, "The Jewel in the Crown." *South Asian Review* 8 (1984): 133–137.

———. "Paul Scott's India: *The Raj Quartet*. *Critique* 20 (1978): 100–110.

———. "Psychological Defenses and Thwarted Union in *The Raj Quartet*." *Literature and Psychology* 31 (1981): 75–87.

———. "Staying On after the Raj." Review of *Staying On*. *Journal of South Asian Literature* 17 (1982): 225–229.

Williams, R. J. P. "Presenting the Raj: The Politics of Representation in Recent Fiction on the British Empire." Ph.D. diss., University of Nottingham, England, 1988.

Zorn, G. Jean. "Talk with Paul Scott." *New York Times Book Review*, August 21, 1977, p. 31.

General Sources

Allen, Charles, ed. *Plain Tales from the Raj: Images of British India in the Twentieth Century*. London: Andre Deutsch and B.B.C., 1975.

Belsey, Catherine. *Critical Practice*. London and New York: Methuen, 1980.

Beveridge, William Henry. *India Called Them*. London: G. Allen and Unwin, 1947.

The Bhagavadgita. Trans. Kees W. Bolle. Berkeley: University of California Press, 1979.

Brown, Norman O. *Life against Death: The Psychoanalytical Meaning of History*. New York: Vintage Books, Random House, 1959.

Collins, Larry, and Dominique LaPierre. *Freedom at Midnight*. New York: Simon and Schuster, 1975.

Edwardes, Michael. *The Last Years of British India*. 1963. Reprint. London: New English Library, 1967.

Eliot, T. S. "Four Quartets" and "The Hollow Men." *The Complete Poems and Plays, 1901–1950*. New York: Harcourt, Brace, 1952.

Farrell, J. C. *The Siege of Krishnapur*. New York: Harcourt Brace Jovanovich, 1973.

Forster, E. M. *Howards End*. London: Edward Arnold, 1932.

———. *A Passage to India*. New York: Harcourt, Brace and World, 1952.

Freud, Sigmund. "The Excretory Functions in Psychoanalysis and Folklore." In *Sigmund Freud: Collected Papers*, ed. James Strachey, 5:88–91. London: Hogarth Press and the Institute of Psychoanalysis, 1971.

———. "Leonardo da Vinci and a Memory of His Childhood" and "On the Universal Tendency to Debasement in the Sphere of Love." Trans. Alan Tyson. In *The Standard Edition of the Complete Psychoanalytical Works of Sigmund Freud*, 11:63–137 and 177–190. London: Hogarth Press and the Institute of Psychoanalysis, 1964.

———. "The Relation of the Poet to Daydreaming." In *Sigmund Freud: Collected Papers*, trans. Alix and James Strachey, 4:173–183. London: Hogarth Press and the Institute of Psychoanalysis, 1971.

———. "Some Psychological Peculiarities of Obsessional Neurotics: Their Attitudes Towards Reality, Superstition and Death." Part B of "A Case of Obsessional Neurosis." In *Sigmund Freud: Collected Papers*, trans. Alix and James Strachey, 3:365–372. London: Hogarth Press and the Institute of Psychoanalysis, 1971.

Frye, Prosser Hall. "Romance and Tragedy." In *The Idea of Tragedy*, ed. Carl Benson and Taylor Littleton, pp. 26–29. Glenview, Illinois: Scott, Foresman, 1966.

Greenberger, Alan J. *The British Image of India: A Study in the Literature of Imperialism, 1880–1960*. London: Oxford University Press, 1969.

Holland, Norman N. "Unity Identity Text Self." *PMLA* 90 (1975): 813–822.

Hutchins, Francis. *The Illusion of Permanence: British Imperialism in India*. Princeton: Princeton University Press, 1967.

———. *India's Revolution: Gandhi and the Quit India Movement*. Cambridge: Harvard University Press, 1973.

Johnson, Stephen M. *Humanizing the Narcissistic Style*. London: W. W. Norton, 1987.

Jones, Ernest. "Anal-Erotic Character Traits." In *Papers on Psycho-Analysis*. 3d ed. London: Balliere, Tindall and Cox, 1923.

Jung, Carl G. "The Dreamlike World of India" and "What India Can Teach Us." In *Civilization in Transition*. Trans. R. F. C. Hull. New York: Random House, 1964.

Kipling, Rudyard. "The Bridge Builders." In *The Day's Work*, pp. 1–47. London: Macmillan, 1964.

———. *Kim*. Garden City, New York: Doubleday, Doran, 1901.

———. "On the City Wall." In *Indian Tales*. New York, 1890.

———. *Plain Tales from the Hills*. Garden City, New York: Doubleday, Page, 1930.

———. *Soldiers Three*. Garden City, New York: Doubleday Page, 1927.

———. *Wee Willie Winkie*. London: Macmillan, 1951.

Klein, Melanie. *Love, Guilt, and Reparation, and Other Works, 1921–1945*. International Psychoanalytic Library, no. 103. London: Hogarth Press and the Institute of Psychoanalysis, 1975.

———. *Our Adult World and Other Essays*. New York: Basic Books, 1963.

Kohut, Heinz. "Introspection, Empathy, and the Semi-Circle of Mental

Health." *International Journal of Psycho-Analysis* 63 (1982): 395–407.

Kramer, Dale. *Thomas Hardy: The Forms of Tragedy.* Detroit: Wayne State University Press, 1975.

Krieger, Murray. "Tragedy and the Tragic Vision." In *The Tragic Vision: Variations on a Theme in Literary Interpretation.* New York: Holt, Rinehart, and Winston, 1960.

Krutsch, Joseph Wood. "The Modern Temper." In *The Idea of Tragedy,* pp. 63–68. Glenview, Illinois: Scott, Foresman, 1966.

Lukacs, Georg. *The Historical Novel.* Trans. Hannah and Stanley Mitchell. New York: Humanities Press, 1965.

Malgonkar, Manohar. *The Princes.* New York: Viking, 1963.

Mannoni, Otare. *Prospero and Caliban: The Psychology of Colonization.* Trans. Pamela Powesland. Introd. Philip Mason Woodruff. New York: Praeger, 1956.

Martin, Jay. "Infant Development: Fictive Personality and Creative Capacity." In *Frontiers of Infant Psychiatry,* ed. Justin D. Call, Eleanor Galenson, and Robert L. Tyson, 2:111–120. New York: Basic Books, 1964.

Mason, Philip. *Prospero's Magic. Some Thoughts on Class and Race.* London: Oxford University Press, 1962.

Masters, John. *Bhowani Junction.* New York: Ballantine Books, 1954.

———. *Nightrunners of Bengal.* New York: Viking, 1951.

Menon, Vapal Pagunni. *The Integration of the Indian States.* Princeton: Princeton University Press, 1957.

Miller, Alice. *The Drama of the Gifted Child: A Search for the True Self.* Trans. Ruth Ward. New York: Basic Books, 1981.

Miller, Arthur. "Tragedy and the Common Man." In *The Idea of Tragedy,* ed. Carl Benson and Taylor Littleton, pp. 68–71. Glenview, Illinois: Scott Foresman, 1966.

———. "Introduction to the Collected Plays." In *Arthur Miller's Collected Plays.* New York: Viking, 1957.

Mosley, Leonard. *The Last Days of the British Raj.* New York: Harcourt, Brace, and World, 1961.

Orwell, George. *Burmese Days.* New York: New American Library, 1963.

———. "Rudyard Kipling" and "Shooting an Elephant." In *A Collection of Essays by George Orwell.* Garden City, New York: Doubleday, 1954.

Sencourt, Robert. *India in English Literature.* London: Simpkin, Marshall, Hamilton, Kent, 1925.

Singh, Khushwant. *Train to Pakistan.* New York: Grove Press, 1956.

Spear, Percival. *A History of India.* Vol. 2. Rev. ed. Harmondsworth, England: Penguin, 1978.

Wilson, Edmund. *The Wound and the Bow.* New York: Oxford University Press, 1965.

Woodruff, Philip (Mason). *The Founders of Modern India.* Vol. 1 of *The Men Who Ruled India.* New York: St. Martin's Press, 1954.

———. *The Guardians.* Vol. 2 of *The Men Who Ruled India.* New York: St. Martin's Press, 1954.

Index

Names of characters in novels are italicized; titles of books are in boldface italics.